SERVICE DELIVERY TO RURAL OLDER ADULTS
OLDER ADULTS

Research, Policy, and Practice

R. Turner Goins, Ph.D., is an Associate Professor in the Department of Community Medicine and in the Center on Aging, West Virginia University, Robert C. Byrd Health Sciences Center. She received her PhD in Gerontology from the University of Massachusetts Boston in 1997 and completed a National Institute on Aging Post-Doctoral Fellowship at Duke University's Center for the Study of Aging and Human Development. The major focus of Dr. Goins' research has been on health and access to health care for rural older adults. From 2000–2002, she extended her program of research to include American Indian and Alaska Native (AI/AN) elders during a two-year grant with the Native Elder Research Center, University of Colorado Health Sciences Center. As the recipient of a five-year career development award from the National Institutes of Health, National Institute on Aging, Dr. Goins continues to examine physical disability and long-term care needs among older American Indians.

Dr. Goins has published over 30 journal articles and monographs on a wide range of gerontological topics, including issues related to health care access in rural areas, long-term care needs among rural elders, and the functional health of older AI/ANs. In addition to her career development award, Dr. Goins is currently the Principal Investigator on three grants, including a project entitled "Rural Healthy Aging Network," funded by the Centers for Disease Control and Prevention, and "Tribal Long-Term Care: Barriers to and Best Practices in Policy and Programming," funded by the Office of Rural Health Policy. She is an Expert Member on both the Rosalynn Carter Institute's Panel on Rural Caregiving and the Center for Substance Abuse Prevention, Substance Abuse, and Mental Health Services Administration. Dr. Goins is a Study Section Member, Health Systems Research, Agency for Healthcare Quality and Research and serves on the editorial boards of the *Journal of Applied Gerontology, Journals of Gerontology: Social Sciences*, and *Journal of Native Aging & Health*. She is a Fellow of the Gerontological Society of America.

John A. Krout, Ph.D., is Professor of Gerontology and Director of the Gerontology Institute at Ithaca College. He has written over 50 book chapters and articles, and published in a wide range of academic journals, such as *The Gerontologist, Research on Aging, International Journal of Aging and Human Development,* and *Journal of Gerontology,* and has made over 125 presentations at national and state conferences. He has received over a dozen grants to support his research program in rural aging issues and community-based services for older adults. His books include, *Residential Choices and Experiences of Older Adults* with Elaine Wethington, *The Aged in Rural America, Senior Centers in America, Providing Community-Based Services to the Rural Elderly,* and *Aging in Rural Settings,* with Raymond T. Coward, as well as several bibliographies on rural aging. He has conducted several national studies on senior centers and other services for older adults, focusing on participation, services, resources, and community linkages. All of these have looked at rural-urban differences. Other research interests include: care management, service knowledge and utilization, elder migration, housing, and intergenerational programming.

Dr. Krout has served as a consultant on a number of AoA-funded research and demonstration projects, including the National Resource Center for Rural Elderly. He has served as a member of the delegate council of the National Council on the Aging's National Center on Rural Aging from which he received a Professional Leadership Award in 1993. He is past-president of the State Society on Aging of New York and received that organization's Walter M. Beattie., Jr. Award in 2004. Dr. Krout is a Fellow of the Gerontological Society of America and a charter fellow of the Association of Gerontology in Higher Education and is active in both those organizations.

SERVICE DELIVERY TO RURAL OLDER ADULTS

Research, Policy, and Practice

R. Turner Goins, PhD
John A. Krout, PhD
Editors

SPRINGER PUBLISHING COMPANY
New York

*This book is dedicated to rural older adults from Allakaket,
Alaska to Pink Hill, North Carolina, and all the service providers
who are committed to improving their quality of life.*

Springer Publishing Company, Inc.
11 West 42nd Street
New York, NY 10036

Acquisitions Editor: Helvi Gold
Managing Editor: Mary Ann McLaughlin
Production Editor: Print Matters, Inc.
Cover design by Joanne E. Honigman
Typeset by Compset

06 07 08 09 10/5 4 3 2 1

Library of Congress Cataloging-in-Publication Data

Service delivery to rural older adults: research, policy, and practice / [edited by]
  R. Turner Goins, John A. Krout.
     p.; cm.
  ISBN 0-8261-0227-1
     1. Rural elderly—Services for—United States.   I. Goins, R. Turner.
  II. Krout, John A.

  HV1461.S457 2006
  362.6'3—dc22

                                                         2006042385

Printed in the United States of America by Maple-Vail Book Manufacturing Group.

Contents

Contributors   ix

Preface   xi

Foreword by *Graham D. Rowles, PhD*   xiv

Acknowledgments   xviii

Part I: Overview

1   Introduction: Aging in Rural America   3
    R. Turner Goins and John A. Krout

    Defining Rural   5
    Defining Best Practices   11
    Myths and Realities of Rural Aging   12
    Conclusions   16

2   Service Delivery to Rural Elders: Barriers and Challenges   21
    John A. Krout and C. Neil Bull

    Service Needs of Rural Elders   22
    Services for Rural Elders   24
    Barriers to Rural Services   25
    Planning and Implementing Successful Services 27
    Programs for Rural Elders   29
    Conclusions   31
    Appendix: Rural Programs   34

3   Demographic and Resettlement Impacts on Rural Services   37
    Don E. Bradley and Charles F. Longino, Jr.

    Method   40
    Results   42
    Discussion   47
    Conclusions   50

4   Service Issues Among Rural Racial and Ethnic   55
     Minority Elders
     R. Turner Goins, Jim Mitchell, and Bei Wu

         African Americans   56
         American Indians and Alaska Natives   61
         Hispanics   66
         Conclusions   69

Part II: Health Service Provision and Policy Issues

5   Health and Nutrition in Rural Areas   79
     Joseph R. Sharkey and Jane N. Bolin

         Rural Older Adults and Health Problems   80
         Chronic Disease Management   84
         Rural Older Adults and Nutritional Health   86
         Self-Management of Nutritional Health   89
         Challenges to Nutrition and Health Issues   92
         Best Practices or Model Programs   93
         Conclusions   93

6   Rural Hospitals and Long-Term Care: The Challenges   103
     of Diversification and Integration Strategies
     Andrew F. Coburn, Stephenie L. Loux, and Elise J. Bolda

         Rural Long-Term Care and the Role of Rural Hospitals   104
         The Evolving Role of Rural Hospitals in Long-Term Care 107
         Hospital Strategies: Diversification, Networking, and 112
             Service Integration
         Integrating Acute and Long-Term Care in Rural Areas   113
         Conclusions   118

7   Changes in the Medicare Program: Meeting   123
     New Challenges in Rural Health Care Delivery
     Keith J. Mueller and Timothy D. McBride

         Principles for Analyzing Changes in Medicare   124
         Best Practices to Optimize Gains from the MMA   132
         Conclusions   137

Part III: Selected Services

8   Caregiving in a Rural Context   145
     Donna L. Wagner and Kelly J. Niles-Yokum

         Informal Caregiving and Well-Being of Older Persons   146
         Is Caregiving Different in a Rural Area?   148

    Interface Between Formal and Informal Care   152
    Creating a Supportive Context for Rural Caregiving   154
    Rural Caregiving Initiatives   155
    Conclusions   158

9   Housing for Rural Elders: Policies, Practices,   163
and Prospects
*W. Edward Folts, Kenneth B. Muir, James R. Peacock,
Bradley Nash, Jr., and Katherine L. Jones*

    Demography of Rural Aging   164
    Federal Housing Policies and Rural Elders   166
    Best Practices   171
    Barriers to Rural Housing   176
    Conclusions   177

10   Transportation and Aging: Challenges in Rural America   183
Helen Kerschner

    Transportation Needs   183
    Destination Needs   184
    Service Availability   184
    Transportation Service Challenge   185
    Five Transportation Solutions   188
    Conclusions   194

Part IV: Moving Forward: Technology and System Change

11   Transforming Rural Health Care: The Role of Technology   201
Linda Redford and Ryan Spaulding

    Current Issues in Rural Health Care   202
    Applications of Technology in Health Care   204
    Use of Technology in Education for Rural Health Professionals   208
    Barriers to the Use of Technology   213
    Conclusions   218

12   Public Policy and Rural Aging   223
David K. Brown and Robert Blancato

    Federal Programs   224
    Devolving Federal Roles to the States   228
    Policy Innovations   230
    Economic Development: Key to Service Delivery   231
    Recommendations   233
    Conclusions   235

13   Summary and Conclusions   239
     John A. Krout and R. Turner Goins

        Setting the Stage   240
        Setting the Stage: Summary   241
        Population Dynamics   242
        Population: Summary   246
        Health, Nutrition, and Health Care Financing Policy   247
        Health and Health Care: Summary   250
        Selected Services   251
        Services: Summary   253
        Technology: Summary   253
        Conclusions   254

        Index   259

Contributors

Robert Blancato, MPA
Matz, Blancato & Associates
Washington, DC

Elise J. Bolda, PhD
University of Southern Maine
Institute for Health Policy
Edmund S. Muskie School of
    Public Service
Portland, ME

Jane N. Bolin, PhD, JD, RN
Texas A & M University
    Health Science Center
School of Rural Public Health
College Station, TX
Texas A & M University
    Health Science Center
School of Rural Public Health
Bryan, TX

Don E. Bradley, PhD
East Carolina University
Thomas Harriot College of
    Arts & Sciences
Department of Sociology
Greenville, NC

David K. Brown, PhD
West Virginia University
Robert C. Byrd Health
    Sciences Center
Department of Community
    Medicine
and Center on Aging
Morgantown, WV

C. Neil Bull, PhD
University of Missouri– Kansas City
Kansas City, MO

Andrew F. Coburn, PhD
University of Southern Maine
Institute for Health Policy
Edmund S. Muskie School of
    Public Service
Portland, ME

W. Edward Folts, PhD
Professor and Chair
Department of Sociology
    and Social Work
Appalachian State University
Boone, NC

R. Turner Goins, PhD
West Virginia University
Robert C. Byrd Health
    Sciences Center
Department of Community
    Medicine
and Center on Aging
Morgantown, WV

Katherine L. Jones, BA
Appalachian State University
Department of Sociology &
    Social Work
Boone, NC

Helen Kerschner, PhD
Beverly Foundation
Pasadena, CA

John A. Krout, PhD
Ithaca College
Ithaca, NY

Charles F. Longino, Jr., PhD
Wake Forest University
Winston-Salem, NC

Stephenie L. Loux, MS
University of Southern Maine
Institute for Health Policy
Edmund S. Muskie School of
  Public Service
Portland, ME
University of Southern Maine
Maine Rural Health Research
  Center
Portland, ME

Timothy D. McBride, PhD
Department of Health
  Management and Policy
School of Public Health
St. Louis University
St. Louis, MO
University of Missouri–St. Louis
St. Louis, MO

Jim Mitchell, PhD
East Carolina University
Center on Aging, Division of
  Research
School of Medicine
Greenville, NC

Keith J. Mueller, PhD
University of Nebraska
  Medical Center
RUPRI Center for Rural Health
  Policy Analysis
Omaha, NE

Kenneth B. Muir, PhD
Appalachian State University
Department of Sociology &
  Social Work
Chapell Wilson Hall
Boone, NC

Bradley Nash, Jr., PhD
Appalachian State University
Department of Sociology &
  Social Work
Boone, NC

Kelly J. Niles-Yokum, MPA
University of Maryland,
  Baltimore County
Center for Aging Studies
Baltimore, MD

James R. Peacock, PhD
Appalachian State University
Department of Sociology &
  Social Work
Boone, NC

Linda Redford, RN, PhD
University of Kansas Medical
  Center
Landon Center on Aging
Kansas City, KS

**Joseph R. Sharkey, PhD,
  MPH, RD**
Texas A & M University System
  Health Science Center
School of Rural Public Health
College Station, TX

Ryan Spaulding, PhD
Center for Telemedicine and
  Telehealth
University of Kansas Medical
  Center
Kansas City, KS

Donna L. Wagner, PhD
Towson University
Gerontology Program
Health Sciences Department
Department of Gerontology
Towson, MD

Bei Wu, PhD
West Virginia University
Robert C. Byrd Health Sciences
  Center
Department of Community
  Medicine
and Center on Aging
Morgantown, WV

Preface

The origins of this book can be found within the Plan of Action on Rural Aging, a project funded by the Administration on Aging from September 2001 to January 2003. The objectives of this initiative were to work collaboratively with local senior service providers to create and evaluate six rurally based demonstration projects and to develop a report based on these projects. The projects addressed needs in the areas of health promotion, caregiving, housing, and health care transportation. One of the main outcomes was to build models to influence positive change in rural service delivery and ultimately improve the overall health and quality of life for older persons in these rural areas. At the conclusion of the demonstration projects, a report was written entitled "Best Practices in Service Delivery to the Rural Elderly," in which variations of the majority of the chapters collected in this book were originally published (Ham, Goins, & Brown, 2003).

The 13 chapters included here represent an attempt to provide a comprehensive discussion of contemporary challenges experienced by older rural residents and their communities in accessing and providing services. In addition, many of the chapters provide details about programs and services which have been successful and may serve as models for others to consider. The information provided in the chapters is intended for researchers, policymakers, planners, and practitioners. This book also provides a useful overview of issues relevant to rural aging for educators and students in the fields of gerontology, public health, public policy, public administration, and social work, to name a few. The chapters are organized into four sections. The first section focuses on providing the reader an overview of the subject matter. Chapter 1, "Introduction: Aging in Rural America," provides a discussion about what is rural about rural aging, key definitions and concepts, and myths and realities of rural aging. Chapter 2, "Service Delivery to Rural Elders: Barriers and Challenges," provides an overview of the existing barriers to the development and provision of services to rural elders. Chapter 3, "Demographic and Resettlement Impacts on Rural Services," is an in-depth examination of migration patterns to/from rural areas and the service implications of these patterns. Chapter 4, "Service Issues Among Rural Racial and Ethnic Minority Elders," focuses on three prevalent older minority populations in rural America and describes their experiences with accessing health services.

The second section presents information on health services and related policy issues. Chapter 5, "Health and Nutrition in Rural Areas," discusses the chronic health and nutritional problems common among older rural adults. Chapter 6, "Rural Hospitals and Long-Term Care: The Challenges of Diversification and Integration Strategies," examines the changing roles of hospitals in rural communities with respect to providing long-term care services. Chapter 7, "Changes in the Medicare Program: Meeting New Challenges in Rural Health Care Delivery," applies the Rural Policy Research Institute principles to examine the Medicare Prescription Drug, Improvement, and Modernization Act and outlines best practices that can be used to ensure a smooth transition to the new coverage.

The third section focuses on important selected services in rural America including informal caregiving, housing, and transportation. Chapter 8, "Caregiving in a Rural Context," reviews the existing research literature on rural caregiving, discusses issues unique to caregiving in rural America, and concludes with practice concepts that support rural caregivers. Chapter 9, "Housing for Rural Elders: Policies, Practices, and Prospects," outlines the housing needs of rural older adults, federal housing policies which affect them, promising practices to ensure adequate housing options, and barriers to securing adequate housing for older adults residing in rural communities. Chapter 10, "Transportation and Aging: Challenges in Rural America," addresses the challenges faced by rural residents and providers to meeting older adults' transportation needs and presents innovative solutions.

The final section of the book focuses on enhancing health care delivery through technology and public policies and provides concluding remarks about service delivery in rural areas. Chapter 11, "Transforming Rural Health Care: The Role of Technology," provides a detailed discussion of technology and how it can be used to alleviate problems in accessing needed care for older rural adults. Chapter 12, "Public Policy and Rural Aging," examines federal and state public policies and programs that affect services and presents ideas for improving the responsiveness of these policies and programs to meet the needs of older rural adults. Chapter 13, "Summary and Conclusions," provides a summary of all the chapters and future directions.

The editors wish to extend their thanks to and deep regard for the work of the many people who contributed to this book's development.

We are particularly indebted to those authors whose work is included here for both their willingness to consider our editorial suggestions and for helping to meet our production deadlines.

REFERENCES

Ham, R. J., Goins, R. T., & Brown, D. K. (Eds.). (2003, March). *Best practices in service delivery to the rural elderly: A report to the Administration on Aging*. Morgantown, WV: West Virginia University Center on Aging.

Foreword

In August of 2005, I moved to the country, relocating to a log home on 6.7 acres off a winding rural road 15 miles from Lexington, Kentucky. The move signaled achievement of a lifelong dream. At last, entering my 60th year, I was able to achieve my aspiration of living where I could look out of my window and not be able to see a neighbor's house. I am now able to savor the warm tranquility of a September evening and hear the sound of the birds without the distraction of a cacophony of bumper-to-bumper traffic or the blaring of emergency vehicle sirens. I can build a fire with logs hewn on my own property, pick pears off my own trees, and plant firs in preparation for a single-tree annual Yuletide harvest. Bucolic bliss!

There is a price. As I grow older and become frail and more vulnerable, my separation from the city may become problematic. When I have to give up driving, it is probable that I will begin to encounter difficulties in accessing services. The gift of solitude and the ability to commune with nature may gradually be overridden by the curse of isolation. Traveling for groceries will become a more taxing venture. It will likely become more difficult to get to the doctor. My inclination to make trips to the city will wane as enthusiasm for the theater is tempered by the thought of driving home in the black darkness with the prospect of a sudden confrontation with glaring headlights. As I grow frailer, the need for home care may arise. It is likely that needed access to higher levels of medical and long-term care services will become ever more difficult and costly in a rural environment where the trend is increasingly toward the closure of local hospitals, the departure rather than addition of providers, and longer waits for care.

Of course, I can rationalize. By the time I encounter these constraints, the miracles of the Internet and telemedicine will have become available in even the most remote areas. I will be able to benefit from advances in surveillance and safety monitoring that will allow me to continue to live safely in a "smart" home. Indeed, it will be possible to transcend reliance on physical proximity as the determinant of service access.

I have made a residential choice and I am willing to live with the consequences, whatever these may be. But the large majority of more than 10 million nonmetropolitan Americans age 60 years or older have made no such choice (Rogers, 2002). Through accident of birth and lifelong residence, they have found themselves living their later years in an environment of "accepted rural disadvantage" where barriers of availability, accessibility, affordability, awareness, appropriateness, and adequacy limit and often preclude the receipt of needed services. In contrast to my circumstances of relative affluence, many of these elders lack resources to access or pay for services that might enable them to overcome the challenges of distance and isolation. How can we support these people to enable them to remain at home and thrive? Should we?

In this thoughtful volume, Turner Goins, John Krout, and their contributors seek to provide a context for addressing these questions as they explore inadequate health care structures, barriers, and challenges to the delivery of services to rural elders, the impact of rural demographic change and migration, and the particular problems faced by racial and ethnic minority elders. Against this backdrop, more detailed in-depth analyses of nutrition, health service delivery, rural hospitals, long-term care, caregiving, housing, and transportation as components of rural support systems not only provide telling insight into the complexity and interdependency of the issues but also incorporate description of a wide array of strategies and directions that have been and might be taken in alleviating the problems. Some of these alternatives are well documented and have been implemented with variable levels of success. Many more, particularly those developed in the concluding section of the book, which considers the actual and potential role of technology and the critical influence of federal and state public policies increasingly obsessed with controlling costs, point in exciting new directions. They suggest the potential for transformation of the rural service delivery landscape.

As readers of this volume will discover, there are a plethora of options for such a transformation—demonstration projects that reflect deep understanding of the issues and creativity in addressing them. These include initiatives to provide mobile health screening, parish nurse networks affiliated with churches, volunteer driver programs, rural caregiver training demonstration projects, targeted rural home repair programs, swing-bed programs in rural hospitals, and models for the integration of acute and long-term care services. Although these options provide cause for celebration, optimism must be tempered by an awareness of political realities. In most rural communities, there remain many options but few choices. There do not appear to be either the dollars or the political will to implement such strategies throughout rural America.

The lack of inclusion of rural realities in many federal policy approaches—a pervasive underlying motif of Goins and Krout's anthology —is particularly distressing. Although each of the chapters in this volume provide crucial insight on some aspect of the dilemmas of giving service to rural elders, in the long run, and placed in broader context, the issue boils down to two fundamental interrelated questions—the value we place on facilitating the option of continued rural residence for elders and the degree to which we are willing, either as a society or individually, to sustain and shoulder the cost of this option.

Consider the issue on several interwoven levels. First, on a purely economic level, it is clear that rural residence is costly and uneconomic both for society and the individual. From a societal perspective, the costs of distance, inefficiencies of spatial dispersion, and the absence of economies of scale that preclude the adequate provision of specialty medical care, emergency services, rehabilitation programs, and many other services make rural residence irrational. As William Miernyk (1967) wrote four decades ago in his "Needed: Appalachian Ghost Towns" essay, it does not make sense for society to invest in maintaining myriad small, low-density, and dispersed communities. It is much more efficient and economically viable to concentrate resources in a small number of central places that consolidate resources within urban growth poles. Also, for the economically rational elder it makes no sense to remain far from potential sources of support.

Second, on a sociocultural level, we become concerned with questions of lifestyles and values. Rural and agrarian values including independence, self-reliance, interpersonal obligation (social capital accumulated from lifelong residence), community responsibility, and localism (even parochialism) are deeply ingrained in American culture. But with the collapsing of distance and the homogenization of lifestyles and culture through mass communication these essential features of rurality are becoming increasingly artificial and commodified. Is a distinctive culture of aging in rural places a romanticized but essentially defunct historical legacy or does it remain a viable way of life amid an ever-changing contemporary rural landscape where few remain in agrarian occupations?

Third, on a moral level, we become concerned with social justice and the principle of equal access that has long permeated our thinking about service provision. Indeed, the notion of equity remains a cornerstone of Medicare policy. What is the obligation of society to provide services for persons like me who have chosen to relocate to a rural setting? Far more important, what about elders who were born in and have spent their entire lives in a rural setting? Does society have an obligation to provide services to rural elders regardless of cost? Or are these elders personally responsible for the consequences of their place of birth? Is there a moral imperative for elders to give up rural residence as part of a larger social contract, much in the same way that some have argued for the duty of elders to die (Harwig, 1997)?

For society, the issues are embedded in political economy. But for the individual, in a free society, the question boils down to one of personal choice. Here I feel some affinity with the rural Kansas residents cited by Scheidt and Norris-Baker (1993, p. 338) who were willing to accept the prospect of being unable to reach help in time should they fall ill rather than move to the city.

> Although a number of the older residents expressed concerns about the quality and accessibility to healthcare, there is a pragmatic acceptance of these circumstances, even when there may be mortal risks. One recent widow from Plainsville recounted the history of her husband's fatal illness with pneumonia, including their dependence on others to reach the hospital, and the physician's attribution of her husband's death to the inability to transfer him to a regional medical center because of a winter storm. She accepted these problems as simply part of living in a rural town, where there had been "no doctoring" for 50 years or more, and expressed no concern about risks to her own health from this lack of services.

With the increasing sophistication and diversity of rural service delivery options, the advent of more viable health information technologies and the expansion of home telemonitoring, interactive televideo (even telepsychiatry), and Internet options described in this volume, it may be possible to obviate the potentially fatal consequences of such cruel choices. Turner Goins and John Krout have done us a wonderful service by providing a comprehensive and richly textured set of essays that will both assist and encourage us to ponder such a future. As I sit here on my porch and watch the setting of the sun, I certainly hope that this is exactly what you, the reader, will do.

Graham D. Rowles, PhD
Georgetown, Kentucky

REFERENCES

Harwig, J. (1997). Is there a duty to die? *Hastings Center Reports, 27*(2), 34–42.

Miernyk, W. (1967, Spring). Needed: Appalachian ghost towns. *Appalachian Review,* pp. 14–20.

Rogers, C. C. (2002). The older population in 21st century rural America. *Rural America, 17*(3), 2–10.

Scheidt, R. J., & Norris-Baker, C. (1993). The environmental context of poverty among older residents of economically endangered Kansas towns. *Journal of Applied Gerontology, 12,* 335–348.

Acknowledgments

Turner Goins would like to extend her deepest gratitude to Mindi Spencer, Sarah Fitch, Josh Byrd, and Deb MacDonald for their support and assistance.

Both editors would like to thank their families for support and understanding of the time we spent working on this book. We would also like to thank Helvi Gold and the staff at Springer Publishing.

PART I

Overview

CHAPTER ONE

Introduction

Aging in Rural America

R. Turner Goins and John A. Krout

The study of rural aging is a culmination of work by gerontologists and professionals from a number of disciplines, with the field of rural sociology holding a particularly central place. The area where gerontology and rural sociology converge is a common interest in how the environment affects aging and how community dynamics affect the behavior and life circumstances of rural individuals. For many researchers interested in older rural adults, the question is, "What is rural about rural aging?" Although the study of older adults in rural settings has recently emerged as a subspecialty within gerontology, more research is needed to allow us to fully answer this question. Given difficult measurement issues with respect to *rural*, we cannot always be certain about residential differences in outcomes. Further, there is a general lack of consistency in the available information and only a modest effort to fund rural research at the level needed.

The literature is more consistent in stating that social and health services are less available and accessible to rural compared to urban elders. Further, the characteristics and resources of both rural elders and rural communities need to be considered in the development and implementation of these services. An exploration of trends in service provision is a major goal of this book. The issue is not whether rural older adults have greater service needs compared to their urban counterparts; rather, the main issue is that rural older people and communities have unique and varied characteristics that must be considered when planning and providing services.

The study of rural places has never taken center stage among gerontologists, nor have aging and the needs of older adults been a priority among social scientists who study rural matters. Relative to other topics in gerontology, the study of the circumstances of older people living in rural America has received little attention. A dozen books and reports have focused exclusively on this topic (e.g., Atchley & Byerts, 1975; Bull, 1993; Coward, Bull, Kukulka, & Galliher, 1994; Coward & Krout, 1998; Coward & Lee, 1985; Gesler, Rabiner, & DeFriese, 1998; Kim & Wilson, 1981; Krout, 1986; Krout, 1994; Peterson & Maiden, 1993; Shenk, 1998; Youmans, 1967), and over the past 20 years, a small cadre of gerontologists from a variety of disciplines have conducted research concerning issues related to rural older adults. There are good reasons for building a better understanding of what it means to be old in a rural setting, including:

- Our nation has rural economic, political, and cultural roots;
- About two thirds of the nation's counties are nonmetropolitan;
- Twenty to 24% of the nation's older people are rural;
- Nationwide, rural areas have a greater proportion of adults age 65 years or older;
- Understanding rural aging helps us understand aging in general;
- Research has shown that rural elders face significant and sometimes unique challenges to maintaining well-being; and
- Policy makers and program planners need to take rural realities and diversity into account when developing and implementing services for older adults.

Given this, more resources need to be directed to meeting the needs of rural elders. Moreover, governmental policies and programs should pay particular attention to addressing the underlying causes of the rural disadvantage and developing, implementing, and supporting effective services. This book is intended to discuss services for rural elders. The authors set out to identify those aspects of rural environment, people, and organizations that are important to consider when designing and implementing programs to help rural older adults.

Although additional research is needed to help us understand what is rural about rural aging, we offer six dimensions critical to understanding the relationship between aging and living in rural places:

- Compositional: This refers to the socio-demographic profile of a rural community. These characteristics include age, gender, race/ethnicity, and socioeconomic status.
- Cultural: Culture is defined as a system of shared beliefs, values, customs, and behaviors among groups of individuals. Culture is transmitted from generation to generation and can influence relationships, living arrangements, and social and health behaviors.
- Behavioral: Behaviors can include engaging in health-related activities such as physical activity, maintaining a nutritional diet, or both; how one interacts with others; and propensity to use services. Behavior or accepted behavioral patterns can vary by community.
- Organizational: Community organizations can include social clubs, local government, and congregations. The presence or absence of community organizations can affect the resources available to provide support to rural elders.
- Social and Economic Resources: These resources refer to the community's economic infrastructure and the capacity to create and sustain social and health services at the local level.
- Ecological: This dimension includes an area's size, density, proximity to urban areas, the remoteness of rural places, and features of the natural environment.

While most researchers use this last dimension as the frame of reference to describe rural issues, questions of socio-demographics, culture, behavior, organizations, and resources are also important to consider. The exact composition of and the role these six dimensions have on the aging experience vary by community. An objective of this book is to encourage the reader to consider aspects in all six dimensions when contemplating what is rural about rural aging. In the development of an empirical body of literature, it is necessary to first make certain that variables or constructs of interest are clearly defined. The purpose of this next section is to provide an overview of definitions and concepts relevant to the study of rural services.

DEFINING RURAL

When we think of what rural is or how to define rural, most often we rely on the components listed in the ecological dimension (i.e., size, population density, etc.). This is probably due to the fact that it is easier and less controversial to define rural this way rather than defining rural in less objective and uniform ways. An operational definition provides the exact manner in which a variable is measured. Specifying the construct and the way it is measured is essential for research, but limitations to these definitions exist. Definitions may oversimplify or fail to fully capture the concept of interest, or they may rely on defining a concept based on a single measure (Kazdin, 2003). Providing the steps to define key variables will allow other researchers to evaluate and potentially replicate a research study. Moreover, the general value of a research project depends on how well the variables are defined. Terms such as "rural" and "nonmetropolitan" are often used in the literature and are essential to the development of research and practice in this area. In addition, these terms are frequently used interchangeably. Inconsistency in the definitions of these and other terms has important conceptual implications for empirical research on service delivery to rural older adults.

Problems related to the different definitions of rural have been well-documented, and research on rural issues produces different results depending on which definition is used. According to the Rural Policy Research Institute (n.d.), there is no standard definition of rural used in research and policy making. Table 1.1 provides a description of some of these terms, which have been developed for statistical purposes and targeting of federal funds. The two most common definitions used in research and policy are the U.S. Census Bureau's use of community size and density to determine rural areas and the Office of Management and Budget's (OMB) use of population size and density to designate counties as nonmetropolitan. According to the U.S. Census Bureau, urban is defined as metropolitan areas and nonmetropolitan areas with a population of at least 2,500 total residents incorporated as cities, villages, boroughs, and towns. Rural is any area not defined as urban. The Census also provides a definition of farm as any place from which $1,000 or more of agricultural products were sold or normally would have been sold during a year (U.S. Census Bureau, 1995).

Historically, the OMB has used the terms Metropolitan Statistical Areas and Nonmetropolitan Statistical Areas to categorize areas. Relatively recently, the OMB released a new version of their classification system that uses Core Based Statistical Areas (CBSAs) to classify areas. CBSAs are geographic areas with at least one core population of 10,000 or more, with adjacent territory that has a high degree of social and economic integration with the core as measured by commuting ties. CBSAs have two categories: Metropolitan Statistical Areas and Micropolitan Statistical Areas. Metropolitan Statistical Areas are based on urbanized areas of a population of

TABLE 1.1 Common Terminology and Descriptions of Rural

Terminology	Agency	Description
Metropolitan Statistical Area (MSA) and Nonmetropolitan Statistical Area (NonMSA)	U.S. Office of Management and Budget	MSAs contain: (a) At least one central county with either a place with a population of 50,000 or more, or an urbanized area and total MSA of 100,000 or more; or (b) One or more outlying counties that have close economic and social relationships (i.e., commuting) with the central county. A NonMSA is any area that does not fit these criteria.
Core Based Statistical Areas (CBSAs) and Outside CBSAs[a]	U.S. Office of Management and Budget	2000 revision to the previous system, which identifies CBSAs comprising two categories: Metropolitan areas, based around at least one U.S. Census Bureau defined urbanized area of 50,000 or more, and micropolitan areas, based around at least one urban cluster of 10,000 to 49,999. A metropolitan area with a single core of at least 2,500,000 population can be subdivided into component metropolitan divisions. Counties that are not included in a CBSA are referred to as "Outside CBSAs."
Rural and Urban[b]	U.S. Census Bureau	Defines urban as all territory, population, and housing units in places of population 2,500 or more incorporated as cities, villages, boroughs (except in AK and NY), and towns (except in the six New England States, NY, and WI). This excludes the rural portions of "extended cities," in U.S. Census designated places of 2,500 or more, or in other territory included in urbanized areas. Territory, population, and housing units not classified as urban are classified as rural. These can be further divided into farm areas, defined as any place from which $1,000 or more of agricultural products were sold or normally would have been sold during the year under consideration, and nonfarm areas.
Rural-Urban Continuum Codes[b]	U.S. Department of Agriculture, Economic Research Service	Categorizes counties on a scale of 0–9 by degree of urbanization and nearness to a metropolitan area. For non-metropolitan counties, this classification system indicates the size of the urban population in a county and the county's proximity to a metropolitan area.

TABLE 1.1 (Continued)

Terminology	Agency	Description
Urban Influence Codes[b]	U.S. Department of Agriculture, Economic Research Service	Categorizes counties on a scale of 0–9 based on the size of the MSA in the case of metropolitan counties, and adjacency to MSAs and size of largest city in the case of nonmetropolitan counties. The counties are classified by the population of the cities within each county, rather than the degree of urbanization.
1989 County Typology Codes[b]	U.S. Department of Agriculture, Economic Research Service	Classifies nonmetropolitan counties based on economic and policy traits. Primary economic activity includes the following nonoverlapping types: Farming-dependent, mining-dependent, manufacturing-dependent, government-dependent, services-dependent, and nonspecialized. The five overlapping policy types include retirement-destination, Federal lands, commuting, persistent poverty, and transfer-dependent.
Census Tracts[b]	U.S. Census Bureau	Uses the Census tract, the smallest geographic building block for which reliable commuting data are available, to classify areas as rural. The Census tract is used instead of the county-level of analysis.
Isolated Rural Areas[b]	H. F. Goldsmith, U.S. Office of Management and Budget	Also known as the Goldsmith Modification, this uses U.S. Census tracts to identify rural areas in Large Metropolitan Counties (LMCs), or counties with at least 1,225 square miles. Rural areas in LMCs are Census tracts with: (a) No persons living in central areas (i.e., urbanized areas), or (b) No persons living in cities of population 25,000 or more. Isolated rural areas are defined as rural areas in the central area, or rural areas in which <15% of the population commuted to work in the central area, or rural areas in which >15% commuted to work in the central area, if 45% of the labor force commuted 30 minutes or more to work.
Frontier Areas[b]	Frontier Education Center	Describes an area (county or U.S. Census tract) with extremely low population density, usually fewer than 6 people per square mile. Frontier Areas are isolated rural areas characterized by considerable distances from central places, poor access to market areas, and relative isolation between people in large geographic areas.

Nonmetro Commuting Zones (CZs) and Labor Market Areas (LMAs)[c]	U.S. Department of Agriculture, Economic Research Service	CZs and LMAs are based on economic and labor force activities. Nonmetro CZs and LMAs do not contain a Metropolitan Area and are ranked based on the size of the largest city, town, or Census Designated Place. Three subcategories are used: Small Town/Rural, Small Urban Center, and Large Urban Center. Three subcategories are also used to describe Metro CZs and LMAs: Small Metro Center, Medium Metro Center, and Major Metro Center.
Rural-Urban Commuting Area Codes[d]	U.S. Department of Agriculture, Economic Research Service	The 2000 codes are based on the theoretical concepts used by the Office of Management and Budget to define county-level metropolitan and micropolitan areas (density, urbanization, and daily commuting). These 10 codes use U.S. Census tracts instead of counties to provide a different and more detailed delineation of metropolitan and nonmetropolitan settlement based on the size and direction of primary commuting flows.

[a]Office of Management and Budget. (2000b). *Final report and recommendations from the Metropolitan Area Standards Review Committee to the Office of Management and Budget concerning changes to the standards for defining metropolitan areas.* Retrieved November 10, 2005, from http://www.whitehouse.gov/omb/inforeg/metro2000.pdf

[b]Rural Policy Research Institute. (n.d.). *Defining rural: Definitions of rural areas in the U.S.* Retrieved November 10, 2005, from http://www.rupri.org/resources/context/rural.html

[c]U.S. Department of Agriculture. Economic Research Service. (2003b). *Measuring rurality: Commuting zones and labor market areas.* Retrieved November 10, 2005, from http://www.ers.usda.gov/briefing/rurality/lmacz/

[d]U.S. Department of Agriculture. Economic Research Service. (2005a). *Measuring rurality: Rural-urban commuting area codes.* Retrieved November 10, 2005, from http://www.ers.usda.gov/briefing/Rurality/RuralUrbanCommutingAreas/

50,000 or more. Micropolitan Statistical Areas are based on urban clusters with a population between 10,000 and 49,999. Central counties of a CBSA have at least 50% of their population in urban areas of at least 10,000 persons or have within their boundaries at least 5,000 persons in a single urban area of at least 10,000 persons. Outlying counties of a CBSA must have at least 25% of employed residents work in the central county or counties of the CBSA or have at least 25% of the employment in the county accounted for by workers who reside in the central county or counties of the CBSA. Counties that do not fall within CBSAs are considered Outside Core Based Statistical Areas (Office of Management and Budget, 2000a). This revision of metropolitan criteria reduced the 2000 nonmetropolitan population from 55 to 49 million persons (U.S. Department of Agriculture, 2003a).

The problem with using different definitions is that the residential areas classified as rural and nonmetropolitan do not perfectly overlap (i.e., a community classified as rural in one study could be considered metropolitan in another). To demonstrate, when these two definitions were compared for the 2000 U.S. Census, findings indicated that 72% of the population was classified as both urban and metropolitan and 10% was classified as rural and nonmetropolitan. Further, 11% were classified as rural and metropolitan and 7% were urban and nonmetropolitan (Hart, Larson, & Lishner, 2005). Most counties, whether metropolitan or nonmetropolitan, contain a combination of urban and rural populations (Isserman, 2005).

Applying inappropriate definitions can affect not only research outcomes but policy analyses and allocation of federal funds for services. These measures were established for political and statistical purposes—for counting people. Definitions of place are the basis for targeting finite resources to underserved rural populations. The OMB definition is used to assess eligibility and reimbursement for numerous federal programs, including Medicare. It is difficult to have a definition of rural America that reflects the unique characteristics of rural compared to urban areas. Further, the growth of suburbia has blurred the lines between rural and urban communities. There is no perfect definition of rural, and the appropriateness of one term over another will vary according to the purpose of the project. Rural areas are not homogeneous nationwide; rural Montana is not like rural Florida, which in turn is not like rural New York or rural Alaska. Definitions can obscure important problems that may be unique at the local level. Therefore, it is important for researchers and policy makers to thoughtfully consider the definition they use and the implications of this decision.

DEFINING BEST PRACTICES

There has been a growing interest in learning more about services and programs that are considered "best practices," "promising practices," or "models for practice" as a way to identify what works. Many of the chapters included in this book present the latest information with respect to best practices in service provision to rural older adults. Best practice is a term that has emerged from the private sector and, like *rural*, is a difficult concept to define. There is no single best practice; best practices need to be adapted to fit a particular organization or agency. In general, the best practice philosophy focuses on developing organizational culture, which is directed to the pursuit of excellence. A related term, *benchmarking*, refers to the continual comparison and measurement of an organization's programs, services, or both and involves working with others from the same field who are known for their excellence (McBride, Stubbings, & Legge, 1998). Benchmarking and best practice are similar in that they both promote continuous improvement.

A service or a program that represents the benchmark is the one to which others are compared. The benchmark program or service in a given area must be under continuous review with sustained efforts to improve practice. Services and programs must be properly evaluated for specified outcomes during the review process, and it is during this evaluation when individual best practice models are most relevant. Increasingly, the evaluation of funded services and programs has been redefined to include outcomes as well as program inputs and processes. This has led to a focus on the creation of performance measurements and monitoring systems.

Two conceptualizations pertaining to best practice have been cited in the literature as particularly helpful. One of the objectives of the *Rural Healthy People 2010* Project, funded by the Federal Office of Rural Health Policy, was to present community-based Models for Practice to address 12 rural health priority areas identified via a nationwide survey of rural health leaders (Gamm & Hutchinson, 2004; Gamm, Hutchinson, Bellamy, & Dabney, 2002). Models for Practice combine elements of best practices and model programs. These elements include innovation, measurement and assessment, and reproducibility across rural settings (Gamm, Hutchinson, Dabney, & Dorsey, 2003). In the late 1990s, the National Rural Health Alliance (NRHA) of Australia singled out three critical drivers of best practice: (1) benchmarking, (2) client focus, and (3) staff empowerment. The NRHA identified these drivers because of their importance in assisting rural health services in achieving best practice in health care delivery (Hulme, 1998).

Much of the work in this area from both the private sector and other countries can be applied to better understand social and health service delivery in rural America. Taking both the *Rural Healthy People 2010*'s and the NRHA of Australia's conceptualizations into account, there appear to be eight key components of best practice for service delivery:

1. New or novel program or service that meets an identified need.
2. Benchmarking.
3. Programs that blend funding streams to sustain the program or service.
4. New and integrative staffing coalitions formed across agency lines.
5. New coalitions between agencies which have not worked together before.
6. Client or patient focus.
7. Reproducibility.
8. Evidence-based successful outcomes.

Some programs that are considered a best practice may have all of these components while others may only possess some of these components. In this book, many of the chapters present information on programs that are known to be effective for rural service delivery and can be used as models for other rural communities to consider.

MYTHS AND REALITIES OF RURAL AGING

Rural America

Common beliefs about rural America are rooted in stereotypes and myths. Research in this area has identified three general patterns of reasoning that guide our thoughts regarding rural issues. "Rural utopia" associates rural America with beautiful natural areas, farmland, and self-sufficient, hard-working, happy people with a healthy way of life not tainted by stereotypical urban vices. Rural utopia is the term most commonly used in discussions about rural America. "Rural dystopia" associates rural areas with negative stereotypes such as uneducated residents who possess little ambition. Third, "Rural systems" draws a parallel between rural communities and more populated areas with respect to economics, social relationships, and institutions, while still attributing rural areas with unique characteristics such as the presence of small towns and farms. This third pattern of reasoning is considered more realistic than the preceding views, although it is also the least common (Aubrun & Grady, 2003).

In 2001, 242 interviews were conducted with persons residing in rural, urban, and suburban America to examine their view of rural living. The findings suggest that these individuals view rural America as having a distinct identity and culture in the four following ways—economy, values, environment, and atmosphere. First, respondents indicated that they see rural America as being primarily an agricultural economy. Second, respondents believed that rural America centers on family, with strong religious values and sense of self-reliance and sufficiency. Third, the study participants suggested that rural America is characterized by beautiful landscapes populated with animals and family farms. Lastly, the respondents indicated that rural America provides a relaxed way of life and rural residents are friendlier compared to their more urbanized counterparts (W.K. Kellogg Foundation, 2001). In truth, these descriptions of rural America do not apply to all rural communities. Rural America is diverse—and growing more so—with some rural communities exemplifying all of these characteristics, others possessing some of these characteristics, and still others having none of these characteristics.

Older Adults in a Rural Setting

Not only is there a generally poor understanding of rural America, many persons also have an inaccurate picture of rural older adults. Some prevailing myths, outlined by Krout (1994), include stereotypes that rural elders:

- Live on farms and are a homogenous group;
- Are in better physical and mental health due to hard work, good food, healthy rural lifestyles, and "living in the country;"
- Are more active;
- Are better able to make ends meet and to take care of themselves;
- Live in adequate housing (i.e., there are no homeless);
- Are surrounded by large and supportive kin networks who are always willing and able to help;
- Have less need for health and social services; and,
- Can get everything they need in the local country store.

Research indicates that the reality is far different. In fact, rural elders can be seen as facing a "double jeopardy" because they face the challenge of being both old and living in a rural place (Krout, 1986). Double jeopardy refers to the dual challenges of being older and residing in a remote area with limited resources and services. The reality is that rural elders:

- Do not live on farms (with some exceptions);
- Are very diverse;
- Have fewer recreation and leisure opportunities available;
- Have lower incomes than their urban counterparts;
- Have lower Social Security payments, smaller savings, less widespread pension coverage, fewer opportunities for part-time work, and infrequent enrollment in Supplemental Security Income;
- Are more likely to own their own home, but these homes are more likely to be older and have substandard features;
- Lack transportation alternatives and are much more likely to rely on private vehicles;
- Have access to a smaller number and more narrow range of home- and community-based services, especially services for the severely impaired;
- Have no more—probably less—contact with adult children because they live farther apart, which can lead to problems for long-distance caregiving;
- Have diets that are too high in fat and lacking in important nutrients, as well as limited food choices;
- Are found to be no more or less satisfied with their circumstances than urban elders;
- Are less healthy than metropolitan residents and more likely to rate their health as poor;
- Have to travel farther for every day goods and services; and,
- Have higher rates of a number of chronic diseases (non-farm) and more acute conditions (farm).

Although rural areas and their residents vary across the United States, a brief aggregated demographic description of rural older adults is a useful place to start when trying to understand the realities of rural aging. Persons age 65 years or older constitute 12.4% of the total United States population. Nonmetropolitan areas have a higher proportion of persons age 65 years or older compared to metropolitan areas, 14.6% compared to 11.9% (U.S. Department of Agriculture, 2005b). The proportion of older adults in nonmetropolitan and metropolitan areas is more similar when examining persons age 85 years or older (1.8% vs. 1.4%, respectively) (Golant, 2004). While older adults in rural areas make up a larger percentage of the total population than older adults in urban areas, in actual counts there are more older adults in urban areas. In general, as size of place and proximity to urban areas increases, the concentration of older adults decreases. In 2001, the nonmetropolitan median age was 38 and the metropolitan age was 34 (Rogers, 2002). The reason for the greater concentration of older adults in rural areas is mostly a result of (1) aging-in-place, which refers to living where one has lived for many years, (2) younger persons seeking jobs in more urban areas and leaving the older adults behind, and (3) in-migration of older adults in search of a retirement destination (Rogers, 1999).

Women age 65 years or older make up similar proportions of the older population in both nonmetropolitan and metropolitan areas (55.8% vs. 57.8%). Close to 31% of persons age 65 years or older are widowed in both nonmetropolitan and metropolitan areas. With respect to race and ethnicity in nonmetropolitan areas among those age 65 years or older, 92.4% are White, 6.2% are African American, 2.6% are Hispanic, and less than 1% are American Indian, Alaska Native, or Asian. Although rural America is becoming more diverse, urban America currently has greater racial and ethnic diversity (see Table 1.2).

Nonmetropolitan poverty rates are the lowest they have been since 1980. Over the past five years, nonmetropolitan poverty rates have been at 14.2% or lower (U.S. Department of Agriculture, 2005c). However, socioeconomic indicators such as educational attainment, poverty rates, and annual household incomes of older adults residing in rural areas have consistently demonstrated lower socioeconomic status compared to their urban peers (Adams & Duncan, 1992; Iceland, 2003). Research has found that poverty rates increase as rural areas become more remote (Miller, Crandall, & Weber, 2002). Further, persistent poverty is predominantly a rural problem (Mosley & Miller, 2004; Rowles & Johansson, 1993). Of the 382 counties with poverty rates of 20% or greater every decade since 1959, 95% are rural (Miller, Crandall, & Weber, 2002).

TABLE 1.2 Percentage of Persons Age 65 Years or Older by Race/Ethnicity and Residence: Current Population Survey, 2004

Ethnicity	Nonmetropolitan	Metropolitan
White	92.4	86.0
African American	6.2	9.7
Hispanic	2.6	7.0
American Indian/Alaska Native	0.6	4.1
Asian	0.8	0.03

U.S. Department of Agriculture. Economic Research Service. (2005b). *Briefing room. Rural population and migration: Rural elderly.* Washington, DC: Government Printing Office.

CONCLUSIONS

Service delivery to specific older adult populations, especially those who experience access difficulties, has always been an important focus of gerontology. The services discussed in this book are those that, taken together, are integral to aging well in any environment. They form a substantial compilation of services intended to meet the needs of older adults. Many of these services facilitate living at home as independently as possible but run the gamut of assisting with self-care to more traditional institutional-based health care. Rural older adults are often susceptible to experiencing barriers to services for a number of reasons. Rural areas are typically described as having a poorly developed and fragile economic infrastructure, which is associated with fewer services and service providers (Schur & Franco, 1999). In addition to infrastructure, there are substantial physical barriers to receiving services in rural areas (Auchincloss & Hadden, 2002), such as limited transportation, difficult terrain, and long distances to services (Braden & Beauregard, 1994; Bull, Krout, Rathbone-McCuan, & Shreffler, 2001; Goins, Williams, Carter, Spencer, & Solovieva, 2005; Schur & Franco, 1999). There are few economies of scale, and thus a single provider can often dictate cost and quality of services (Rogers, 1999). Lastly, some studies have suggested that a pervasive culture unique to rural America, characterized by a sense of independence and a suspicion of change from the outside, may affect propensity to use services (Bull et al., 2001; Goins et al., 2005; Schoenberg & Coward, 1998; Wilkinson, 1991).

Rural older adults are in need of accessible health and social services, yet characteristics of the rural environment have often impeded the success of programs in rural areas. The rural environment is not a problem per se, but it is a context from which it is possible to better understand service access disparities. Programs designed for urban areas typically do not translate well into rural areas, and resources for developing and providing services are not as plentiful in rural areas as they are in urban. Rural communities can work to overcome service barriers by being creative and resourceful when seeking funding for the development of new programs. It is important to encourage innovation to increase the effectiveness and efficiency of services in rural areas and to implement supplemental services that rely on the development of local resources. Rural communities may benefit from viewing persons traditionally not perceived as service providers to better address the needs of their older adults. For instance, postal employees, newspaper carriers, or trash collectors may be able to work with local programs and agencies to identify in-need or at-risk older adults. Current funding resources should also be examined to develop the most cost-effective approach to service provision.

Looking to the future, it will be critical to identify the strengths of the rural environment as a way to help facilitate change. It is not enough to look at the older adult without also considering the social, political, and economic system that shapes his or her behaviors and access to resources. A feeling of communality is present in rural areas and this sociocultural identity is strengthened by a sense of membership and shared cultural values (Israel, Schulz, Parker, & Becker, 1998). Thus, more and more programs are working towards providing older rural adults with home- and community-based services that are sensitive to their particular circumstances. The home- and community-based approach addresses concerns at the local level and builds on strengths, resources, and relationships within the community. Although there is a tendency to focus on the deficits of rural communities, it is crucial for rural communities to take inventory of their own strengths and unique assets when designing or redesigning services. Rural settings, just like urban settings, present both opportunities and challenges; these factors interact with those of the individual and family to determine the well-being of older adults. The capacity to provide a variety of needed services, the nature of those services, and receptivity on the part of rural residents must all be seen within the context of the environment.

REFERENCES

Adams, T. K., & Duncan, G. J. (1992). Long-term poverty in rural areas. In C. M. Duncan (Ed.), *Rural poverty in America* (pp. 63–93). New York: Auburn House.

Atchley, R., & Byerts, T. (Eds.). (1975). *Rural environments and aging.* Washington, DC: Gerontological Society of America.

Auchincloss, A. H., & Hadden, W. (2002). The health effects of rural-urban residence and concentrated poverty. *Journal of Rural Health, 18*, 319–336.

Aubrun, A., & Grady, J. (2003). *The Agrarian myth revisited: Findings from cognitive elicitations.* Providence, RI: Cultural Logic, LLC.

Braden, J., & Beauregard, K. (1994). *Health Status and Access to Care of Rural and Urban Populations. National Medical Expenditure Survey Research Findings 18.* Rockville, MD: Agency for Health Care Policy and Research, U.S. Department of Health and Human Services. AHCPR publication 94-0031.

Bull, C. N. (Ed.). (1993). *Aging in rural America.* Newbury Park, CA: Sage.

Bull, C. N., Krout, J. A., Rathbone-McCuan, E., & Shreffler, M. J. (2001). Access and issues of equity in remote/rural areas. *Journal of Rural Health, 17*, 356–359.

Coward, R. T., Bull, C. N., Kukulka, G., & Galliher, J. M. (Eds.). (1994). *Health services for rural elders.* New York: Springer Publishing.

Coward, R. T., & Krout, J. A. (Eds.). (1998). *Aging in rural settings: Life circumstances and distinctive features.* New York: Springer Publishing.

Coward, R. T., & Lee, G. R. (Eds.). (1985). *The elderly in rural society: Every fourth elder.* New York: Springer Publishing.

Gamm, L., & Hutchinson, L. (2004). *Rural Healthy People 2010:* Evolving interactive practice. *American Journal of Public Health, 94,* 1711–1712.

Gamm, L. D., Hutchison, L. L., Bellamy, G., Dabney, B. J., & Dorsey, A. M. (Eds.). (2003). *Rural Healthy People 2010: Volume 1.* College Station, TX: Texas A&M University System Health Science Center, School of Rural Public Health, Southwest Rural Health Research Center.

Gesler, W. M., Rabiner, D. J., & DeFriese, G. H. (Eds.). (1998). *Rural health and aging research: Theory, methods, and practical applications.* Amityville, NY: Baywood.

Goins, R. T., Williams, K. A., Carter, M. W., Spencer, S. M., & Solovieva, T. (2005). Perceived barriers to health care access among rural older adults: A qualitative study. *Journal of Rural Health, 21,* 206–213.

Golant, S. M. (2004). The urban-rural distinction in gerontology: An update of research. In H. W. Wahl, R. Scheidt, & P. Windley (Eds.). *Annual review of gerontology and geriatrics: Issue on aging in context: Socio-physical environments* (Vol. 23, pp. 280–312). New York: Springer Publishing.

Hart, L. G., Larson, E. H., & Lishner, D. M. (2005). Rural definitions for health policy and research. *American Journal of Public Health, 95*(7), 1149–1155.

Hulme, A. L. (1998). *Best practice in rural community health services.* Unpublished manuscript. Centre for Development and Innovation in Health, Victoria, Australia.

Iceland, J. (2003). *Poverty in America.* Berkeley, CA: University of California.

Israel, B. A., Schulz, A. J., Parker, E. A., & Becker, A. B. (1998). Review of community-based research: Assessing partnership approaches to improve public health. *Annual Review of Public Health, 19,* 173–202.

Isserman, A. M. (2005). In the national interest: Defining rural and urban correctly in research and public policy. *International Regional Science Review, 28,* 465–499.

Kazdin, A. E. (2003). *Research design in clinical psychology* (4th ed.). Boston: Allyn & Bacon.

Kim, P. K., & Wilson, C. (Eds.). (1981). *Toward mental health of the rural elderly.* Washington, DC: University Press of America.

Krout, J. A. (1986). *The aged in rural America.* Westport, CT: Greenwood.

Krout, J. A. (Ed.). (1994). *Providing community-based services to the rural elderly.* Thousand Oaks, CA: Sage.

McBride, T., Stubbings, K., & Legge, D. (1998). *Quality improvement in municipal public health practice.* Draft copy. Centre for Development and Innovation in Health, Victoria, Australia.

Miller, K. K., Crandall, M., & Weber, B. A. (2002). *Persistent poverty and place: How do persistent poverty and poverty demographics vary across the rural urban continuum?* Paper presented at Measuring Rural Diversity, a conference sponsored by the U.S. Department of Agriculture, Economic Research Service, the Southern Rural Development Center, and the Farm Foundation, Washington, DC: Nov. 21–22.

Mosley, J. M., & Miller, K. K. (2004, March). *What the research says about . . . spatial variations in factors affecting poverty.* Rural Poverty Research Center (Research Brief 2004-1).

Office of Management and Budget. (2000a). Standards for defining metropolitan and micropolitan statistical areas. *Federal Register, 65*(249), 82228–82238.

Office of Management and Budget. (2000b). *Final report and recommendations from the Metropolitan Area Standards Review Committee to the Office of Management and Budget concerning changes to the standards for defining metropolitan areas.* Retrieved November 10, 2005, from http://www.whitehouse.gov/omb/inforeg/metro2000.pdf

Peterson, S., & Maiden, R. (1993). *The public lives of rural older Americans.* Washington, DC: University Press of America.

Rogers, C. C. (1999). *Changes in older populations and implications for rural areas.* Washington, DC: U.S. Department of Agriculture. Economic Research Service. Rural Development and Research Report No. 90.

Rogers, C. C. (2002). The older population in 21st century rural America. *Rural America, 17*(3), 2–10.

Rowles, G. D., & Johansson, H. K. (1993). Persistent elderly poverty in rural Appalachia. *Journal of Applied Gerontology, 12,* 349–367.

Rural Policy Research Institute. (n.d.). *Defining rural: Definitions of rural areas in the U.S.* Retrieved November 10, 2005, from http://www.rupri.org/resources/context/rural.html

Schur, C. L., & Franco, S. J. (1999). Access to health care. In T. C. Ricketts, (Ed.) *Rural health in the United States* (pp. 25–37). New York: Oxford University Press.

Schoenberg, N. E., & Coward, R. T. (1998). Residential differences in attitudes about barriers to using community-based services among older adults. *Journal of Rural Health, 14,* 295–304.

Shenk, D. (1998). *Someone to lend a helping hand: Women growing old in rural America.* Amsterdam, Netherlands: Gordon & Breach.

U.S. Census Bureau. (1995). *Urban and rural definitions.* Retrieved November 14, 2005, from http://www.census.gov/population/censusdata/urdef.txt

U.S. Department of Agriculture. Economic Research Service. (2003a). *Measuring rurality: New definitions in 2003.* Retrieved November 9, 2005, from http://www.ers.usda.gov/Briefing/Rurality/NewDefinitions/

U.S. Department of Agriculture. Economic Research Service. (2003b). *Measuring rurality: Commuting zones and labor market areas.* Retrieved November 10, 2005, from http://www.ers.usda.gov/briefing/rurality/lmacz/

U.S. Department of Agriculture Economic Research Service. (2005a). *Measuring rurality: Rural-urban commuting area codes.* Retrieved November 10, 2005, from http://www.ers.usda.gov/briefing/Rurality/RuralUrbanCommutingAreas/

U.S. Department of Agriculture. Economic Research Service. (2005b). Briefing room. *Rural population and migration: Rural elderly.* Washington, DC: U.S. Government Printing Office.

U.S. Department of Agriculture. Economic Research Service. (2005c). *Rural America at a glance, 2005.* Washington, DC: U.S. Government Printing Office.

W. K. Kellogg Foundation. (2001). *Perceptions of rural America.* http://www. wkkf.org/pubs/FoodRur/pub2973.pdf

Wilkinson, K. P. (1991). The rural-urban variable in community research. In *The community in rural America* (pp. 41–66). New York: Greenwood.

Youmans, E. G. (1967). *Older rural Americans: A sociological perspective.* Lexington, KY: University of Kentucky.

CHAPTER TWO

Service Delivery to Rural Elders

Barriers and Challenges

John A. Krout and C. Neil Bull

Social scientists interested in analyzing rural communities and populations have consistently reported a rural disadvantage when it comes to the availability, accessibility, and adequacy of health and social services (Gamm, Hutchison, Dabney, & Dorsey, 2003; Glasgow, Morton, & Johnson, 2004). This disadvantage appears to affect all age groups, with older populations being particularly impacted because of a lifetime of service disadvantage and due to an increased need for such services (Ricketts, Johnson-Webb, & Randolph, 1999). The nature, causes, and impacts of this service disadvantage are many and complex. One major underlying factor is that, with some exceptions, many rural areas have experienced population losses since World War II (National Advisory Committee on Rural Health and Human Services, 2004; Ricketts, Johnson-Webb, & Randolph, 1999). Declines in access to health and economic services, corporate centralization in health care, changes in health care delivery and policy (managed care), and flat federal funding for many home- and community-based services have all constricted the availability of services to elders in rural areas. Twentieth-century transportation changes have increasingly left rural America behind. For economically and socially advantaged elders, these things are not quite so problematic. For disadvantaged elders, they can significantly impact quality of life (Krout, 1986, 1998).

Unfortunately, gerontological researchers have not given much priority to understanding rural aging issues or the impact of residential environments on older persons in general and have shown only a modest amount of interest in examining the causes and consequences of the service deficits faced by rural older persons. Few national studies have been conducted on this topic and much of the information related to it is not readily available to researchers and policy makers as it is contained in agency reports, not in published journals. Nonetheless, enough research has been done to allow us to piece together a fairly consistent picture of the problems rural elders face in accessing appropriate and effective health and social services. This chapter provides an overview of what is known about service needs of rural elders, gaps in services for rural elders, barriers to service availability, and factors that need to be considered in developing and implementing successful programs for rural elders.

SERVICE NEEDS OF RURAL ELDERS

Researchers have long noted that older adults living in rural areas have significant, unique, and often unmet needs. Rural elders experience deficits in income, housing, transportation, and health (Bull, 1993; Coward, 1979; Coward, Bull, Kukulka, & Galliher, 1994; Krout, 1986, 1994a; New York State Senate, 1980; Schooler, 1975; Youmans, 1967). For example, nearly 30% of substandard housing in nonmetropolitan areas is occupied by older adults, as contrasted with 17% in metropolitan areas (Belden, 1993). Even with the slow rise in rural housing values in some areas, the value of rural property is still much lower and outstanding mortgages still higher for rural areas. This disparity means the family home cannot be expected to produce enough capital for older adults to purchase condominiums, smaller houses, or rent apartments when retirement occurs. Transportation issues have long been identified as particularly problematic in rural areas. In most rural places, the automobile is the only means of transportation (Bull, 1993), and for rural elders who do not drive this means reliance on family, friends, and neighbors. The loss of a driver's license can be particularly devastating to a rural elder. Few if any rural older adult transit programs do more than focus on trips to meal sites, medical facilities, or shopping. No improvement in accessibility as an alternative to the automobile is on the horizon, thus increasing isolation is to be expected (Bull & Bane, 2001). Finally, although the health status of rural elders varies considerably, many researchers report a rural disadvantage compared to urban elders (Coward, McLaughlin, Duncan, & Bull, 1994).

These conditions translate into service needs that are often less likely to be met because of geographic isolation and distance to providers, fewer community resources and infrastructure to support services, and sociocultural factors that disincline rural elders from using available services (Krout, 1994a). Over the years, a considerable body of literature has accumulated that indicates that despite these needs, rural elders are disadvantaged compared to their urban counterparts in terms of the availability and accessibility of home- and community-based services. Further, the service needs of older rural adults have been obscured by stereotypes about rural places and people that suggest these service needs are no greater or different than those of old people living in other environments.

We would argue that with fewer personal resources, poorer health, older housing, and communities that provide fewer social and health options, rural elders face significant problems of "environmental press" (Lawton & Nahemow, 1973). Environmental press refers to the demands placed on an individual by natural and built environments. Environment refers to the immediate living environment such as the type and adequacy of housing, as well as neighborhood and community characteristics and resources. In regards to rural places, greater distances between services and individuals, poorer quality housing, and fewer transportation options are examples that can be seen as aspects of environmental press. The impact or press of the environment is seen in relation to the physiological, psychological, and social competencies and resources of individuals. As described in the environmental docility hypothesis, individuals who have lower competencies are more likely to experience higher levels of press (Lawton & Nahemow, 1973). Given the overall poorer health and fewer economic resources of rural elders, this population, in general, can be seen as facing higher levels of environmental press. This translates into a greater need for services.

One important factor underlying this environmental press is the economic vulnerability of rural older persons and their communities. With respect to work and retirement, lower incomes among rural versus urban older adults are a pattern that has slowly continued to worsen (Dorfman, 1998). After retirement, the greatest disadvantage is seen among nonfarm elders, older women, and the single elders who are more likely to be dependent on Social Security and need help from Supplemental Security Income. Income from continued labor force participation is low, estimated at around only 20% of the rural older population (Dorfman & Rubenstein, 1994). As a result, poverty rates are higher among nonmetropolitan compared to metropolitan elders—14.2% versus 10.8% in 1995, and 50% were considered low income in nonmetropolitan areas versus 38% of metropolitan dwellers (Coburn & Bolda, 1999). The major reason for this income disadvantage is the lifelong employment trajectory followed by many rural people. Aside from major traumatic events such as sudden illness or death of a spouse, longer-term causes of poverty among older adults can be seen as the accumulation of life-course events. In rural areas, the lack of well-paying jobs and the gradual decline in choice of occupation can have serious long-term effects on pensions, Social Security, upkeep of housing, and lifetime savings. Chronic unemployment and underemployment has made the nonfarm population vulnerable to entering old age with much-diminished resources. The lack of the full range of educational opportunities and the dearth of well-paying jobs has led to an increase in school dropouts. Too often, those who do graduate lack marketable skills that are needed in the modern world of computers and telecommunications.

SERVICES FOR RURAL ELDERS

The realities of rural aging translate into a variety of service needs. These needs include, but are not limited to, housing repairs and options, long-term care, nutrition, health and mental health care, income support and job opportunities, transportation options, recreation and leisure, health promotion and disease prevention, education and training opportunities, and programs to support family caregivers such as respite and adult day care (Bull, 1993; Coward, et al., 1994; Krout, 1994a, 1998). One of the most consistent findings of rural gerontology research over the years, however, has been that rural older persons generally have access to a smaller number and narrower range of home- and community-based services and service professionals to meet these needs than urban dwellers. A broad spectrum of services is either unavailable or inadequate including adult day care (especially medical), mental health, home health, transportation, respite care, geriatric assessment, and affordable housing options (Krout, 1998; Schlenker, Powell, & Goodrich, 2002).

Although considerable variation exists between rural communities in the richness and diversity of services for older persons and the rural–urban service gap has diminished for some services in some areas in the last 20 years, a significant number of rural communities are still disadvantaged. National surveys conducted by the lead author in the early 1990s of Area Agencies on Aging (AAA) (Krout, 1991) and senior centers (Krout, 1994b), as well as work by others on in-home services (Nelson, 1994), have documented this disadvantage. Rural areas also suffer from a dearth of key health care practitioners (Coward, et al., 1994) and have a much lower ratio of health care professionals per population than found in urban places.

As a result, the continuum of care in rural communities is very uneven and suffers from service gaps. Often, few alternatives exist for those who cannot live independently but do not require institutionalization (e.g., home- and community-based services or housing options). The one exception to this picture is that of nursing home beds, where rural areas have a distinct per capita advantage over urban ones (Coward, Duncan, & Uttaro, 1996). This advantage may be the result of a system fault, however. That is, without accessible and appropriate community-based service options or willing and able informal care providers, rural elders with long-term care needs who cannot remain at home, lack adequate informal care, or both may find themselves with few choices other than entering a nursing home or relocating to a larger community where services are available. In summary, we argue that the rural service disadvantage includes:

- fewer recreation and leisure opportunities;
- lack of transportation alternatives and much greater reliance on private vehicles;
- access to a smaller number and more narrow range of community-based practitioners and services, especially for the severely impaired;
- lack of housing and long-term care options;
- lack of training for professionals on rural appropriate practice and service delivery; and
- lack of rural program models anchored in evidence-based practice.

BARRIERS TO RURAL SERVICES

A number of factors have been identified as underlying the development and sustainability of services for rural elders. First, even though there has been a national emphasis on rural economic development, there has been little incentive for industries that can produce high wage employment to move into rural areas. In fact, it is much more likely that such industries will continue to develop in the suburban rings of industrial metropolitan areas (McLaughlin & Jensen, 1993). This continued spatial development is likely to perpetuate the life-course cycle of low wages and underemployment, leading to continued cohorts of rural older adults below the poverty line.

Second, geographic isolation is a major barrier to rural service providers (LaSala, Hopper, Rissmeyer, & Shipe, 1997). Access problems, most notably the dearth of transportation options for elders in need of services delivered outside the home, and the challenges for service provision created by distance and low population densities, are often identified as underlying many rural service network problems. Public transportation (bus, train, and taxi) matters are continuing to worsen as less and less service is provided. Exacerbating this strain are the shrinking of small-town services and the concomitant growth of regional service and shopping centers (Bull, 1998). These changes have meant that travel distances, most often measured in time, have grown (Bull, Howard, & Bane, 1991).

Third, rural human service infrastructures are slowly eroding as reductions continue in the number and size of hospitals, pharmacies, schools, and, as previously mentioned, transportation services (Hartley, Bird, & Dempsey, 1999). The lack of private practitioners in the mental health service areas has meant that only public services are available, often consolidated at multipurpose service sites, thus decreasing accessibility due to distance and lack of transportation. In addition, the lack of high-technology equipment and trained personnel to run and service it has made many rural older adults bypass rural hospitals and clinics to go to urban areas for services (Shreffler, Capalbo, Flaherty, & Heggem, 1999). The use of volunteers to assist paid staff has become more difficult as more women, the traditional volunteers, work full-time and the rural youth has continued their out-migration, thus depleting the pool of rural volunteers (Broomhall & Johnson, 1994).

Finally, economies of scale are difficult to obtain in the provision of services in rural areas. Frequently, rural service providers cannot put services out for competitive bidding because they are available through only a single supplier. Therefore, providers must use this sole supplier, who can dictate both quality and price. In addition, as part of the distance problem, the costs of long-distance telephone calls, travel time, and gasoline can overtake lower wage scales (Bull & Bane, 2001).

To summarize, the following factors have been identified as barriers to providing services to rural elders (Krout, 1994a, pp. 16–17):

- general constriction of rural economic viability brought about by national trends in the concentration of capital in large corporations;
- overall stagnant rural population growth with large areas of the rural Midwest experiencing depopulation;

- lack of economies of scale, which increases the cost of rural service delivery;
- lack of individual resources to pay for and community/organizational resources to develop services that reflect these trends;
- lack of attention in the private and public sectors to designing service delivery models and strategies specifically for rural areas and populations;
- lack of training opportunities for rural practitioners;
- lack of professional incentives for practitioners to stay in or relocate to rural communities;
- tendency among policy makers and some professionals to try to scale down urban programs for rural populations;
- lack of attention to and understanding of the often unique circumstances and challenges faced by rural practitioners and a need for different, or additional, skills and knowledge for successful rural practice;
- lack of adequate funding through the Older Americans Act and other federal programs;
- lack of integration of existing resources at national and state levels that can help meet rural aging needs;
- regulatory and reimbursement policies that impede the creation, delivery, and survivability of rural community-based services;
- lack of research on rural aging issues necessary to inform policy and practice;
- lack of funding for evaluation of the cost and effectiveness of programs serving rural elders; and
- lack of interpreters or translators for the increasing number of older immigrants as they seek to access services.

PLANNING AND IMPLEMENTING SUCCESSFUL SERVICES

Despite the challenges and barriers, many rural areas have services that do meet a wide variety of needs. The aging services network, in particular, has responded to the challenge despite resource limitations and increasing demands on its personnel (Krout, 1994a). One way to plan and evaluate services for rural elders is to gauge how well a particular service, or perhaps more appropriately, a bundle of related services address the following: availability, accessibility, affordability, awareness, appropriateness, and adequacy (Krout, 1994a). Examining these terms in more detail illustrates the complexity of rural service provision.

Availability relates to:

- number and diversity of formal services and providers;
- qualified human and social service professionals;
- basic and high tech equipment; and
- general lack of human services infrastructure.

Accessibility relates to:

- adequate, appropriate and affordable transportation systems;
- population density—geographic isolation;
- cultural and social isolation, especially of the vulnerable;
- terrain and weather; and
- political isolation and lack of policy input.

Affordability relates to:

- economic resources to support services (economic development), pay for match;
- economies of scale;
- poverty and lack of income to access services, cost share; and
- challenges to rural economies in a multi-national economy.

Awareness relates to:

- levels of service awareness and knowledge;
- information dissemination and service referral; and
- levels of literacy and educational opportunities.

Appropriateness refers to:

- fit of service models and approaches with values and expectations of rural people and communities, levels of service awareness and knowledge;
- services that address underlying needs; and
- recognition of rural reliance on self-remedies.

Adequacy refers to:

- skill of rural professionals;
- evidence that services are effective and address needs successfully;
- data that support evidence-based practice; and
- lack of training programs and technical assistance.

When planning and delivering rural services, it is useful to consider the distinctive rural features of the population to be served, the social and physical environment where the population lives, and provision of services to that population (Coward, DeWeaver, Schmidt, & Jackson, 1983). Distinctive features of rural client populations include demographics; attitudes, beliefs, and values; educational attainment; economic patterns; and health and mental health issues. Distinctive features of rural environment include topography and terrain, population distribution, cultural enclaves, community organization and services, and housing. Distinctive features of the provision of rural services include educational preparation and training of providers, knowledge and skills of providers, attributes and values of providers, and task environment. We have previously noted some of these, and in a number of cases, the distinctive "ruralness" of the features, create real challenges for service providers and planners.

Successful programs need to be tailored to the specific circumstances of the community, population, and service milieu. Certainly, general program models can find success in a variety of rural settings but need to be adjusted to individual communities in order to be effective. The three distinctive features noted above serve as a good starting point when deciding how a program needs to be modified to be successful. Successful programs also take advantage of and support community, social, cultural, and organizational systems, especially indigenous helping networks such as church, family, and neighboring. It is essential to not look at rural communities as only presenting obstacles but to look at them as also providing resources and solutions. Programs can and should be changed to fit the community, because doing otherwise is unlikely to work. Flexibility, coordination of resources, innovation, and a good dose of common sense are also generally required (Krout, 1994a, 2003).

PROGRAMS FOR RURAL ELDERS

Over a decade ago, the author surveyed several hundred rural AAA to learn about their operation, the needs of rural elders in their planning and service areas, and the services they supported to meet those needs (Krout, 1989, 1994b). Out of this research came a profile of some 80 programs in rural areas across the United States that were seen by AAA staff to be effective and sustainable (Krout, 1990). These programs included:

- caregiver education that involves public health nurses and church parishioners;
- transportation using paid "volunteer" neighbors and family rather than the fixed route, van approach;

- partnerships between schools, hospitals, and nutrition programs to lower food costs;
- multi-county housing coalitions that tap into federal dollars for home repair and modification; and
- partnerships between nursing homes, senior centers, and hospitals to build congregate housing.

Several years ago, a number of these programs were re-surveyed. Many of them were still in operation and had expanded. A few had ceased to function due to a lack of funding or because other programs had developed similar services (Krout, 1994b). Descriptions of several of these programs are found in Appendix A. More recent studies have identified other successful approaches (National Council on the Aging, 2001).

Future Research

There are many unanswered questions about service delivery to rural elders that need to be investigated. To begin with, adequate information is not available, or at least easily accessed, that speaks to the use of community-based services by rural elders and the level of unmet need and demand for these services. Although local AAA have data on the use of programs that they fund, local and state variations in services and data collection make assessing need nationally quite difficult. Information on the cost of service provision to rural elders is particularly lacking despite its relevance for policy and funding decisions at all levels of government. Existing evaluation data on programs to rural elders are scarce, so little is known empirically about the outcomes of rural services or what program approaches work under what conditions. We have little evidence-based practice for rural elders. Likewise, we know very little about the best ways to educate and prepare practitioners for work in rural communities and with rural elders. Far too little research has been conducted on the strategies that are most effective in helping rural communities (including families, business, and private and public agencies) find solutions to rural service needs.

A variety of factors underlie these research gaps. They include a multiplicity of federal and state agencies with responsibility for policy and programs that affect rural elders; the jumble of rural definitions used by researchers and agencies; the lack of a coherent rural policy at the federal level; the lack of recognition of the importance of and need for rural research among federal and foundation funders; and the lack of a strong political advocacy base for rural research (the efforts of a number of professional organizations notwithstanding). It is unlikely the dearth of research on service delivery to rural elders will improve any time soon unless there are changes in these underlying factors.

We suggest a number of steps to increase the amount and quality of research on rural aging services. First, the U.S. Congress should authorize (and fund) the Administration on Aging (AoA) or some other federal agency to develop a white paper to pull together the best and most current data and thinking on the rural aging service needs, best practices, barriers to providing services, and strategies to overcome those barriers. As part of this process, all federal agencies that fund programs for older adults should examine and report the degree to which and how well they believe their programs meet the needs of rural elders. Second, state aging offices should be directed by the AoA to conduct a similar process and develop a similar document that can be used by state policy makers to better direct resources to local rural aging issues. Third, the federal government (through the AoA, Department of Health and Human Services, Office of Rural Health Policy, or a similar agency) should make rural aging services a priority and partner with national foundations and advocacy groups to develop a 10-year plan to improve the quality and quantity of research on rural service delivery to older adults. Fourth, additional resources should be provided to the aging services network for program evaluation and dissemination of rural best practices. Finally, federal and state agencies, as well as foundations and other private entities that fund research on aging, should be encouraged by the federal government and aging advocacy organizations to fund research on rural aging services.

CONCLUSIONS

It is clear that too many rural elders lack access to home- and community-based services and do not have a full range of consumer choice. Much of the problem lies in a lack of insufficient resources and access issues, but the development and implementation of successful and appropriate program responses to the needs of rural elders is constrained by myths that obscure the reality of aging in rural places. A variety of other factors also contributes to this disadvantage and operates as barriers to developing programs. First, there is minimal national interest in rural elders and low priority for rural aging issues. Second, funding for national rural health, housing, and transportation programs is inadequate. Third, there is a lack of rural-focused or sensitive education in gerontology, health, and human service training programs. Fourth, we lack the research on rural aging issues necessary to inform policy and practice. Fifth, too little funding has been available for the evaluation of the cost and effectiveness of programs serving rural elders. Finally, a lack of integration of existing knowledge and resources at national and state levels hinders the optimal benefit of the resources that are available.

Successful program approaches do exist, but little evaluation research has been conducted on their operation, and the training of professionals for rural practice is lacking. Flexibility, innovation, and public and private collaboration have and will remain important ingredients for local responses to local needs. Federal and state agencies can serve rural elders best by providing more recognition of rural needs, more dollars, more flexibility, and more education and training resources. A greater commitment to rural aging, along with innovation and public and private collaboration will be important ingredients to the success of these local responses.

REFERENCES

Belden, J. N. (1993). Housing for America's rural elderly. In C. N. Bull (Ed.), *Aging in rural America* (pp.7l–83). Newbury Park, CA: Sage.

Broomhall, D. E., & Johnson, T. G. (1994). Economic factors that influence educational performance in rural communities. *American Journal of Agriculture Economics, 76,* 567–577.

Bull, C. N. (Ed.). (1993). *Aging in rural America.* Newbury Park, CA: Sage.

Bull, C. N. (1998). Aging in rural communities. *National Forum, 78,* 38–41.

Bull, C. N., & Bane, S.D. (2001). Program development and innovation. *Journal of Applied Gerontology, 20*(2), 184–194.

Bull, C. N., Howard, D. M., & Bane, S. D. (1991). *Challenges and solutions to the provision of programs and services to rural elders.* Kansas City, MO: University of Missouri, National Resource Center for Rural Elderly.

Coburn, A. F., & Bolda, E. J. (1999). The rural elderly and long-term care. In T. C. Ricketts (Ed.), *Rural health in the United States* (pp. 179–189). New York: Oxford University Press.

Coward, R. T. (1979). Planning community services for the rural elderly: Implications from research. *The Gerontologist, 19,* 275–282.

Coward, R. T., Bull, C. N., Kukulka, G., & Galliher, J. M. (Eds.). (1994). *Health services for rural elders.* New York: Springer Publishing.

Coward, R. T., DeWeaver, K. L., Schmidt, F. E., & Jackson, R. W. (1983). Mental health practice in rural environments: A frame of reference. *International Journal of Mental Health, 12*(1–2), 3–24.

Coward, R. T., Duncan, P. R., & Uttaro, R. (1996). The rural nursing home industry: A national perspective. *Journal of Applied Gerontology, 15,* 153–176.

Coward, R. T., McLaughlin, D. K., Duncan, R. P., & Bull, C. N. (1994). An overview of health and aging in rural America. In R. T. Coward, C. N. Bull, G. Kukulka, & J. Galliher (Eds.), *Health services for rural elders* (pp. 1–32). New York: Springer Publishing.

Dorfman, L. T. (1998). Economic status, work, and retirement among the rural elderly. In R. T. Coward & J. A. Krout (Eds.), *Aging in rural settings* (pp.47–66). New York: Springer Publishing.

Dorfmann, L. T., & Rubenstein, L. M. (1994). Paid and unpaid activities and retirement satisfaction among rural elders. *Physical and Occupational Therapy in Geriatrics, 12,* 45–63.

Gamm, L. D., Hutchison, L. L., Bellamy, G., Dabney, B. J., & Dorsey, A. M. (Eds.). (2003). *Rural healthy people 2010: A companion document to Healthy People 2010. Volume 1.* College Station, TX: Texas A&M University System Health Science Center, School of Rural Public Health, Southwest Rural Health Research Center.

Glasgow, N., Morton, L. W., & Johnson, N. (2004). *Critical issues in rural health.* Ames, IA: Blackwell.

Hartley, D., Bird, D., & Dempsey, P. (1999). Rural mental health and substance abuse. In T. Ricketts (Ed.), *Rural health in the United States* (pp. 159–178). New York: Oxford University Press.

Krout, J. A. (1986). *The aged in rural America.* Westport, CT: Greenwood.

Krout, J. A. (1989). Area Agencies on Aging: Service planning and provision for the rural elderly. *Final Report to the Retirement Research Foundation.* Fredonia, NY: Author.

Krout, J. A. (1990). *Meeting the needs of the rural elderly: Eighty program profiles.* National Resource Center for Rural Elderly, Kansas City, MO: University of Missouri at Kansas City.

Krout, J. A. (1991). Rural Area Agencies on Aging: An overview of activities and policy issues. *Journal of Aging Studies, 5,* 409–424.

Krout, J. A. (Ed.). (1994a). *Providing community-based services to the rural elderly.* Thousand Oaks, CA: Sage.

Krout, J. A. (1994b). Community size differences in senior center programs and participation: A longitudinal analysis. *Research on Aging, 16,* 440–462.

Krout, J. A. (1998). Services and service delivery in rural environments. In R. T. Coward & J. A. Krout (Eds.), *Aging in rural settings: Life circumstances & distinctive features* (pp. 247–266). New York: Springer Publishing.

Krout, J. A. (2003). Rural elders: Meeting their needs. In R. Ham, R. T. Goins, & D. K. Brown (Eds.), *Best practices in service delivery to the rural elderly* (pp. 43–54). Morgantown, WV: West Virginia University Center on Aging.

LaSala, K. B., Hopper, S. K., Rissmeyer, D. J., & Shipe, D. P. S. (1997). Rural health care and interdisciplinary education. *Nursing and Health Care Perspectives, 18,* 292–298.

Lawton, M. P., & Nahemow, L. (1973). Ecology and the aging process. In C. Eisdorfer & M. P. Lawton (Eds.), *The psychology of adult development and aging* (pp. 619–674). Washington, DC: American Psychological Association.

McLaughlin, D. K., & Jensen, L. (1993). Poverty among older Americans: The plight of nonmetropolitan elders. *Journals of Gerontology: Social Sciences, 48,* 544–554.

National Advisory Committee on Rural Health and Human Services. (2004). *The 2004 report to the secretary: Rural health and human service issues.* Washington, DC: USDHHS.

National Council on the Aging. (2001). *Together we care: Helping caregivers find support.* Washington, DC: Author.

Nelson, G. M. (1994). In-home services for rural elders. In Coward, R. T., Bull, C. N., Kukulka, G. & Galliher, J. M. (Eds.), *Health services for rural elders* (pp. 65–83). New York: Springer Publishing.

New York State Senate. (1980). *Old age and ruralism: A case of double jeopardy, report on the rural elderly.* Albany, NY: New York State Senate.

Ricketts, T. C., Johnson-Webb, K. D., & Randolph, R. K. (1999). Populations and places in rural America. In T. C. Ricketts (Ed.), *Rural health in the United States* (pp. 7–24). New York: Oxford University.

Schlenker, R. E., Powell, M. C., & Goodrich, G. K. (2002). Rural-urban health care differences before the Balanced Budget Act of 1997. *Journal of Rural Health, 18*, 359–372.

Schooler, K. (1975). A comparison of rural and non-rural elderly on selected variables. In R. Atchley & T. O. Byerts (Eds.), *Rural environments and aging.* Washington, DC: The Gerontological Society of America.

Randall, T. (1993). Rural health care faces reform too: Providers sow seeds for better future. *Journal of the American Medical Association, 270*, 419–421.

Shreffler, M. J., Capalbo, S., Flaherty, R. J., & Heggem, C. (1999). Community decision-making about critical access hospitals: Lessons learned from Montana's medical assistance facility program. *Journal of Rural Health, 15*(2), 182–190.

Youmans, E. G. (1967). Health orientations of older rural and urban men, *Geriatrics, 22*, 139–147.

APPENDIX: RURAL PROGRAMS

This appendix provides information on several of the many rural programs described by Krout (1990). The information was collected by interview in 1989 and updated in 2001.

Health—Mobile Screening

Ulster County Area Agency on Aging, 110 Development Court, Kingston, NY 12401-2959 (845)340-3456.

The county health department, the AAA, and three hospitals worked to get state funding for the purchase of a 28-foot mobile, health-screening recreational vehicle (RV). This vehicle is equipped to provide a variety of health checks (blood pressure, vision, hearing, glaucoma, etc.) in rural communities. The objective is to provide health screenings, identify isolated elders, and increase the visibility of health programs and outreach efforts. The planning and service area is one county of 1,150 square miles with a largest community of 24,000.

In 2001, the program, called Care-A-Van, was still going strong. A Registered Nurse from Kingston Hospital and a Licensed Practitioner Nurse from the AAA office staff the RV. These two drive the van to various locations throughout the county to do health and medical screenings for rural elders. They serve 800 to 900 clients per year and expect to serve even more in the future because of a grant just received to do diabetic screenings. A grant has been received from the state legislature to upgrade the van. Another small grant makes it possible for people to visit an optometrist and get glasses if a screening by the nurses determines this may be necessary, and if the client cannot pay for the appointment, glasses, or both.

Health Promotion and Screening

Health Ministries ICARE, 2408 590th Street, Newell, IA 50568 (712) 288–5826, www.ncn.net/-hmicare.

This program uses local churches in a parish nurse network. Churches donate space for a program staffed by 12 volunteer RNs who regularly provide health and wellness information, education, and referral as well as blood pressure screening, etc. The parish nurses receive special training for the program. The church does not provide the service but works with and legitimizes it. Two manuals on the program are available at cost. This project was originally collaborated between an AAA, local churches, and health and social agencies. It covers nine counties and 4,800 square miles where the largest community is 11,000 people.

By 2001, the program was run by an individual and now has sites in hospitals as well as churches and provides blood pressure screenings, health and wellness information, and health education.

Transportation Volunteers

Director of Volunteer Transportation, Madison, County Office for the Aging, PO Box 250, Route 20, Morrisville, NY 13408-0250 (315) 684–7870.

This program serves persons age 60 years or older and provides transportation for medical appointments, emergency transport, benefit program appointments, hospital visitation, and necessities (shopping). Volunteer drivers are recruited from each township in the Planning and Service Area to provide transportation for older adults in those townships. Requiring a half-time paid coordinator, recruitment of these drivers is seen as the most important part of the program. All drivers carry "no fault" insurance and the AAA carries additional liability insurance. The program has 150 volunteer drivers who often provide social interaction and support beyond transportation. It serves one county of 650 square miles where the largest community has 10,800 people. In 2001, the program was still functioning and busy. Drivers for the program are still all volunteers and are paid for mileage.

CHAPTER THREE

Demographic and Resettlement Impacts on Rural Services

Don E. Bradley and Charles F. Longino, Jr.

The major nationwide migration trend since the industrial age in the United States is the movement from rural to urban locations. Yet urban migrants and their progeny did not forget their rural roots. Even in Thomas Jefferson's time, many urban dwellers, weary of the hassles of city life, longed for the tranquility and aesthetic charms of the countryside. Indeed, the agrarian myth—the belief in the special virtue of agrarian society and life—has played an important part in American history and in American cultural mythology. A generation ago, surveys were still showing that the majority of Americans would prefer to live in small towns or rural areas if suitable jobs were available there (Dillman, 1979). For much of the last century, those with such predilections had to satisfy themselves with weekend outings and vacations to rural recreational areas.

In the 1960 Census, 133,000 interstate retirees indicated a recent move to a nonmetropolitan community; 170,000 more moved from within their states (Frey, 1992; Longino, 1990). By 1960, retirement was becoming institutionalized in the United States, and the rapid economic growth after World War II provided a heightened sense of security in old age. For most people of retirement age, employment opportunities were no longer salient in location decisions. These older migrants were the vanguard of the more general migration turnaround in the 1970s, when young and old alike contributed to the 20th century's first *net* migration increases for nonmetropolitan regions (Fuguitt & Tordella, 1980; Longino, 1982).

The reasons for the rural migration turnaround are not well understood, nor documented in the literature. For many young adults, the "rural renaissance" may have been encouraged by the movement of manufacturing jobs from the North to towns and small cities in Sunbelt locations, where wages were lower and labor unions were fewer. In addition, an unknown number of young persons were part of the back-to-the-land movement of the 1970s, a movement that rejected the rat race of urban life for a simpler, less stressful and more self-sufficient lifestyle available in rural locations.

The net population flow to rural America, however, was short-lived. The flight of manufacturing to third-world locales, where wages were even lower, coupled with stagflation and rising interest rates during the late 1970s, effectively ended the population turnaround. It ended at least insofar as young adults were concerned. About 1.5 million persons age 20 to 29 years left nonmetropolitan counties during the extended recessionary periods of the early 1980s, which again had higher levels of unemployment and poverty than those being experienced in more urban and suburban metropolitan counties (Longino & Smith, 1998).

The slow dance of rural depopulation is well known, as is the brief and dramatic nonmetropolitan migration turnaround one generation ago. What is not well understood, however, is the fascinating dynamic tension in that dance between old age and youth, and how retirement migration is affecting parts of rural America. The discussion to follow begins by posing two key questions. First, are older adults more likely than those of working age to choose a rural destination? Second, how are urban to rural movers different from rural elders aging-in-place? We address these questions empirically using individual-level data from the 2000 U.S. Census. Discussion of results gives specific attention to the implications of retirement migration for rural communities.

Why would a disproportionate number of older adults move to rural areas?

Employment opportunities available in urban areas that pull young adults from rural communities have less influence on the migration of retirees, whose income streams may be independent of residential location. Retirees thus have greater freedom to act on their preferences. Retirees may prefer rural retirement settings for any number of reasons, including a low cost of living. Previous research suggests that at least among the "young old" there is a tendency to move away from areas with high living costs (Kallan, 1993). Along these lines, older homeowners in areas where housing stock has appreciated considerably over the past several decades may choose to sell their homes in order to fund a new life in a cheaper housing market (Steinnes & Hogan, 1992).

On economic grounds, rural living might be attractive to retirees. In addition, migrants may move to escape a range of other problems associated with urban areas such as crime, traffic, and pollution (Haas & Serow, 1997). Moreover, the slower pace of life offered by rural communities and small towns may be quite attractive to some older adults living in urban areas (King, Warnes, & Williams, 2000).

What kinds of older adults are likely to be attracted to rural retirement destinations?

Retired persons are far less likely to migrate than are younger adults (Longino, 1995). Later-life movers are in short, a select group. There is a selectivity process beyond age, however, that draws migrants to particular types of destination. Thus, not only are movers likely to be different from nonmovers, but we also anticipate that urban to rural movers will differ from rural to urban movers.

Among older adults, movers may be positively or negatively selected. In the broadest possible terms, it is important to distinguish those who move because they can from those who move because they must. *Amenity migrants* relocate in order to maximize access to recreational and cultural opportunities and tend to be relatively young, healthy, and prosperous. *Assistance migrants* by contrast are often motivated by negative life circumstances (e.g., low income, declining health, death of a spouse) and often move closer to family members. In response to severe health problems, *disability migrants* may be forced to move into institutional settings usually where adult children are close at hand (Litwak & Longino, 1987; Walters, 2000).

The nature of the ties between movers and a receiving community condition the kinds of individuals attracted to a region (e.g., King, Warnes, & Williams, 2000). As a simple example, golf course communities will attract a disproportionate number of golfers. Those rural areas that offer scenic beauty (e.g., mountains, beaches, lakes, and rivers) and those that are adjacent to urban centers are likely to attract a relatively large number of *amenity migrants*.

Rural areas offering fewer services and attractions will nevertheless be attractive to native sons and daughters who moved away in search of employment. Among other factors, *provincial return migrants* may be pulled to rural areas by residual family and social ties. In addition, retirement income generated in urban areas may be expected to support a comfortable lifestyle in less expensive rural receiving communities. *Provincial return migrants* are motivated by lifestyle considerations and are generally relatively young and healthy, though somewhat less affluent, than other *amenity migrants* (see Longino & Serow, 1992).

But what about older adults moving out of rural areas in favor of more densely populated areas? The rural to urban migration stream is likely to include a disproportionate number of *assistance migrants* and *disability migrants*. When young adults leave rural communities in search of employment and economic opportunity, they leave behind parents and older family members. As a result, senior adults in rural areas may have no one to care for them, resulting in pressure to move closer to younger family members (Van der Geest, Mul, & Vermeulen, 2004). Given that most of the job expansion in recent decades has occurred in urban areas and that urban areas offer superior health care facilities, a substantial portion of older adults moving from rural to urban areas are likely to fit the profiles of *assistance* and *disability* migrants (see Litwak & Longino 1987; Rowles 1983).

METHOD

Data

Our analysis depends on individual-level data from the 2000 U.S. Census; the five-percent Public Use Microdata Sample (PUMS). For the United States, the PUMS offers a representative sample of housing units and their residents as well as persons living in group quarters. The five-percent PUMS is a stratified subsample drawn from the full census sample; the housing units and individuals randomly selected to receive the long form questionnaire. Via a four-stage process the Census Bureau has assigned each individual record in the PUMS a weight, allowing us to generate estimates of population counts across characteristics of interest.

The five-percent PUMS offers several key advantages over alternative data sources, the most obvious of which are those associated with its size. Given that long-distance mobility is relatively rare among older adults, smaller national samples may offer few cases for analysis, an especially important limitation where interest is directed towards a subset of older movers (e.g., those moving into and out of outlying areas).

In order to protect the confidentiality of respondents, the PUMS offers only limited geographic information. The smallest geographic units defined in the PUMS data are Public Use Microdata Areas (PUMAs), constructed to include no less than 100,000 persons. As such, PUMAs lack unit-character and may be constructed from parts of counties or groups of counties. Though other data products from the 2000 Census offer selected summary tabulations at geographic levels down to the Census Tract, it is not possible to isolate older movers using these Summary File datasets (i.e., SF1, SF2, SF3, SF4).

Measures

In the analysis to follow, individuals age 60 years or older who report having moved across state lines within the past five years are counted as retirement migrants, consistent with existing research (e.g., Longino, 1995). Measuring the rural/urban character of sending and receiving areas is of central importance for our analysis. In the 2000 Census, urban territory is comprised of "core census block groups or blocks that have a population density of at least 1,000 persons per square mile and surrounding census blocks that have an overall density of at least 500 people per square mile" (U.S. Bureau of the Census, 2003).

In order to measure the rural/urban status for places of origin and destination we use data from the Census Bureau's Population and Housing Tables that tabulate the percent of each PUMA's population residing in urban territory, based on SF1 from the Census (see PHC-T-36). By merging the percentage urban onto the PUMS file we are able to link individual records to a PUMA-level measure of rural-urban status. Territory, people, and housing units outside urban zones are classified as rural.

To create a descriptive profile we employ a number of relevant variables, including age, widowhood, college educated, and income from all sources (e.g., earnings, investments, pension, and Social Security). The person in whose name the home is owned or rented and his or her spouse is treated as householder, which is employed here as an indicator of independent living.

There were two two-part items in the 2000 Census on disability. We include a measure of mobility disability indicating that the person is housebound, that is, has difficulty getting out of the house even to go to the grocery store or doctor's office. We also include a general measure of self-care disability, which indicates difficulty with routine tasks such as dressing, bathing, and moving about within the home. These disabling conditions are not fleeting, but must have lasted for six months or longer.

RESULTS

Are older migrants especially likely to be leaving urban areas?

Table 3.1 provides weighted totals across categories of percent rural for the PUMA of origin. From these findings it is apparent that the majority, about 56%, leave relatively urbanized PUMAs, which equates to an estimated 1.17 million persons. As is evident in the second column, the origins of retirement age movers 60 years or older, are similar to those of their working age counterparts 25–59 years. At each level of percent rural, working age and retirement age interstate migrants are equally represented with one exception. Retirement age migrants are somewhat more likely to originate from a highly rural PUMA, 9.62% as compared to 6.97% for working age migrants. This finding may simply reflect a greater tendency for older adults to live in rural areas as compared to younger individuals. So, although migrants of all ages tend to originate in more densely populated areas, older migrants are more likely to come from less densely populated areas. This finding has not been previously noticed in the research literature.

Are older migrants especially likely to settle in rural or outlying areas?

Percentages based on weighted totals are provided in Table 3.2 across categories of percentage rural with respect to the destination PUMA. Findings suggest that retirement age movers are substantially less likely to settle in urban PUMAs, accounting for an estimated 44.6%

TABLE 3.1 PUMA of Origin Percentage Rural: Comparing Working Age and Retirement Age Interstate Migrants

Percentage rural	Percentage of age 60+ movers	Percentage of age 25–59 movers
≤10% Rural	55.82	58.11
>10 to ≤40% Rural	20.18	20.95
>40 to ≤60% Rural	14.38	13.97
>60% Rural	9.62	6.97
Percentage Total	100.00	100.00
Weighted Total	2,096,841	12,837,555

Source: 2000 U.S. Census, 5% PUMS

Figures represent 100% weighted estimates

TABLE 3.2 Destination PUMA Percentage Rural: Comparing Working Age and Retirement Age Movers

Percentage rural	Percentage of age 60+ movers	Percentage of age 25–59 movers
≤10% Rural	44.55	53.96
>10 to ≤40% Rural	27.84	24.24
>40 to ≤60% Rural	16.33	13.42
>60% Rural	11.28	8.38
Percentage total	100.00	100.00
Weighted total	2,096,841	12,837,555

Source: 2000 U.S. Census, 5% PUMS

Figures represent 100% weighted estimates

of interstate migrants age 60 years or older but roughly 54% of their working age counterparts. Moreover, at each subsequently higher level of percent rural, older migrants are overrepresented as compared to those age 25–59 years. These results are consistent with the idea that older migrants prefer less densely populated destinations. We do not know at this point, however, whether those older individuals moving into rural areas are arriving from an urbanized or a relatively rural PUMA.

Do older migrants from urban areas prefer rural retirement settings?

A partial answer to this question is provided by results presented in Table 3.3, which cross-tabulates percent rural for origin PUMA as compared to destination PUMA for both retirement age and working age interstate migrants. Of the estimated 1,170,472 retirement age interstate migrants originating in urbanized PUMAs, an estimated 50% relocated to a different urbanized PUMA as compared to 61% of working age migrants. In fact, across nearly all categories of percent rural with respect to PUMA of origin, older adults are under represented in urban destinations and overrepresented in semi-urban, semi-rural, and rural destinations. One exception is among rural origin movers where working age (16.66%) migrants are slightly more likely to select rural destinations than their counterparts age 60 years or older (15.76%).

Still it is important to point out that highly urban PUMAs attract a substantial portion of older movers, ranging from a third of those originating in rural PUMA's to about half of those originating in urban PUMA's. Moreover, reading along the diagonal from top-left to bottom right, the majority of older movers chose destinations at least as urbanized as the PUMA of origin. To say it differently, only a minority of

TABLE 3.3   Percentage Rural Cross-Tabulated by Destination PUMA and Origin PUMA

| | | | Percentage rural PUMA of origin | | | | | | |
| | Urban | | Semi-urban | | Semi-rural | | Rural | |
Location	Age 60+ migrants	Age 25–59 migrants	Age 60+ migrants	Age 25–59 migrants	Age 60+ migrants	Age 25–59 migrants	Age 60+ migrants	Age 25–59 migrants
Urban (≤10%)	50.38	60.56	40.01	48.83	35.78	42.78	33.31	36.72
Semi-Urban (>10 to ≤40%)	25.97	22.37	29.87	26.57	30.98	27.68	29.70	25.92
Semi-Rural (>40 to ≤60%)	14.23	10.81	17.75	15.37	19.24	17.72	21.23	20.70
Rural (>60%)	9.42	6.25	12.36	9.23	14.00	11.82	15.76	16.66
Percentage total	100.00	99.99	99.99	100.00	100.00	100.00	100.00	100.00
Weighted total	1,170,472	7,459,665	423,159	2,689,225	301,450	1,793,913	201,760	894,752

Source: 2000 U.S. Census, 5% PUMS

Figures represent 100% weighted estimates

interstate migrants of retirement age move to a location more rural than the one they are leaving.

Magazines focusing on retirement lifestyles tend to picture retirees in rural small town settings. We see from the data described here that these images may gloss over important complexity with respect to settlement patterns among later-life interstate migrants. The Jeffersonian ideal may have colored our expectations, but the reality is different. What could contribute to this discrepancy?

Several factors may grant older migrants leaving urban areas for less densely populated destinations a particularly high profile. First, as a function of sheer category size, urban-origin movers to rural and semi-rural areas comprise a substantial portion of all older migrants into those kinds of zones. Of the estimated 236,561 retirement age migrants arriving in rural areas, approximately 47% originated in urban PUMAs. Similarly, about 49% of the 342,501 older migrants arriving in semi-rural PUMAs had previously resided in an urban PUMA. Second, at least some portion of those moving from urban areas to less densely populated zones will be attracted to a limited number of amenity-rich retirement destinations. In this way, the respective migration flows are expected to be highly channelized, perhaps raising the proportion from urban origins in these popular retirement locations (Longino, 1995). Third, urban-to-rural migrants may have a disproportionate impact on receiving communities as compared to other kinds of migrants given a distinctive socio-demographic profile.

Table 3.4 profiles three groups of older adults defined on the basis of mobility status: Nonmovers, urban-to-rural migrants, and rural-to-urban migrants. Compared to rural nonmovers, urban-to-rural migrants are younger, less likely to be widowed, more likely to have a college education, and tend to have higher incomes. Within the urban-to-rural migrant stream we distinguish those returning to their native state as an imperfect operationalization of *provincial return migration*. This proves to be an important distinction, as returning natives compared to non-native urban-to-rural migrants appear more likely to be widowed, less well-educated, and report lower amounts of income. Broadly speaking, these findings are consistent with the kinds of differences we would expect to find between *provincial return migrants* and other kinds of *amenity migrants*.

The rural-to-urban migrant category is partly distinguished by age composition; an estimated 40% are age 75 years or older as compared to 35% of rural nonmovers and 25% of urban-to-rural migrants. In addition, rural-to-urban migrants are more likely than nonmovers and urban-to-rural migrants to report a mobility or self-care disability. Rural-to-urban movers were also more likely to be widowed. It is important to

TABLE 3.4 Selected Characteristics Across Groups of Elders Defined by Mobility Status

Variable	Rural aging-in-place	Urban to rural in-migrants			Rural to urban out-migrants
		Total	Native	Non-native	
Weighted total	1,017,847	110,212	37,304	72,908	67,207
Age					
60–64	23.8%	35.9%	36.0%	35.8%	22.9%
65–74	41.0%	39.0%	39.7%	38.7%	37.2%
75+	35.2%	25.1%	24.3%	25.5%	40.0%
Physical Disability					
Mobility disability	20.5%	19.8%	21.5%	18.9%	24.7%
Self-care disability	10.4%	11.5%	13.2%	10.7%	14.3%
Widowed	27.9%	21.9%	24.2%	20.8%	33.5%
Completed college	9.4%	20.2%	16.1%	22.4%	21.4%
Per capita income	$20,528	$24,843	$21,529	$26,539	$25,889
Householder	93.7%	80.6%	80.5%	80.7%	73.3%

Source: 2000 U.S. Census, 5% PUMS

Figures represent 100% weighted estimates

note that the findings presented in Table 3.4 suggest that compared to rural nonmovers, rural-to-urban migrants are more than twice as likely to have a college education and on average report substantially higher personal incomes. In short, rural-to-urban migrants are older, report higher rates of disability and widowhood, but do not appear to lack for economic resources.

Unsurprisingly, those who move, regardless of the rural or urban character of their movement, are less likely to be living independently (81% and 73%), when compared with those who are aging-in-place in rural locations (94%). Of those who change environments, however, it is the stream of migrants who are leaving rural communities for metropolitan areas who carry a heavier load of residential dependency. Consistent with expectations, some of these may be moving to be closer to their transplanted adult children living in cities and nearer to more accessible health care and social services. These are not isolated findings but are generally agreed on in the literature, particularly for long-distance movers. The pattern has held for the past three census decades (Longino, 1990).

DISCUSSION

Migration impact is a theme that permeates the literature on rural older adult migration. Is retirement migration a boon or burden to rural host communities? The consensus seems to be that because retired migrants to rural communities are, on the whole, younger, healthier, and relatively more affluent than the overall retiree population; their presence benefits host communities (Longino, 2001).

The issue of migration impact is a complicated one. Understanding it requires bringing into play three of the issues already discussed in this chapter: the sociodemographic characteristics of the older migrants, the character and purpose of their move, and the impact that their migration has on the age structure of rural areas. Case studies of Appalachian rural retirement communities by Rowles and Watkins (1993) emphasize the heterogeneity of both retirees and retirement destinations. Thus, the impact of migration depends, in part, on how different the migrants are from the local population.

It is important to keep in mind that older persons are less likely than younger persons to migrate in the first place. Those who do so for enhanced amenities tend to be the relatively affluent, healthy, and youthful among retirees. The economic presumption is that retiree migration represents a transfer of resources and consumption from the area of origin to that of destination. The belief that fuels rural development interests in retirement migration is that these migrants will contribute more to the economic base of rural communities through consumption and payment of taxes than they consume in the form of public services. The relative affluence and stable incomes of migrating retirees are thought to both increase shrinking rural populations and boost employment and incomes.

The literature on this subject provides support for this belief. On the whole, older migrants, whether durable or seasonal, tend not to put an undue burden on local services. There are several factors at work here. First, migrants tend to pay their fair share of state and local taxes because they are likely to own their homes and have better than average incomes for their age category. At the same time, older adults are less likely to make use of the most expensive government service—public education.

Second, older in-migrants command income streams generated outside the region (e.g., Social Security or private pension), so that local consumption transfers funds into local economies. These funds recirculate, creating demand for new goods and services across a range of sectors, for example, construction, real estate, retail, and health care. Moreover, retired migrants do not come as competitors in local labor markets. Rather, they create employment in service industries for younger adults. Further, most *amenity migrants* tend to be covered by some combination of private insurance and Medicare so that the health care demands of older in-migrants often result in the transfer of additional funds into regional economies (Longino & Bradley, 2006; Reeder, 1998; Sastry, 1992; Serow 2003).

The Economic Research Service of the U.S. Department of Agriculture (USDA) and Cornell University cosponsored a study of the impact of retirement migration on rural communities in the 1980s (Reeder & Glasgow, 1990). The findings of the study suggest that although the promotion of retirement migration can be a viable rural economic development option, retirement migration is not necessarily an unmitigated blessing as there may be problems down the road as migrants age-in-place.

Overall, the results suggest that retirement migration does tend to boost populations. The 481 counties designated by the USDA as retirement counties grew faster than the population in metropolitan areas and growth tripled that of other nonmetropolitan counties. Furthermore, it is important to note that this population growth does not come at the expense of further distortions to the age structure because retirement counties also tend to be counties that keep and even attract young adults.

As an additional caveat, although migration encourages job growth, it does not tend to increase per capita income or contribute to economic stability in host communities. The presence and activity of migrants tend to create service sector jobs, and some jobs produced by retirement income, such as health care and transportation, are high wage ones. But many of these jobs created in the service sector require lower skills and bring with them lower average earnings. Reeder (1998), in discussing this study, however, says that median family income is higher in retirement counties because the income of retiree newcomers reduces unemployment and underemployment.

There is a third qualification to the rosy scenario of positive economic impact. As noted, retired migrants do tend to pay their fair share of local taxes, but such migrants also place demands on public services such as roads and public protection services that bring added costs to local governments (Rowles & Watkins, 1993). Of equal importance, older in-migrants may come to represent a powerful force in local politics. Conflict can result where the interests of long-term residents and newcomers are at odds. For example, like other tax payers without children, older in-migrants may be less likely to support increased funding for public schools (e.g., MacMannus, 1997; McHugh, Gober, & Borough, 2002; Reeder, Schneider, & Green, 1993).

Glasgow and Reeder (1990), who studied these issues the most closely, conclude that retiree migration as a tool of rural economic development has both strength and potential, but they worry that a concentration of retirees could dampen efforts to improve local education and highways, possibly offsetting an area's long-term economic prospects. It is not uncommon for writers who examine this issue to speculate that the aging of the population may leave a future residual of heavy health care and service needs.

The problem with this argument is that it assumes that nothing will change in the future except the aging of the population. Observers of the rural scene know that this is very unlikely to be true. In the first place, some ailing migrants, especially if they have lost their spouses, will move to be near to their children, taking away some pressure on health resources in their rural communities. Such counterstream return migration can be observed at the state level, carrying older and sicker retirees northward from popular destination states like Florida.

How this works on the local level, unfortunately, has not yet been studied. It seems likely that many older migrants will prefer to remain in their adopted rural communities, or will be unable to out-migrate for financial or other reasons. In all probability, the demand for social and medical services will gradually increase in rural retirement counties as amenity-motivated migrants continue to age-in-place. However, in many cases the types of services needed, such as transportation assistance and light housekeeping, generate only modest costs.

The short-term impact of retiree migration on service delivery in rural communities is positive. They contribute their money to the tax coffers and provide some work as volunteers in community-based services. Further, they use few age-related services themselves. The long-term impact may be greater. At this point, however, it is very difficult to assess the relative degree of this impact.

When old age is combined with poverty, poor health, and isolation from family members, the impact on services is negative and substantial. The wild card is continued migration. Having demonstrated their resourcefulness in moving to a rural community in the early years of retirement, there is always the possibility that many of these same persons, when faced with health and family support deficits, would adjust by moving again. In the meanwhile, migration to rural areas by retirees will continue.

As a final point, it should be clear that not all rural areas can hope to attract affluent retirees. Rural retirement counties, those that are important destinations of retirement migration, also have greater success in holding on to their young adults and even attracting other young in-migrants. The reason for this connection may be summed up in one word: adjacency. These rural counties tend to be adjacent to metropolitan counties (Longino, 1995). Proximity to a city can be supportive of lifestyles that were developed and nurtured in cities before the move, while the slower pace and smaller scale of small town life substantially reduces the negative side of city living. This is equally true for the young and old.

Long-term out-migration of young adults is characteristic of the more remote rural counties that are overwhelmingly dependent upon agriculture. Some rural counties are fortunate to have scenic beauty, such as mountains, lakes, and rivers, and are relatively close to urban centers. Tourism, as well as retirement migration, into such adjacent counties creates jobs in service industries for young adults. Among these adjacent counties, those with the largest proportions of their populations living in towns or places with populations of less than 2,500, appear to be the fastest growing (Reader & Glasgow, 1990). New residents capture the best of both worlds; the benefits of small-town life and the close proximity to the entertainment, recreation, shopping, and services that a large population base demands.

CONCLUSIONS

No radical shifts in current migration trends are seen on the horizon. High amenity areas attract retirees as a function of the local tourist industry. Few migrants settle in towns that they have never been in before. Most have established a relationship with the community long before retirement through vacationing or visiting local friends, some of whom may be friends who are also retired migrants (King, Warnes, & Williams, 2000).

There are some near-term population trends, however, that may influence the number of persons available to migrate (Longino, 1998). What will happen to rural communities with large retired migrant settlements, for example, when the proportion of older persons in the United States nearly stops growing, at least momentarily, as it will in the coming decade? It is the continued migration of retirees that rejuvenates and enriches the local retired population because those who enter are younger and often have better retirement incomes than previous migrants now aging-in-place.

We are now entering the period when people born during World War II are retiring. Those were times of very low fertility rates, the trough before the baby boom. People born in 1938 are age 68 in 2006. Growth of the retiring population will level off, as will the number of retired migrants. When the young "recruits" to retirement counties level off, the in-place population will appear to age rapidly. How will this phenomenon influence rural communities? Will pessimism about long-term retiree migration impact increase as a result? No one knows for certain. However, when the baby boom begins retiring after 2008, the older population will seem to get younger for the next 18 years. This perception should hold equally in rural or urban locations. The doom-saying about the eventual burden of older migrants aging-in-place will have to wait for the 2030s and later. By then, the increased burden of later-life aging brought by the aging baby boom will be felt everywhere. At that time, the smaller number in rural areas will make its share of this burden also seem small by comparison.

Rather than fading away with the ascendancy of the urban population, its culture and economy, the agrarian myth retains its hold on Americans even today. The fantasy of the rural getaway, the little place in the mountains or by the lake, the cottage or the mobile home with the scenic view, is still powerful for many urban professionals. As a result, rural retirement migration may accelerate as the baby boom generation approaches later middle age and retirement. Certainly the number of retirees will increase as the baby boom retires. Judging from Table 3.3, about half of those who move from highly urbanized locations will tend to move to less crowded places.

There are many popular places to retire that are not well known because they tend to recruit from nearby cities. They may not even show up on lists of interstate migration destinations because most of their new residents are from within state. As the baby boom retires, however, these places will become more highly visible. This rising visibility of attractive retirement destinations will beg the question of a new rural renaissance fed by retirees. It would be safer to guess that most of these locations are simply riding the wave of baby boom retirement, which will begin receding only one decade after its incipient rise.

REFERENCES

Dillman, D. (1979). Residential preferences, quality of life, and the population turnaround. *American Journal of Agricultural Economics, 61*, 960–966.

Frey, W. F. (1992). Metropolitan redistribution of the U.S. elderly: 1960–70, 1970–80, 1980–90. In A. Rogers (Ed.), *Elderly migration and population redistribution* (pp. 123–142). London: Belhaven.

Fuguitt, G. V., & Tordella, S. J. (1980). Elderly net migration: The new trend of nonmetropolitan population change. *Research on Aging, 2*, 191–204.

Glasgow, N., & Reeder, R. J. (1990). Economic and fiscal implications of nonmetropolitan retirement migration. *Journal of Applied Gerontology, 9*, 433–451.

Haas, W. H. III, & Serow, W. J. (1997). Retirement migration decision making: Life course mobility, sequencing of events, social ties and alternatives. *Journal of the Community Development Society, 28*, 116–130.

Kallan, J. E. (1993). A multilevel analysis of elderly migration. *Social Science Quarterly, 74*, 403–416.

King, R., Warnes, A. M., & Williams, A. (2000). *Sunset lives: British retirement migration to the Mediterranean.* New York: Berg.

Litwak, E., & Longino, C. F., Jr. (1987). Migration patterns among the elderly: A developmental perspective. *The Gerontologist, 27*, 266–272.

Longino, C. F., Jr. (1982). Changing aged nonmetropolitan migration patterns, 1955 to 1960 and 1965 to 1970. *Journal of Gerontology, 37*, 228–234.

Longino, C. F., Jr. (1990). Geographic mobility and family caregiving in nonmetropolitan America: Three-decade evidence from the U.S. Census. *Family Relations, 39*, 38–43.

Longino, C. F., Jr. (1995). *Retirement migration in America.* Houston, TX: Vacation.

Longino, C. F., Jr. (1998). Geographic mobility and the baby boom. *Generations, 22*, 60–64.

Longino, C. F., Jr. (2001). Geographical distribution and migration. In R. H. Binstock & L. K. George (Eds.), *Handbook of aging and the social sciences* (5th ed., pp. 103–124). San Diego, CA: Academic.

Longino, C.F., Jr. & Bradley, D. E. (2006). Internal and international migration. In R. H. Binstock & L. K. George (Eds.), *Handbook of aging and the social sciences* (6th ed. pp. 76–93). San Diego, CA: Elsevier.

Longino, C. F., Jr., & Serow, W. J. (1992). Regional differences in the characteristics of elderly return migrants. *Journal of Gerontology: Social Sciences, 47*, S38–S43.

Longino, C. F., Jr., & Smith, M. H. (1998). The impact of elderly migration on rural communities. In R. Coward and J. A. Krout (Eds.), *Aging in rural settings: Life circumstances and distinctive features* (pp. 209–226). New York: Springer Publishing.

MacMannus, S. (1997). Selling school taxes and bond issues to a generationally diverse electorate: Lessons from Florida referenda. *Government Finance Review, April,* 17–22.

McHugh, K., Gober, P., & Borough, D. (2002). The Sun City wars. *Urban Geography, 23,* 627–648.

Reeder, R. J. (1998). *Retiree-attraction policies for rural development.* (Agriculture Information Bulletin No. 741). Washington, DC: U.S. Department of Agriculture.

Reeder, R. J., & Glasgow, N. L. (1990). Nonmetro retirement counties' strengths and weaknesses. *Rural Development Perspectives, 6,* 12–18.

Reeder, R. J., Schneider, M. J., & Green, B. L. (1993). Attracting retirees as a development strategy. In D. L. Barkley (Ed.), *Economic adaptation: Alternatives for nonmetropolitan areas.* Boulder, CO: Westview.

Rowles, G. D. (1983). Between worlds: A relation dilemma for the Appalachian elderly. *International Journal of Aging and Human Development, 17,* 301–314.

Rowles, G. D., & Watkins, J. F. (1993). Elderly migration and development in small communities. *Growth and Change, 24,* 509–538.

Sastry, M. L. (1992). Estimating the economic impacts of elderly migration: An input-output analysis. *Growth and Change, 23,* 54–79.

Serow, W. J. (2003). Economic consequences of retiree concentrations: A review of North American studies. *The Gerontologist, 43,* 897–903.

Steinnes, D. N., & Hogan, T. D. (1992). Take the money and sun: Elderly migration as a consequence of gains in unaffordable housing markets. *Journal of Gerontology: Social Sciences, 47,* S197–S203.

U.S. Census Bureau. (2003). Census 2000, Public Use Microdata Samples (PUMS), United States, Technical Documentation.

Van der Geest, S., Mul, A., & Vermeulen, H. (2004). Linkages between migration and the care of frail older people: Observations from Greece, Ghana, and The Netherlands. *Ageing & Society, 24,* 431–450.

Walters, W. H. (2000). Types and patterns of later-life migration. *Geografiska Annaler, 82B*(3), 129–147.

CHAPTER FOUR

Service Issues Among Rural Racial and Ethnic Minority Elders

R. Turner Goins, Jim Mitchell, and Bei Wu

In the literature to date, rural older adults who identify as part of a racial or ethnic minority group have been largely ignored. Most often discussions of racial and ethnic diversity typically focus on metropolitan areas. A review of the existing research on health and service access among these subgroups suggests that relative to older Whites in rural areas, racial and ethnic minority elders experience a disproportionate amount of disparities. Although rural areas have less racial and ethnic diversity than urban areas, we have seen rural America become more diverse over the past decade (Johnson, 2003). As the racial and ethnic profile of rural areas becomes less homogenous, service providers are faced with the challenge of how to best serve a new clientele.

According to Krout (1986), rural older adults are in double jeopardy with respect to accessing services because they have two characteristics that place them at risk for health and service access disparities—residing in a rural area and being older. Rural older adults who are also members of racial and ethnic minority groups can be said to face *triple* jeopardy, which makes these individuals especially vulnerable to poor health and service barriers. In light of what we know, it is important to improve our understanding of service provision among rural minority elders. This chapter focuses on three racial and ethnic minority populations: African

Americans, American Indians[1] and Alaska Natives, and Hispanics. Geographically, African Americans are concentrated in the Southeast, with American Indians and Hispanics concentrated in the West and Midwest (Randolph, Gaul, & Slifkin, 2002). We chose these three populations because they are the most predominant of all racial and ethnic minority populations in rural America.

AFRICAN AMERICANS

Historically, migration is the demographic dynamic that has most influenced the distribution and characteristics of the United States African-American population. Beginning with the forced migration of Africans to this continent as slaves, slavery continued to be the dominant force in the concentration in the population of persons of African descent throughout the country until emancipation during and after the Civil War. According to Lemann (1992), following sporadic movement of sometimes rather large numbers of emancipated persons of African descent to the West, the Great Migration of African Americans from the rural South to the cities of the North began in the 1890s, accelerated during World War I with significant decline in European immigration, and lasted until the 1970s. This migration was precipitated by Southern pushes—including diminished need for farm labor resulting from agricultural mechanization, Southern urban blight, and an oppressive racial climate—and Northern pulls—including the need for unskilled laborers to fill manufacturing jobs in the rapidly industrializing Northeast and Midwest. Tolnay's (1998) analysis points out that African-American migrants were generally better educated than those who did not migrate but their educational attainment was generally lower than that of the Northern-born African-American population in the destination areas.

Frey (2004) uses Census data to show that this Great Migration began reversing in the late 1970s. Economically vibrant urban areas in Southeastern states and Texas began to attract large numbers of young college-educated and empty nest upper middle-income older African Americans from Northeastern and Midwestern urban locations. De-industrialization and urban decay in Northern locations pushed college-educated African Americans to Southern urban areas that were

---

[1]In 1977 the National Congress of American Indians and the National Tribal Chairmen's Association, the two largest national political organizations representing American Indians and Alaska Natives, issued a joint resolution that, in the absence of a specific tribal designation, the preferred term of reference to the indigenous peoples of North America is American Indian or Alaska Native.

increasingly attractive because of family ties, high-tech development and knowledge-based industries, recreation, and urban and suburban development. This "brain drain" to Southern urban areas will likely affect the socioeconomic composition of the African-American population in Southeastern destination locations, but the demographic profiles and life chances of African-American older people living in largely Southern rural locations will likely change very little. It will take decades for efforts during the 1980s and 1990s to reduce the disparity by race and ethnicity in high school graduation—among a myriad of socioeconomic markers—to result in improved life chances among African-American older people living in Southern rural areas. Frey (2004) shows that this recent return migration of African Americans does not include rural (or urban) areas of the "Deep South," suggesting that the compromised life chances that pushed African Americans north in earlier decades persist today (cf., Kelley-Moore & Ferraro, 2004).

Two over-riding issues of equal importance pertaining to older African Americans living in rural areas persist. First, data to guide policy and targeted intervention are lacking. Second, the mix of home- and community-based services for this population continues to be inadequate. The published research comparing noncondition-specific health outcomes between older African Americans and Whites illustrates the insufficiency of data to guide public policy and intervention. Table 4.1 shows that virtually all studies rely on data sets gathered with support from federal agencies, and outcome measures vary considerably, depending on the interest and agenda of the sponsoring organization.

This comparison illustrates, first, that outcomes used across studies of secondary data vary widely for obvious reasons, making summary conclusions difficult. Second, given the numbers of African Americans in these samples combined with variability in the living situations among older African Americans across regions of the country, across states, and among counties and small geographic areas within states, the claim that these samples represent African-American older adults is questionable. Studies that include numbers that are sufficiently large, such as Lee and colleagues (1997), are limited geographically. Additionally, virtually all of the studies cited employ multivariate predictive modeling in the analysis of variables affecting the health-related outcome of choice. With up to 10 independent variables included and controlled statistically in such models in combination with skewed distributions according to socioeconomic characteristics in the older African-American population, cell sizes can become precariously small, threatening statistical power to detect non-random differences by race.

Add to this mix the issue of rural residence, and the adequacy of data becomes even more problematic. The older African-American rural

TABLE 4.1 Published Studies Comparing Noncondition-Specific Health Outcomes Between Older African Americans and Whites

Author(s)	Data source	Samples[a]	Variables
Mutchler & Burr (1991)	1984 Census survey of income and program participation	8,955 W 848 AA	Race, self-rated health, ADL limitations, mobility index, bed days, hospital days, medical visits
Escarce, Epstein, Colby, & Schwartz (1993)	CMS Part B Medicare annual beneficiary file and health insurance skeleton eligibility write-off file	1,109,954 W 94,086 AA	Race, 32 medical procedures and diagnostic tests
Miller, McFall, & Campbell (1994)	1982–1984 National Long Term Care survey	3,891 W 473 AA	Race and change in subjective health
Ferraro & Farmer (1996)	1971–1975, 1982–1984 & 1987 NHANES I	5,968 W 873 AA	Race, chronic illness, serious illness, restricted activity, subjective health
Lee, Gehlbach, Hosner, Reti, & Baker (1997)	Medicare claims data from 10 states and the District of Columbia	287,885 W 288,008 AA	Race, office visits, hospital treatment phase, 84 medical treatments
Miller, Campbell, Furner, Kaufman, Li, Muramatsu, & Prohaska (1997)	Health interview survey aging supplement, National Long Term Care survey, National Medical Care Expenditure survey	555,513 W 421 AA	Race, doctor visits, hospital visits, hospital days
Ferraro & Kelley-Moore (2001)	NHANES I	5,782 W 814 AA	Race, self-rated health, mortality
Kersting (2001)	Longitudinal study of aging	6,921 W 555 AA	Race, change in self-rated health, mortality

[a]Abbreviations denote Whites (W) and African Americans (AA).

ADL, Activities of Daily Living; CMS, Centers for Medicare and Medicaid Services; NHANES I, National Health and Nutrition Examination Survey I.

population is concentrated regionally in the South and Southeastern portions of the country (Coward, Netzer, & Peek, 1998; Probst, Moore, Glover, & Samuels, 2004). Over 90% of older rural African Americans live in the South, and over three quarters of these live in only seven states (Louisiana, Mississippi, Alabama, Georgia, South Carolina, North Carolina, and Virginia) (Coward et al., 1998). It has been suggested that the regional concentration of the older rural adult African-American population reflects historic patterns perpetuated by the ownership of land. Like many rural regions of the country, the trend towards labor force downsizing and shifting factory and assembly-line production overseas has led to the out-migration of younger adults out of rural areas, leaving economically vulnerable minority older adults behind (Probst et al., 2004). Consequently, representation of the diversity of older African Americans in secondary data sources is limited not only by sample size but also by the lack of disproportionate or weighted sampling schemes to capture the relevance of rural residence in the lives of older African Americans.

Because of the data limitations described previously, research comparing service availability between older African Americans and Whites by residence is relatively scarce. Studies tend to focus upon the effect of either race and ethnicity or residence separately, seldom together (Mueller, Ortega, Parker, Patil, & Askenazi, 1999). In spite of this, however, some conclusions about service availability seem evident. First, because of limited funding and the increased per unit of service expense of delivering Older Americans Act-supported services to rural areas, African-American rural older adults tend to be underserved, from a human capital perspective. This statement refers to recipients as well as those delivering services. At times, penetration of services into rural areas is limited by bureaucratic service delivery regulations. For example, the requirement that home-delivered meals be delivered by volunteers in combination with persistently long lists of people awaiting assistance limits penetration of this particular program beyond the city limits of small and larger municipalities.

The question of human capital and access to services is pertinent to the former occupations of older African-American rural residents. According to Gibbs (1996), 68% of rural African Americans are in jobs classified as high-poverty, resulting in financial deficits that accumulate with age and impact the ability to pay for needed assistance through often economically untenable private providers and the likelihood of having health insurance (Monheit & Vistnes, 2000). Not only does the work history and the resultant benefits of those in need of services limit access among African-American elders, but so does the mix of services available in rural areas. Compared to nonrural older residents, those living in rural locations have a smaller number and less variety of services available to them (Coward & Cutler, 1989; Krout, 1994; Nelson, 1994) and the range of health personnel, including medical specialists, is more restricted in rural compared to nonrural locations (Coward, Duncan, & Netzer, 1993).

Similar to the work on racial and ethnic differences in health services use among older persons, the significance for rural residence for home- and community-based service use emerges when available services are differentiated by type. There are generally fewer home- and community-based services available to older people living in rural areas but disproportionately more nursing home beds than in nonrural areas. Consequently, nursing home use rates per capita, controlling for age, are higher in rural than in urban areas (Shaughnessy, 1994). Some have suggested that the greater availability of hospital and nursing home beds in rural areas depresses the demand for and use of home- and community-based service alternatives (Kenney & Dubay, 1992). These services are allocated differently, however, and the reasons that there are fewer community-based services in rural compared to urban areas likely mirror those contributing to the lack of specialty medical care. Strategies for overcoming barriers to providing the full range of services for rural older residents have been described in other publications (e.g., Krout, 1998).

As stated previously, only a few studies include a number of older rural African Americans sufficient to look at the interaction of race and ethnicity with residence while controlling other variables on the use of home- and community-based services (e.g., Mitchell, Matthews, & Griffin, 1997; Mitchell & Krout, 1998). Studies drawn from the behavioral model generally find the interaction effect of race and ethnicity and residence on the use of home- and community-based services to fall short of statistical significance. Further, when the effect of other predisposing, enabling, and need indicators are controlled, either race and ethnicity significantly affects the use of specialty medical care in the expected direction and residence has no effect (Mitchell et al., 1997) or rural and small-town older African-American residents are more likely than others to use discretionary as opposed to non-discretionary (e.g., medical) services (Mitchell & Krout, 1998).

A growing body of literature also suggests that African-American elders in general, and rural residents in particular, are less likely than Whites to receive specialized medical care (AMA Council on Ethical and Judicial Affairs, 1990; Dressler, 1993; Mitchell et al., 1997), to adhere to long-term preventive prescription drug regimens (Mitchell, Matthews, Hunt, Cobb, & Watson, 2001), and less likely to use more complex health care services (Dunlop, Manheim, Song, & Chang, 2002). All of these combine to impact survival and premature mortality. Clearly, more work, including geographically weighted representative samples across a variety of health and other services, is needed to better understand the implications of rural residence for the health and well being of older adults. This work should include a number of races and ethnicities across a variety of residential locations and consistency across outcome measures sufficient to sort out more conclusively the joint effects of race and ethnicity and residence on the lives of older people.

AMERICAN INDIANS AND ALASKA NATIVES

Enumeration of American Indians and Alaska Natives (AI/ANs) has always been confounded by many factors, including variations in self-identification, isolation, mobility, and rapid change (Sandefur, Rindfuss, & Cohen, 1996). According to the 2000 U.S. Census, there are approximately 2.5 million people who identify solely as AI/AN. Older AI/ANs are a rapidly growing subset of the AI/AN population; approximately 300,000 older adults were identified in the 2000 U.S. Census, a 26% increase over the past decade. Generally, AI/ANs are a younger racial and ethnic group compared to the overall United States, with older adults comprising a relatively smaller proportion of the population. Adults age 65 years or older comprise 11% of the AI/AN population, but 21% of the general population and 23% of the White population (Indian Health Service, 1997). Although AI/AN elders are a relatively small group, they are among the fastest growing groups of minority elders, exceeding the growth rates of older African Americans and Whites between 1980 and 1990.

When discussing this population, it is important to note its heterogeneity. As of December 2003, there were 562 federally recognized tribes, speaking over 200 languages (Bureau of Indian Affairs, 2003). Older AI/ANs live in all 50 states including the District of Columbia. Census data show that the AI/AN elder population is highly concentrated, with approximately half living in three states: Oklahoma, California, and Arizona (Ogunwole, 2002). Older AI/AN adults are the most rural of all non-White elders, with about half living in rural areas and often in small reservation communities (Baldridge, 2001; John, 1999). Long-term residential stability is a striking characteristic of older rural AI/ANs. The vast majority who live on reservations report that they have always lived there. Rural residence among AI/AN elders has also been found to increase with age (John & Baldridge, 1996).

Growing evidence suggests that chronic and degenerative diseases among AI/ANs are increasing and represent substantial health care costs (Indian Health Service, 2001; Kramer, 1997). Based on an examination of the Public Use Microdata Sample from the 1990 U.S. Census, Hayward and

Heron (1999) determined that the time AI/ANs live with a disease or multiple diseases has increased while the time spent with a disease(s) among the majority population has decreased. Consequently, these researchers suggest that longer life for AI/ANs means more years of disability. Although this study found that African Americans experience the greatest disadvantage of shorter life and longer periods of health impairment, AI/ANs' levels of impairment and length of inactive life are the highest among all of the racial and ethnic groups. Although older AI/ANs' comparatively low mortality in old age means more years of life than most other non-White groups, this study estimated that they can expect 50–60% of those years to be spent with disabilities. Unadjusted prevalence estimates suggest that AI/AN elders experience some of the highest physical disability rates of any racial or ethnic group in the United States (Goins, Spencer, Roubideaux, & Manson, 2005; Hayward & Heron, 1999; Waidmann & Liu, 2000). Data from the 1992–1996 Medicare Current Beneficiary Survey, for example, indicated that 30.1% of AI/AN Medicare beneficiaries had at least one activity of daily living limitation compared to 17.0% of Whites (Waidmann & Liu, 2000). The prevalence of disabling chronic diseases presents challenges to the health care system to provide services for persons with long-term care needs. Overall, there has been minimal effort to understand these issues within Indian Country.

Rurally located AI/AN tribes and villages share the difficulties of service provision typically found in rural America but also experience unique delivery issues. AI/AN elders living on reservations and in Alaska Native villages face rural access problems, including a lack of services and a shortage of jobs which provide health and retirement benefits. Distinctive cultural issues, including limited proficiency in English, compound both the problems of poverty and of rural access to care. Beyond language barriers and the need for translators, Western medical providers are often unaware of tribal social and family structure, cultural beliefs about health and illness, traditional Indian medicine, and appropriate and respectful ways of interacting with elders (Baldridge, 2001).

The most basic premise of the public policy goal of equal access includes a commitment to ensure individuals access to publicly financed services regardless of whom they are or where they live. Six major obstacles have been identified that inhibit the development of long-term care in rural areas, including (1) lack of a clear consensus among consumers, care providers, and social policy analysts about what a system would contain and how it should be organized; (2) difficulty of recruiting and retaining professional personnel; (3) problems of integrating a variety of services into a coordinated system; (4) limited models of long-term care that capture the needs and characteristics of rural communities; (5) how to finance the services; and (6) the overall lack of empirical data on the effectiveness of existing programs and organizations that deliver these services (Coward, Netzer, & Peek, 1996). The difficulties associated with providing long-term care in rural areas become even more pronounced when the residents are a racial or ethnic minority group such as AI/ANs. Further, what we know about long-term care specifically for AI/ANs, whether it is best practices or common barriers, is antidotal and has not been systematically studied.

Federally recognized AI/AN tribes have a special political status. The sovereign status of tribal governments, the treaty-making process under which the United States assumed certain responsibilities to tribal governments, and the resulting federal–Indian relationship continue to be powerful influences shaping health care for AI/ANs. One of the most important doctrines of federal Indian law is the trust relationship. Generally speaking, the trust responsibility of the United States is the duty to assist AI/ANs in the protection of property and rights, the underlying purpose being the continued survival of Indian tribes as self-governing entities. Tribes function as permanent political institutions exercising the basic powers of government necessary to fulfill the needs of tribal members. There has been a gradual and sustained movement since 1975 in the direction of increased tribal sovereignty with less emphasis on federal executive direction. This movement has been referred to as self-determination (Kickingbird & Rhoades, 2000).

Indian Health Service (IHS) is a federal agency in the U.S. Department of Health and Human Services that provides free health care to tribally enrolled AI/ANs. The IHS was established in 1955 to raise the health status of AI/ANs who are members or descendants of federally recognized tribes and reside on or near federal reservations and other AI/AN communities. The IHS is a primary responsibility of the federal government as a result of the Transfer Act of 1954 (P.L. 83–568) (Indian Health Service, 1997). IHS provides services to about 1.8 million AI/ANs, principally through the operation of 59 health centers and 33 hospitals. IHS can be reimbursed through the Medicare and Medicaid programs for care rendered to the AI/ANs who are eligible for services (Johnson & Rhoades, 2000). Access to health care in the Indian health system varies with residential location and governmental recognition of tribal status (Brown, Ojeda, Wyn, & Levan, 2000). IHS facilities and resources are targeted specifically in areas where IHS eligibles generally live, including many rural and sparsely populated areas. In addition, IHS is required by law to be only a residual provider of health services (Johnson & Rhoades, 2000). The IHS is not specifically authorized in legislation to provide comprehensive long-term care services, and funds have never been appropriated to the IHS for long-term care. AI/AN elders most often rely on tribally-funded services, Medicaid/State funded services, and Administration on Aging funded services for long-term care or go without. Many tribes have taken on the responsibility of long-term care service provision (Manson, 1989a).

Acting on the recommendation of an informal 1992 Long-Term Care Work Group of IHS, the agency established the Elder Care Initiative in 1996. Currently the Initiative works to advocate within the agency for long-term care and promote in-service training of its health care providers in geriatric health care issues (Baldridge, 2001). In-home or community-based supportive services are usually provided via other sources of funding, including Title III-C, Title VI of the Older Americans Act, and Title XX of the Social Security Act. Furthermore, many federally recognized tribes are choosing self-determination (P.L. 638), giving them full authority over how their IHS allocation will be spent. Consequently, there is no single agency with responsibility for long-term care and no formal coordination among IHS, Bureau for Indian Affairs, and the tribes (Manson & Callaway, 1988). A lack of formal services in rural areas, and the unique status of long-term care provision in Indian Country, creates a precarious situation for rural older AI/ANs.

There are other avenues through which rural AI/ANs can access long-term care services. For example, Medicaid is the principal source of public long-term care financing in the United States. It is the largest public payer of nursing home care and provides increasing amounts of home-based care, usually through a state's use of Medicaid waivers or through the provision of personal care services as an optional Medicaid service. Unlike other Medicaid services, health services provided by either tribal or IHS providers to enrolled tribal members are fully financed by the Federal government (Benson, 2002). At the present time, Medicaid is not only the leading funding source for long-term care for Americans in general, but it also serves as one of the only sources of long-term care for AI/ANs (Dixon, 2002). Health care under Medicaid remains primarily a state responsibility, but between-state home care coverage varies, particularly in definitions of homemaker services. The federal Centers for Medicare and Medicaid Services defines basic rules for Medicaid participation. It can set liberal policies on state waivers for direct funding to tribes, although this flexibility appears to remain unrealized (Benson, 2002). Opportunities do exist for tribes to more fully take advantage of current federal Medicaid and waiver provisions and develop new or improve existing long-term care programs for disabled, rural, tribal members (Dixon, 2002).

A study funded by the Administration on Aging examined issues affecting home- and community-based long-term care service access among AI/ANs. Results indicated that home health care was one of the most frequently needed services among AI/ANs. Further, 88% of the services sometimes, rarely, or never met the need and 36% of services were rarely to never available (Jervis, Jackson, & Manson, 2002). Today, there are only 12 tribally operated nursing homes in the United States (Benson, 2002), which rely predominantly on funding from Medicaid and tribal subsidies. Many tribes would like to have nursing homes but are blocked by state certificate-of-need requirements, Medicaid licensing require-ments, and lack of commercial financing (Dixon, 2001). The lack of al-ternate medical resources, whether private insurance or public programs, may limit rural AI/AN access to specialty medical and long-term care not included as part of IHS benefits. These characteristics make older AI/ANs particularly vulnerable to experiencing disruption in continuity of care. Compared to their rural counterparts, urban AI/AN elders use formal long-term care services at twice the rate. This may be an artifact of availability or that such facilities and services are more profitable in urban areas (Manson, 1989a, 1989b). Tribes have started to express a growing interest in providing home- and community-based long-term care options to keep elders in their homes as long as possible. Some im-portant services funded through Title VI of the Older Americans Act include congregate and home-delivered meals, information and referral, home assistance services, and the relatively new Family Caregiver Support program.

The need for formal long-term care service provision in AI/AN communities has been recognized by certain federal government agen-cies and tribal communities for over 15 years. In 1990, IHS convened a roundtable of experts to discuss the subject (Indian Health Service, 1993). A greater understanding of the barriers to long-term care pro-gram development in Indian Country and disseminating information about promising and best practices will become increasingly impor-tant because in approximately 25 years, the number of AI/ANs age 75 years or older who will need some form of long-term care will at least double (U.S. Census Bureau, 2000). Further, the increased risk for the accompanying expense of treating chronic illness at this age foreshadows a new set of demands on long-term care health systems. AI/ANs suffer more frequent comorbidity of chronic conditions and generally have less access to needed services, which leads to more serious complications. Despite recognizing these circumstances, relatively few inroads have been made with respect to research in this area. In fact, a comprehensive review of 190 population-based health data sets found only 13% contained at least 100 AI/ANs age 65 years or older, and less than 5% of the data sets contained 500 or more (Rhoades, 2006). The lack of relevant, immediately applicable empirical data poses a signifi-cant obstacle to advancement in this area.

HISPANICS

Hispanics are one of the fastest growing populations in the United States. In 2000, 35.2 million Hispanics resided in the United States, which accounted for 12.5% of the total population. The Hispanic population has increased 61% since 1990, compared with 13% growth for the total United States population (U.S. Census Bureau, 2004). Hispanics are the youngest of all racial and ethnic groups. According to the 2000 U.S. Census, Hispanic adults age 65 years and older composed 4.8% of the total Hispanic population, a lower proportion than the 12% of older adults in the total population (U.S. Census Bureau, 2004). Nevertheless, based on the current structure of the Hispanic population, the number and percentage of Hispanic elders will increase dramatically over the next several decades. The majority of the Hispanic population is concentrated in metropolitan areas, especially in the inner cities. Although 6.6% of the Hispanic population reside in rural areas (U.S. Census Bureau, n.d.), Hispanic populations are experiencing significant increase in rural communities (Saenz & Torres, 2003; U.S. Department of Agriculture, 2005). There is some variation of geographic distribution within the Hispanic group. For example, in the southwestern part of this country where the majority of Hispanics are Mexican-American, 20% live in rural areas (Holmes & Holmes, 1995). Subgroups of Hispanic elders and their proportional representations are as follows: Mexican-Americans (49.9%), Cuban-Americans (17.1%), Central and South Americans (11.8%), Puerto Ricans (11.0%), and Other Hispanics (10.1%) (Siegel, 1999). Each of these groups is distinct in terms of their economic status, educational attainment, and immigration history.

Rural Hispanic elders report greater prevalence and incidence of activities of daily living (ADL) limitations, instrumental activities of daily living (IADL) limitations, and cognitive impairment than their non-Hispanic White counterparts (Bryant, Shetterly, Baxter, & Hamman, 2002; Mulgrew et al., 1999). In addition, rural Hispanic elders are significantly more likely to need IADL assistance (Shetterly, Baxter, Morgenstern, Grigsby, & Hamman, 1998). However, studies suggest that rural non-Hispanic White elders are twice as likely as rural Hispanic elders to reside in nursing homes (Baxter, Bryant, Scarbro, & Shetterly, 2001). The majority of rural Hispanic elders with disabilities resides at home and is cared for by their family members. There is also some evidence that family and extended kin play an important role in caring for rural Hispanic elders (Saenz & Torres, 2003).

Previous literature indicates that Hispanic elders and their families have a lower rate of formal service use than the non-Hispanic White population (Delgado & Tennstedt, 1997; Greene & Monahan, 1984; Manton & Hausner, 1987). Studies suggest that both Hispanic elders and their caregivers' characteristics contributed to their low use of formal services. These contributing factors may include low socioeconomic status, large informal support networks, low health insurance coverage, and perceived low level of emotional stress of the caregiver (Angel, Douglas, & Angel, 2003; Ardanda & Knight, 1997; Cox, 1995; John, Roy, & Dietz, 1997; Kosloski, Montgomery, & Karner, 1999; Mui & Burnette, 1994; Wallace, Campbell, & Lew-Ting, 1994; Wallace & Lew-Ting, 1992; Wu, 2000). In addition, factors such as knowledge and awareness of services, language barriers, and cultural preferences are strongly related to formal service use among Hispanic elders (Starrett, Wright, Mindel, & Tran, 1989; Starrett, Todd, & Deleon, 1989).

Over 60% of older Hispanics were born outside the continental United States, and 40% immigrated to the continental United States when they were age 45 years or older (Commonwealth, 1989). Hispanic elders, especially Puerto Rican elders, are characterized by an almost exclusive use of the Spanish language (Sanchez-Ayendez, 1988). Consequently, speaking little or no English is a primary factor in older Hispanics' lack of knowledge about formal service options. Structural barriers of long-term care delivery systems also affect use of home- and community-based long-term care services by Hispanic older adults and their caregivers. Studies have suggested that lack of culturally sensitive services and staff, mistrust of outside services, complication of application forms of services, and lack of insurance coverage are important factors for long-term care service use (Baxter, Bryant, Scarbro, & Shetterly, 2001; Hernandez-Gallegos, Capitman, & Yee, 1993; Yeatts, Crow, & Folts, 1992).

Given the scarcity of data, the pattern of home- and community-based long-term care use among rural Hispanic elders is unclear. Korte (1982), with a small sample of 52 New Mexican Spanish-speaking rural and urban older couples, found that 85% of urban and 96% of rural older parents expected their children to provide care when they were sick. It is likely that Hispanic elders show a lower level of formal service use than their urban counterparts, because rural Hispanic elders rely more on family members to provide care. Using the San Luis Valley Health and Aging Study data found that both rural Hispanic elders and non-Hispanic White elders relied similarly on home-based care (Baxter, Bryant, Scarbro, & Shetterly, 2001). Given the fact that rural Hispanic elders had more ADL and IADL limitations and a lower rate of nursing home admission, the study results suggest that rural Hispanic elders had persistent unmet health care needs.

Despite a high expectation of family support for frail Hispanic elders in American society, several studies concluded that Hispanic families have been unable to meet elders' needs and need greater assistance from formal service agencies (Dietz, 1995; John, Roy, & Dietz, 1997; Wallace, Campbell, & Lew-Ting, 1994). John and colleagues (1997) analyzed the data from the 1988 National Survey of Hispanic Elderly People and found that approximately 19% of Mexican-American females with two or more ADL limitations did not receive any family assistance. However, among those who did not receive help from family members, 61% received some level of assistance from home- and community-based service agencies. In addition, Dietz (1995) found that 57% of those needing care did not receive any assistance from the family with the activities on which data were collected.

As indicated earlier, previous studies have provided some information on community-based long-term care use among the older Hispanic population. However, little is known about service use among the rural Hispanic population in particular, due to a lack of available data to conduct the analysis. There are several large national and regional representative data sets available, including information on formal service use among Hispanics. One example is the 1988 Hispanic Established Populations for Epidemiologic Studies of the Elderly (H-EPESE), which included Mexican-American elders living in the Southwest U.S. Another is the longitudinal study of Asset and Health Dynamics Among the Oldest Old (AHEAD), which oversampled Hispanics in the United States. A 1996 national survey of family caregiving by the National Alliance for Caregiving and AARP also oversampled Hispanic caregivers, yielding a total of 307 Hispanic caregivers. However, given the small percentage of rural Hispanic older respondents in the surveys, it is difficult to conduct meaningful analyses on this subgroup. Few studies have examined formal service use among rural Hispanic older adults (e.g., Baxter, Bryant, Scarbro, & Shetterly, 2001; Korte, 1982). To our knowledge, the San Luis Valley Health and Aging Study is the only large random survey of rural Hispanic elders. The survey examined health and disability, including use of health services and home nursing care, among 798 rural older Hispanics and 614 non-Hispanic Whites in two counties in southern Colorado. Because these studies on rural Hispanic elders' use of formal services were either regional or involved a non-random small sample, it is difficult to generalize study findings. Moreover, the heterogeneity of the Hispanic population makes generalization even more challenging.

Current under use of services coupled with the growing need for services and the declining ability of the Hispanic family to provide adequate long-term care represent serious problems for the well being of Hispanic elders. Too little attention has been paid to rural elders, especially the growing number of rural Hispanic elders. Future research efforts should include over sampling rural Hispanic elders in national surveys. Although there is a growing number of researchers interested in minority aging issues, more are needed with a focus on rural minority aging. Currently, the data available on rural Hispanic older adults is limited to the Southwestern region of the United States. Given the vast geographic variation in terms of service delivery systems and heterogeneity of Hispanic populations, data are needed that will permit an examination of rural Hispanics in other regions as well as nationally. One way to increase the amount of research in this area is to offer special training and funding opportunities. Policies, strategies, and interventions focusing on health promotion among the rural Hispanic population need to be implemented which are informed by research. Several strategies can be applied to better serve this population. First, it is imperative to establish partnerships with Hispanic community organizations to ensure the provision of culturally competent services. Second, recruitment and retention of bilingual and bicultural staff working in agencies is important, especially in areas with a high concentration of Hispanics. Finally, it is important to set service delivery priorities based on the needs of the Hispanic population.

CONCLUSIONS

Some of the health and service issues unique to these three racial and ethnic minority populations have been outlined. Based on the literature reviewed, rural African-American, Hispanic, and AI/AN older adult populations have limited access to necessary formal health services. Barriers to health services for these three populations are both related to their race and ethnicity as well as availability of these services in rural areas. This combination is believed to make them especially vulnerable to experiencing unmet care needs. Rural racial and ethnic minority elders are among the most understudied and underserved of all groups in the United States. For the three populations examined here, the recurring theme is lack of good national data. National data in federal reports provide breakdowns by race and ethnicity and rural and urban residence, although these breakdowns are not provided simultaneously. This is primarily due to a lack of detailed information on these populations. Fortunately, there is growing recognition of the glaring absence of useful national data to allow us to fully understand diversity in rural areas. In 2001, the National Rural Health Association published an Issue Paper calling for improved data collection efforts with rural racial and ethnic minority populations. As stated in this Issue Paper:

> While there are a multitude of data being collected and analyzed nationwide, little pertains to rural minority populations. Thus, the results are not useful in terms of designing programs and initiatives

for these populations. These limitations of data result in barriers that affect programs, services, and efforts focused on health and quality of life issues.

In more recent efforts, the chair of the National Committee on Vital and Health Statistics recommended that the Department of Health and Human Services expand their efforts to obtain sufficient data on racial and ethnic minority populations (Lumpkin, 2003).

Without adequate information, the experiences of rural minority older adults cannot be known. Their difficulties in accessing services cannot be tracked nor can the strengths of rural communities be considered as potential promising practices. Although the effect of racial and ethnic minority status is similar across residence, the combined effects of rural residence, minority status, and older age can result in greater service disadvantage than these characteristics alone. Services developed to improve access and reduce disparities must explore ways they can build on rural strengths (Probst et al., 2004). Improvements in data collection will ultimately inform some of the ways that barriers to services can be reduced or eliminated.

REFERENCES

American Medical Association Council on Ethical and Judicial Affairs. (1990). Black-White disparities in healthcare. *Journal of the American Medical Association, 263*, 2344–2346.

Angel, J. L., Douglas, N., & Angel, R. J. (2003). Gender, widowhood, and long-term care in the older Mexican American population. *Journal of Women & Aging, 15*(2–3), 89–105.

Aranda, M. P., & Knight, B. G. (1997). The influence of ethnicity and culture on the caregiver stress and coping process: A sociocultural review and analysis. *The Gerontologist, 37*, 342–354.

Baldridge, D. (2001). The elder Indian population and long-term care. In M. Dixon & Y. Roubideaux (Eds.), *Promises to keep: Public health policy for American Indians and Alaska Natives in the 21st century* (pp. 137–164). Washington, DC: American Public Health Association.

Baxter, J., Bryant, L. L., Scarbro, S., & Shetterly, S. M. (2001). Patterns of rural Hispanic and non-Hispanic White health care use: The San Luis Valley Health and Aging Study. *Research on Aging, 23*(1), 37–60.

Benson, W. (2002). Long-term care in Indian country today: A snapshot. In B. Finke, Y. Jackson, L. Roebuck, & D. Baldridge (Eds.), *American Indian and Alaska Native roundtable on long-term care: Final report 2002*. Spokane, WA: Kauffman.

Brown, E. R., Ojeda, V. D., Wyn, R., & Levan, R. (2000). *Racial and ethnic disparities in access to health insurance and health care*. Los Angeles, CA:

University of California, Los Angeles Center for Health Policy Research and The Henry J. Kaiser Family Foundation.

Bryant, L. L., Shetterly, S. M., Baxter, J., & Hamman, R. F. (2002). Modifiable risks of incident functional dependence in Hispanic and non-Hispanic White elders: The San Luis Valley Health and Aging Study. *The Gerontologist, 42,* 690–697.

Bureau of Indian Affairs. (2003). Indian entities recognized and eligible to receive services from the United States Bureau of Indian Affairs. *Federal Register, 68,* 68180–68184.

Commonwealth Fund Commission on Elderly People Living Alone. (1989). *Poverty and poor health among elderly Hispanic Americans.* Baltimore: Author.

Coward, R. T., & Cutler, S. J. (1989). Informal and formal health care systems for the rural elderly. *Health Services Research, 23,* 785–806.

Coward, R. T., Duncan, R. P., & Netzer, J. K. (1993). The availability of health care resources for elders living in non-metropolitan persistent low-income counties in the South. *Journal of Applied Gerontology, 12,* 368–387.

Coward, R. T., Netzer, J. K., & Peek, C. W. (1996). Obstacles to creating high-quality long-term care services for rural elders. In G. D. Rowles, J. E. Beaulieu, & W. W. Myers (Eds.), *Long-term care for the rural elderly* (pp. 10–34). New York: Springer Publishing.

Coward, R. T., Netzer, J. K., & Peek, C. W. (1998). Older rural African-Americans. In R. T. Coward & J. A. Krout (Eds.), *Aging in rural settings: Life circumstances and distinctive features* (pp. 167–185). New York: Springer Publishing.

Cox, C. (1995). Meeting the mental health needs of the caregivers: The impact of Alzheimer's disease on Hispanic and African American families. In D. K. Padgett (Ed.), *Handbook on ethnicity, aging, and mental health* (pp. 265–283). Westport, CT: Greenwood.

Delgado, M., & Tennstedt, S. (1997). Making the case for culturally appropriate community services: Puerto Rican elders and their caregivers. *Health and Social Work, 22,* 246–255.

Dietz, T. L. (1995). Patterns of intergenerational assistance within the Mexican American family: Is the family taking care of the older generation's needs? *Journal of Family Issues, 16,* 344–356.

Dixon, M. (2001). Access to care for American Indians and Alaska Natives. In M. Dixon & Y. Roubideaux (Eds.), *Promises to keep: Public health policy for American Indians and Alaska Natives in the 21st century* (pp. 61–87). Washington, DC: American Public Health Association.

Dixon, M. (2002). Opportunities for Medicaid financing of long-term care in American Indian and Alaska Native communities. In B. Finke, Y. Jackson, L. Roebuck, & D. Baldridge (Eds.), *American Indian and Alaska Native roundtable on long-term care: Final report 2002.* Spokane, WA: Kauffman.

Dressler, W. W. (1993). Health in the African American community: Accounting for health inequalities. *Medical Anthropology Quarterly, 7,* 325–345.

Dunlop, D. D., Manheim, L. M., Song, J., & Chang, R. W. (2002). Gender and ethnic/racial disparities in health care utilization among older adults. *Journal of Gerontology: Social Sciences, 57B,* S221–S233.

Escarce, J. J., Epstein, K. R., Colby, D. C., & Schwartz, J. S. (1993). Racial differences in the elderly's use of medical procedures and diagnostic tests. *American Journal of Public Health, 83*, 948–954.

Ferraro, K. F., & Farmer, M. M. (1996). Double jeopardy, aging as leveler, or persistent health inequality? A longitudinal analysis of White and Black Americans. *Journal of Gerontology: Social Sciences, 51B*, S319–S328.

Ferraro, K. F., & Kelley-Moore, J. A. (2001). Self-rated health and mortality among Black and White adults: Examining the dynamic evaluation thesis. *Journal of Gerontology: Social Sciences, 56B*, S195–S205.

Frey, W. H. (2004). The new great migration: Black Americans return to the South, 1965–2000. *The Living Cities Census series.* Washington, DC: The Brookings Institution, Center on Urban and Metropolitan Policy.

Gibbs, R. M. (1996). Trends in occupational status among rural southern blacks. In L. L. Swanson (Ed.), *Minorities in rural areas: Progress and stagnation, 1980–1990* (pp. 28–42). Washington, DC: U.S. Department of Agriculture. (Agricultural Economics Report No. ERSAER731)

Goins, R. T., Spencer, S. M., Roubideaux, Y., & Manson, S. (2005). Differences in functional disability of rural American Indian and White elders with comorbid diabetes. *Research on Aging, 27*, 643–658.

Greene, V. L., & Monahan, D. J. (1984). Comparative utilization of community based long term care services by Hispanic and Anglo elderly in a case management system. *Journal of Gerontology, 39*, 730–735.

Hayward, M. D., & Heron, M. (1999). Racial inequality in active life among adult Americans. *Demography, 36*(1), 77–91.

Hernandez-Gallegos, W., Capitman, J., & Yee, D. (1993). Conceptual understanding of long-term service use by elders of color. In C. M. Barresi & D. E. Stull (Eds.), *Ethnic elderly and long-term care* (pp.204–220). New York: Springer Publishing.

Holmes, E. R., & Holmes, L. D. (1995). *Other cultures, elders years.* Newbury Park, CA: Sage.

Indian Health Service. (1993). *Consensus statement of the roundtable on long-term care for Indian elders.* Rockville, MD: U.S. Government Printing Office.

Indian Health Service. U. S. Department of Health and Human Services. (1997). *Indian health focus: Elders.* Washington, DC: U.S. Government Printing Office.

Indian Health Service. U.S. Department of Health and Human Services. (2001). *Trends in Indian health.* Washington, DC: U.S. Government Printing Office.

Jervis, L. L., Jackson, M. Y., & Manson, S. M. (2002). Need for, availability of, and barriers to the provision of long-term care services for older American Indians. *Journal of Cross-Cultural Gerontology, 17*, 295–311.

John, R. (1999). Aging among American Indians: Income security, health, and social support networks. In T. P. Miles (Ed.), *Full-color aging: Facts, goals, and recommendations for America's diverse elders* (pp. 65–85). Washington, DC: Gerontological Society of America.

John, R., & Baldridge, D. (1996). *The NICOA report: Health and long-term care for American Indian elders. A report by the National Indian Council on Aging to the National Indian Policy Center.* Washington, DC: National Indian Council on Aging.

John, R., Roy, L. C., & Dietz, T. L. (1997). Setting priorities in aging populations: Formal service use among Mexican American female elders. *Journal of Aging and Social Policy, 9*(1), 69–85.

Johnson, K. M. (2003). Unpredictable directions of rural population growth and migration. In D. L. Brown & L. E. Swanson (Eds.), *Challenges for rural America in the twenty-first century* (pp. 19–31). University Park, PA: Pennsylvania State University.

Johnson, E. A., & Rhoades, E. R. (2000). The history and organization of Indian Health Services and systems. In. E. R. Rhoades (Ed.), *American Indian health: Innovations in health care, promotion, and policy* (pp. 74–92). Baltimore: Johns Hopkins University.

Kelley-Moore, J. A., & Ferraro, K. F. (2004). The Black/White disability gap: Persistent inequality in later life? *Journal of Gerontology: Social Sciences, 59B*, S34–S43.

Kenney, G. M., & Dubay, L. C. (1992). Explaining area variation in the use of Medicare home health services. *Medical Care, 30*(1), 43–57.

Kersting, R. C. (2001). Impact of social support, diversity, and poverty on nursing home utilization in a nationally representative sample of older Americans. *Social Work in Health Care, 33*(2), 67–87.

Kickingbird, K., & Rhoades, E. R. (2000). The relation of Indian Nations to the U.S. government. In E. R. Rhoades (Ed.), *American Indian health* (pp. 61–73). Baltimore: John Hopkins University.

Korte, A. O. (1982). Social interaction and morale of Spanish-speaking rural and urban elderly. *Journal of Gerontological Social Work, 4*, 57–66.

Kosloski, K., Montgomery, R. J., & Karner, T. X. (1999). Differences in the perceived need for assistive services by culturally diverse caregivers of persons with dementia. *Journal of Applied Gerontology, 18*, 239–256.

Kramer, B. J., (1997). Chronic disease in American Indian populations. In K. S. Markides & M. R. Miranda (Eds.), *Minorities, aging, and health* (pp. 181–202). Thousand Oaks, CA: Sage.

Krout, J. A. (1986). *The aged in rural America*. Westport, CT: Greenwood.

Krout, J. A. (1994). Community size differences in senior center programs and participation: A longitudinal analysis. *Research on Aging, 16*, 440–462.

Krout, J. A. (1998). Services and service delivery in rural environments. In R. T. Coward & J. A. Krout (Eds.), *Aging in rural settings: Life circumstances & distinctive features* (pp. 247–266). New York: Springer Publishing.

Lee, A. J., Gehlbach, S., Hosmer, D., Reti, M., & Baker, C. S. (1997). Medicare treatment differences for Blacks and Whites. *Medical Care, 35*, 1173–1189.

Lemann, N. (1992). *The promised land: The great black migration and how it changed America*. Philadelphia: McKay.

Lumpkin, J. (2003, March). *Letter to Secretary Thompson on populations-based data for racial and ethnic minorities*. Retrieved November 11, 2005, from www.ncvhs.hhs.gov/030327lt.htm

Manson, S. M. (1989a). Long-term care in American Indian communities: Issues for planning and research. *Gerontologist, 29*, 38–44.

Manson, S. M. (1989b). Provider assumptions about long-term care in American Indian communities. *The Gerontologist, 29*, 355–359.

Manson, S. M., & Callaway, D. (1988). Health and aging among American Indian: Issues and challenges for the biobehavioral sciences. In S. M. Manson, & N. G. Dinges (Eds.), *Behavioral health issues among American Indians and Alaska Natives* (pp. 160–210). Denver, CO: University of Colorado Health Sciences Center.

Manton, K., & Hausner, T. (1987). A multidimensional approach to case mix for home health services. *Health Care Financing Review, 8*(4), 37–52.

Miller, B., Campbell, R. T., Furner, S., Kaufman J. E., Li, M., Muramatsu, N., & Prohaska, T. (1997). Use of medical care by African American and White older persons: Comparative analysis of three national data sets. *Journal of Gerontology: Social Sciences, 52B*, S325–S335.

Miller, B., McFall, S., & Campbell, R. T. (1994). Changes in sources of community long-term care among African American and White frail older adults. *Journal of Gerontology: Social Sciences, 49*(1), S14–S24.

Mitchell, J., & Krout, J. A. (1998). Discretion and service use among older adults: The behavioral model revisited. *The Gerontologist, 38*, 159–168.

Mitchell, J., Mathews, H. F., & Griffin, L.W. (1997). Health and community-based service use: Differences between elderly African Americans and Whites. *Research on Aging, 19*, 199–222.

Mitchell, J., Mathews, H. F., Hunt, L. M., Cobb, K. H., & Watson, R. (2001). Mismanaging prescription medications among rural elders: Effects of socioeconomic status, health status, and medication profile indicators. *The Gerontologist, 41*, 348–356.

Monheit, A. C., & Vistnes, J. P. (2000). Race/ethnicity and health insurance status: 1987 and 1996. *Medical Care Research Review, 57*(Suppl. 1), 11–35.

Mulgrew, C. L., Morgenstern, N., Shetterly, S. M., Baxter, J., Baron, A. E., & Hamman, R. F. (1999). Cognitive functioning and impairment among rural elderly Hispanics and non-Hispanic Whites as assessed by the Mini-Mental State Examination. *Journal of Gerontology: Psychological Sciences, 54B*, 223–230.

Mueller, K. J., Ortega, S. T., Parker, K., Patil, K., & Askenazi, A. (1999). Health status and access to care among rural minorities. *Journal of Health Care for the Poor and Underserved, 10*, 230–249.

Mui, A. C., & Burnette, D. (1994). Long-term care service use by frail elders: Is ethnicity a factor? *The Gerontologist, 34*(2), 190–198.

Mutchler, H. E., & Burr, J. A. (1991). Racial differences in health and health care service utilization in later life: The effect of socioeconomic status. *Journal of Health and Social Behavior, 32*, 342–356.

National Rural Health Association. (2001, April). *The need for standardized data and information systems* (Issue Paper). Retrieved November 10, 2005, from http://www.nrharural.org/advocacy/sub/issuepapers/ipaper19.html

Nelson, G. M. (1994). In-home services for rural elders. In R. T. Coward, C. N. Bull, G. Kukulka, & J. M. Galliher (Eds.), *Health services for rural elders* (pp. 65–83). New York: Springer Publishing.

Ogunwole, S. U. (2002). *The American Indian and Alaska Native population: 2000.* (Census 2000 Brief). Washington, DC: Bureau of the Census, Economics and Statistics Administration.

Probst, J. C., Moore, C. G., Glover, S. H., & Samuels, M. E. (2004). Person and place: The compounding effects of race/ethnicity and rurality on health. *American Journal of Public Health, 94,* 1695–1703.

Randolph, R., Gaul, K., & Slifkin, R. (2002). *Rural populations and health care providers: A map book.* Chapel Hill, NC: University of North Carolina at Chapel Hill, Cecil G. Sheps Center for Health Services Research.

Rhoades, D. A. (2006). National health data and older American Indians and Alaska Natives. *Journal of Applied Gerontology, 25*(1), 9S–26S.

Saenz, R., & Torres, C. C. (2003). Latinos in rural America. In D. L. Brown, & L. E. Swanson (Eds.), *Challenges for rural America in the twenty-first century* (pp. 57–70). University Park, PA: Pennsylvania State University.

Sanchez-Ayendez, M. (1988). Elderly Puerto Ricans in the United States. In S. Applewhite (Ed.), *Hispanic elderly in transition* (pp. 17–31). Westport, CT: Greenwood.

Sandefur, G. D., Rindfuss, R. R., & Cohen, B. (1996). Introduction. In G. D. Sandefur, R. R. Rindfuss, & B. Cohen (Eds.), *Changing numbers, changing needs: American Indian demography and public health* (pp. 1–13). Washington, DC: National Academy.

Shetterly, S. M., Baxter, J., Morgenstern, N. E., Grigsby, J., & Hamman, R. F. (1998). Higher instrumental activities of daily living disability in Hispanics compared with non-Hispanic Whites in rural Colorado. *American Journal of Epidemiology, 147,* 1019–1027.

Siegel, J. S. (1999). Demographic introduction to racial/Hispanic elderly populations. In T. Miles (Ed.), *Full-color aging: Facts, goals, and recommendations for America's diverse elders* (pp. 1–19). Washington, DC: Gerontological Society of America.

Starrett, R. A., Todd, A. M., & Deleon, L. (1989). A comparison of the social service utilization behavior of the Cuban and Puerto Rican elderly. *Hispanic Journal of Behavioral Science, 11,* 341–353.

Starrett, R. A., Wright, R., Mindel, C. H., & Tran, T. V. (1989). The use of social services by Hispanic elderly: A comparison of Mexican American, Puerto Rican and Cuban elderly. *Journal of Social Service Research, 13*(1), 1–25.

Shaughnessy, P. W. (1994). Changing institutional long-term care to improve rural health care. In R. T. Coward, C. N. Bull, G. Kukulka, & J. M. Galliher (Eds.), *Health services for rural elders* (pp. 144–181) New York: Springer Publishing.

Tolnay, S. E. (1998). Educational selection in the migration of southern Blacks, 1880–1990. *Social Forces, 77,* 487–514.

U.S. Census Bureau. (2000). *Projections of the total resident population by 5-year age groups, race, and Hispanic origin with special age categories: Middle series 1999–2000; Middle series 2050–2070.* Retrieved October 5, 2005, from http://www.census.gov/population/projections/nation/summary/np-t4-a.txt

U.S. Census Bureau. (2004). *We the people: Hispanics in the United States.* Washington, DC: Author.

U.S. Census Bureau. (n.d.) *2000 Summary File 4 (SF4) PCT3.* Retrieved March 17, 2005 from http://www.census.gov/Press-Release/www/2003/SF4.html

U.S. Department of Agriculture Economic Research Service. (2005). Rural Hispanics at a glance. Retrieved January 3, 2006, from http://www.ers.usda.gov/publications/EIB8/EIB8.pdf

Waidmann, T. A., & Liu, K. (2000). Disability trends among elderly persons and implications for the future. *Journal of Gerontology: Social Sciences, 55B,* S298–S307.

Wallace, S. P., Campbell, K., & Lew-Ting, C. (1994). Structural barriers to the use of formal in-home services by elderly Latinos. *Journal of Gerontology: Social Sciences, 49*(5), S253–S263.

Wallace, S. P., & Lew-Ting, C. Y. (1992). Getting by at home: Community-based long-term care of Latino elders. *Western Journal of Medicine, 157*(3), 337–334.

Wu, B. (2000). *Supplementing informal care of frail elders with formal services: A comparison of White, Hispanic, and Asian non-spouse caregivers.* Unpublished doctoral dissertation, University of Massachusetts Boston.

Yeatts, D. E., Crow, T., & Folts, E. (1992). Service use among low-income minority elderly: Strategies for overcoming barriers. *The Gerontologist, 32*(1), 24–32.

PART II

Health Service Provision and Policy Issues

Health and Nutrition in Rural Areas

Joseph R. Sharkey and Jane N. Bolin

As life expectancy increases, the burden of chronic health conditions, functional decline, and diminished independence place an unprecedented strain on the resources of individuals, families, caregivers, communities, the health care system, and service providers (Guralnik, Alecxih, Branch, & Wiener, 2002). Conceptual models for loss of function, such as the Disablement Process (see Figure 5.1), show a progressive relationship among the burden of disease, physical and cognitive functional decline, and the development of disability in essential activities of daily living (Verbrugge & Jette, 1994). Predisposing and introduced factors (e.g., demographic, social, lifestyle, behavioral, psychological, environmental, and nutritional) may influence this process (Verbrugge & Jette, 1994). It has been recognized that older adults in rural areas disproportionately grapple with problems that affect this process: high levels of chronic conditions, low levels of available health support, limited personal and community resources, geographic isolation, and poor nutritional health, among others (Auchincloss, Van Nostrand, & Ronsaville, 2001; Jensen, Kita, Fish, & Heydt, 1997; Kaufman, 1998; Sharkey, 2003).

This chapter provides an overview of prevention and management of chronic health problems, especially those that are nutrition-related, and the challenges to achieving and maintaining good physical and

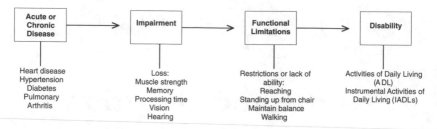

FIGURE 5.1   Framework for progressive loss of function.

nutritional health in older populations who reside in rural areas. We know that personal, structural, and neighborhood characteristics influence differential access to health care and serve as either barriers or enhancements to lifestyle behaviors such as physical activity or healthy eating (Booth et al., 2001; Saelens, Sallis, Black, & Chen, 2003). Additionally, residents of rural and poor areas face the greatest structural and neighborhood disadvantage (Auchincloss et al., 2001). This makes it particularly difficult for formal and informal health and nutrition service providers in rural and remote areas to help older adults to make or maintain lifestyle changes that are critical for the prevention or management of health conditions and functional consequences. Added to this is the challenge to rural service providers of assisting increasing numbers of older persons for longer periods of time to remain independent and living in the community.

RURAL OLDER ADULTS AND HEALTH PROBLEMS

Prevention and treatment of health problems for older Americans who live in small towns and remote areas is an important rural service delivery issue. Health problems include acute and chronic health conditions and other factors linked to the burden of health conditions and functional decline, such as falls, polypharmacy or use of multiple medications, a heightened risk for poor nutrition, and key indicators of existing poor nutritional health—overweight/obesity and low dietary intake (e.g., nutrients, meal patterns, and food groups) (Institute of Medicine, 2000). According to the 2000 U.S. Census nearly 13% of the United States population age 65 years or older, or 7.6 million persons, live in areas designated as rural. Rural populations, particularly those age 65 years or older, are more likely than their urban counterparts to have an activity-limiting chronic illness and to face more difficult barriers in accessing health care (Lewin & Altman, 2000). When one considers that

TABLE 5.1 Comparison of Rates of Chronic Diseases across Urban and Rural Populations

Health Status Indicator	Large MSA[*] (%)	Small MSA (%)	Rural/Remote (%)
Heart disease	10.3	11.8	12.3
Diabetes	6.3	6.7	7.3
Cancer	6.3	7.7	8.0
Symptoms of depression[a]	2.7	3.0	3.4
Hypertension	19.7	21.9	23.5
Emphysema	1.1	1.7	2.1
Stroke	2.1	2.7	2.5
Arthritis	19.2	22.2	22.7

[*]MSA, Metropolitan Statistical Areas.
[a]Combined percentages for sadness, hopelessness, worthlessness and "everything is an effort" experienced all/most of the time.

nearly 78% of Americans age 65 years or older have one or more chronic disease and nearly 50% of them report two or more (Congressional Budget Office, 2005), the availability of health care resources and health care providers becomes critically important because rates of chronic disease are significantly higher among the oldest old (e.g., age 85 or older) Medicare beneficiaries.

According to *Rural Healthy People 2010*, rural populations lag behind their urban counterparts in several health status indicators. Among them, higher rates of uninsured elders, reduced access to primary care services, and higher rates of heart disease, respiratory disease, diabetes, stroke, mental diseases, malnutrition, obesity, substance abuse, and cancer (Gamm, Hutchison, Dabney, & Dorsey, 2003). In this section we examine specific rural-urban differences among persons age 65 years or older with important health status indicators. Table 5.1 shows rates of chronic diseases across urban and rural populations (Lethbridge-Cejku, Schiller, & Bernadel, 2004).

Heart Disease

In general, populations living in rural and remote areas have higher rates of heart disease. Heart disease–related death rates are highest for men and second highest for women who reside in rural areas (Eberhardt et al., 2001). Two frequently occurring antecedents of heart disease and stroke—diabetes and hypertension—are more prevalent in rural communities with rates of hypertension nearly 13% compared to 10% in urban areas (National Rural Health Association, 2005), whereas self-reported diabetes is 17% higher in rural areas than all MSAs (Gamm et al., 2003). In addition, the impact of chronic diseases is compounded for rural minorities, such as African-American and Hispanic seniors, who are more likely than White seniors to have a history of racial or ethnic discrimination, lower educational, lower income levels, and experience additional stress factors. Stress factors can include periods of unemployment, poor health, larger family sizes, marital problems, and single parenthood (McGrath, Keita, Strickland, & Russo, 1990).

Diabetes

Diabetes is also the most common cause of end renal disease and adult blindness and is a major contributor to heart attack, stroke, and foot amputation (CDC, 2004). The rate of cardiovascular disease among women age 75 years or older is more than twice as high among women who have diabetes than it is among women without diabetes. When occurring together, diabetes and cardiovascular disease appear to be responsible for significantly higher morbidity and health-related costs than is the case when either disease appears alone (AHRQ & CDC, 2001). Some studies report that diabetes is as much as 17% higher in rural areas than all MSAs (Gamm et al., 2003). These differences are noteworthy because diabetes afflicts over 90 million Americans and accounts for 70% of all deaths in the United States (American Diabetes Association, 2003; CDC, 2004). Current estimates of the projected financial burden of diabetes exceed $100 billion per year and are expected to grow (American Diabetes Association, 2003; CDC, 2004).

Symptoms of Mental Illness and Depression

Overall, rates of chronic mental illness in the rural older population are also higher than they are in urban areas. Data from a 10-year prospective study of rural elders showed that incidence rates for all dementias and of Alzheimer's disease increased with age; men and those with lesser education had higher rates of possible/incipient dementia (Ganguli, Dodge, Chen, Belle, & DeKosky, 2000). Incidence of mental illness in rural populations is 9.4%, a rate significantly higher than for metropolitan and urbanized areas (Substance Abuse and Mental Health Services Administration, 2001). Data from the National Health Interview Survey, 2002 showed that self-reported symptoms of depression (e.g., sadness, hopelessness, worthlessness, and lethargy) are higher in rural and remote areas compared with MSAs (see Table 5.1). Rates of depression for women are as high as 40% in some rural areas, compared to depression rates of 13–20% of women in urban areas (Hauenstein & Boyd, 1994). In addition, the age-adjusted odds for depressive symptomatology among Hispanic women was twice that of non-Hispanic White women (Swenson, Baxter, Shetterly, Scarbro, & Hamman, 2000). Unfortunately, mental health care providers and counselors are in extremely short supply in rural areas (Place, 2004).

Polypharmacy

Rural elders are users of both a large number of total medications and number of different therapeutic categories of medications. This places them at great risk for polypharmacy and adverse drug reactions (Lassila et al., 1996). This problem is compounded by the convergence of two additional factors: (1) multiple health care providers at varying distance from the individual and (2) limited access to pharmacies and knowledgeable pharmacists. The risk for drug-drug and drug-nutrient interactions is further exacerbated by difficulties in the management of multiple medications and choices that individuals make to restrict their medication use on account of cost (Sharkey, Ory, & Browne, 2005). Falls are a leading cause of serious injury, loss of mobility, functional dependence, disability, and death among older adults. Another consequence of a fall is developing a fear of falling, which causes older adults to restrict their activity levels. Among rural elders, four of five significant risk factors for falls were prescribed medications: painkillers, tranquilizers, arthritis medications, and medications for high blood pressure (Richardson, Hicks, & Walker, 2002).

Among older adults, residents of rural or near-rural areas were much more likely to have activity limitations (73% and 63%, respectively) than elders who reside in metropolitan or near-metropolitan areas (Larson, Machlin, Nixon, & Zodet, 2005). Activity limitations are commonly associated with chronic diseases caused by vascular problems and reduced lung and cardiac capacity. However, physical limitations and impairments are more difficult to treat in rural areas because of reduced numbers of physical therapists and community health centers where rehabilitation and therapy can be received (Place, 2004). The high incidence of disability associated with diseases such as diabetes suggests that access to preventive health care is more difficult due to the scarcity of qualified rural providers, transportation barriers, fewer diagnostic services, fewer pharmacists and pharmacy services, lack of Medicare supplemental insurance, and fewer options for health insurance (Larson et al., 2005). Given health-related costs, loss of functioning and poor quality of life, the problem of prevention and treatment of chronic diseases in the rural older population is a critical rural health policy issue. It is no wonder that rural residents lag behind suburban and urban residents in nearly all health status indicators (Eberhardt et al., 2001). For example, rates of screening for diabetes, cancer, depression, and hypertension are lower in rural populations despite the fact that rates of these diseases are proportionately higher in rural areas (Gamm et al., 2003).

CHRONIC DISEASE MANAGEMENT

Chronic disease management has been defined as an integrated system of monitoring, intervention, and communication with patients, with the goal of managing chronic diseases and promoting self-care in order to decrease the number of acute events that might be expected to occur with a given disease state (Bolin, Gamm, Kash, & Peck, 2005; Disease Management Association of America, 2005; Wagner et al., 2001). Optimally, chronic disease management (see Table 5.2) coordinates health care interventions and communications for populations with conditions in which patient self-care efforts are significant (Disease Management Association of America, 2005; Wagner et al., 2001). A growing literature now supports chronic disease management as an effective method to manage and coordinate the health care needs of high risk populations with chronic health conditions, reducing the incidence of acute events associated with such conditions, thereby reducing the need for expensive care (Bolin, Gamm, Zuniga, Berger, & Kash, 2003a; CDC, 2004; Hogan, Dall, & Nikolov, 2003).

As shown in Figure 5.2, Wagner's chronic care model (Wagner et al., 2001) emphasizes patient self-management to support appropriate care

TABLE 5.2   Components of Chronic Disease Management Programs

1. Population identification processes for locating and working with at-risk groups.

2. Evidence-based best practice guidelines are used at the community and clinical level.

3. Collaborative practice models that include physicians, community care providers, and support-service providers.

4. Patient self-management education (may include primary and secondary prevention, behavior modification programs, and compliance/surveillance).

5. Process and outcomes measurement, evaluation, and management.

6. Routine reporting/feedback loop (communication with patient, physician, health plan and ancillary providers; practice profiling may be part of the feedback loop, as well).

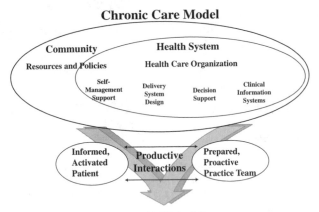

Chronic Care Model

FIGURE 5.2 Wagner's chronic care model.

for chronic diseases and conditions. As pictured, the chronic care model shows that improved outcomes are a result of interactions between the health system and community resources and policies.

The chronic disease model, as an approach to support appropriate care for chronic diseases and conditions, has been embraced by the vast majority of public and private health delivery organizations and is a health policy priority of Medicare and Medicaid programs as well as the Office of Rural Health Policy (Crippen, 2002; Wheatley, 2001). The Medicare Modernization Act, passed on December 8, 2003, included provisions relating to the chronic care improvement within Medicare's fee-for-service programs and included programs for initiation, development, and testing of chronic care improvement programs for chronically ill Medicare beneficiaries.

Rural health care providers may find it difficult to comply with chronic care improvement's disease management initiatives because health care delivery in rural and underserved populations presents many challenges that go well beyond recognized, conventional concerns such as financing, controlling costs, and ensuring quality of care (Bolin, Gamm, Zuniga, Berger, & Kash, 2003b). Rural patients are reported to face greater barriers in accessing treatment, including lack of transportation, fewer health care providers, and lack of pharmacy and laboratory services (Bolin et al., 2003b; Bolin et al., 2005). In fact, only 10% of physicians practice in rural areas; there is a scarcity of minority health care providers; and rural residents are less likely to have a regular primary care physician (Bolin et al., 2003b). Access to health and community support services is important from a rural policy perspective because rural poverty along with reduced numbers of health care providers combine to increase the prevalence and severity of chronic diseases for rural elders.

RURAL OLDER ADULTS AND NUTRITIONAL HEALTH

Nutritional Risk

The level of risk for poor nutritional health is often determined by the administration of a self-reported screening tool such as the Nutrition Screening Initiative's 10-item DETERMINE Checklist (Nutrition Screening Initiative, 1996). This screen identifies 10 nutritional problems (e.g., meal pattern, eating alone, inadequate resources for food, and medication use) and is considered to be a necessary first step in the development and modification of targeted program activities. Based on a scoring algorithm with scores ranging from 0 to 21, putative levels of nutritional risk include "low risk" (scores 0–2), "moderate risk" (scores 3–5), and "high risk" (scores 6–21) for poor nutritional health. Although there have been a number of criticisms leveled at this particular screening tool and the way in which it is administered and used, it still remains the common screen for nutrition risk in Older Americans Act Nutrition Programs (Administration of Aging, 2000). In fact, several studies that used various thresholds for nutritional risk have found nutritional risk correlates with functional decline (Jensen, Friedmann, Coleman, & Smiciklas-Wright, 2001). Using this screening tool, numerous studies identified large proportions of rural older adults as "high risk" for poor nutritional health (Jensen et al., 1997; Marshall et al., 1999; Sharkey & Haines, 2001). Considering the wide range of scores that are included in describing high nutritional risk (scores 6–21), Sharkey and Haines (2001) provided criteria for the trifurcation of the single high-risk category into three levels of increasing higher risk: high risk (scores 6–8), moderate high risk (scores 9–11), and very high risk (scores 12–21). Using this new threshold for being at very high risk for poor nutritional health, Sharkey and Haines (2001) found in a rural North Carolina sample of 245 homebound older adults, 29% of high-risk African Americans and 9% of high-risk Whites were at very high risk. It was also reported that among 883 homebound Mexican-American and non-Mexican-American older adults in the Lower Rio Grande Valley of Texas, 19.4% were at moderately high risk, 40.5% at very high risk, and the odds for being at very high nutritional risk were 49% greater for older individuals who resided in rural areas, independent of other factors (Sharkey, 2004).

Overweight/Obesity

The anthropometric measure of body mass index (BMI) provides a general picture of nutritional health. BMI is defined as weight in kilograms divided by height in meters squared. In most cases, BMI is calculated from an exact measure of weight and stature (or knee height); however, in many reports, the calculation of BMI is based on self-reported height and weight. This presents a challenge to understanding the extent and consequences of obesity in rural older populations. Using self-reported data from a highly rural area of the country—the Appalachia region including a specific examination of West Virginia, which is entirely in Appalachia—investigators report high percentages of overweight adults (BMI 25–29.9 kg/m^2) in Appalachia and West Virginia who are age 55 to 64 years (approximately 38% and 40%, respectively) and age 65 years or older (approximately 34% and 35%, respectively). Among the obese adults (BMI ≥30 kg/m^2) in Appalachia and West Virginia, greater than 20% were age 55 to 64 years and almost 20% were age 65 years or older (Halverson, Ma, Harner, & Hanham, 2004). Ledikwe and colleagues (2004), using exact measures of height and weight in the home, found 44% of their rural Pennsylvania older sample to be overweight and 35% obese (7% were severely obese with a BMI ≥35 kg/m^2). Using measured knee height and weight data from the North Carolina Nutrition and Function Study of 345 homebound older adults, Sharkey and colleagues (2002) found 31% to be overweight and 34.5% to be obese, with 13.6% severely obese. Also using measured height and weight, Jensen and Friedman (2002) found 40% of their study population of 2,634 rural Pennsylvania older adults to be overweight (48% men and 34% women), 27% obese (24% men and 31% women), and 8% severely obese (6% men and 11% women). Finally, in the Lower Mississippi Delta region of Arkansas, Louisiana, and Mississippi, a largely rural and poor area, investigators found using self-reported data collected by telephone that 39.5% of adults age 55 to 64 years, 24.5% of those age 65–74 years, and 18.1% of those age 75 years or older were obese (Lower Mississippi Delta Nutrition Intervention Research Consortium [Delta NIRI], 2004). There are a number of reasons for the concern with high percentages of obesity among rural older adults. Obesity is strongly associated with individual and multiple chronic conditions, such as diabetes, hypertension, heart disease, and with overall functional decline (Delta NIRI, 2004; Jensen & Friedman, 2002; Sharkey, Branch, Giuliani, Haines, & Zohoori, 2004). In addition, living in rural areas, many of which are isolated areas, having to travel long distances for care and experiencing difficulty obtaining transportation exacerbate the burden of obesity and its sequelae (Gesler, Savitz, & Wittie, 1998).

Nutritional Deficiencies

Available methodology, cost, and respondent burden make it difficult to obtain an accurate measure of usual nutrient intake from rural elders. With these limitations in mind, several studies have attempted to document dietary intake in rural older adults. Sharpe and colleagues (2003) found that rural elders, especially single older women, consumed lower intakes in protein, seven vitamins (A, C, E, B_6, B_{12}, riboflavin, and folate), and three minerals (calcium, phosphorus, and magnesium). Sharkey and colleagues (2002) reported low nutrient intakes in individual and multiple nutrients in a sample of rural and urban older adults. Using a subset of 179 participants from the Geisinger Rural Aging Study, Ledikwe and colleagues (2004) reported that 50% of the sample consumed a low-nutrient-dense pattern of eating, which included high intake of bread, cereal, rice, pasta, fats, oils, and sweets. This particular eating pattern was associated with higher levels of total calories and fat and lower levels of intake of protein, carbohydrate, fiber, folate, B_6, B_{12}, vitamins D and E, calcium, iron, and zinc. The individuals most likely to report eating a low-nutrient-dense pattern were older persons who had a higher proportion of abdominal body fat, defined as waist/hip circumference greater than National Institutes of Health risk cutoff.

Other meal patterns, such as number or type of daily meals, are also important. In a study of 556 adults age 55–92 years in two rural counties of Kentucky, Quandt and colleagues (1997) reported that 15% consumed two meals per day, 6% consumed less than two daily meals, 20% did not eat a breakfast meal everyday, and 8% never ate breakfast; an estimated 10.6% of women and 5.3% of men never ate breakfast. In addition, it was believed that changes in meal pattern for these rural elders may be attributed to changes in work, family, and health that occurred over the life course. These new meal patterns have the potential for causing poor nutrition, especially among older persons in rural areas who concomitantly face decreased access to services, goods, and informal care networks. As Sharkey and colleagues (2002) discovered, older adults who did not regularly eat a breakfast meal reported lowest intakes in individual and multiple nutrients. Meal patterns also refer to food group choices. In a study of 1,817 adults in six rural communities in Wyoming, Montana, and Idaho where 63% of participants were at least age 50 years, 45% consumed ≤1 serving of fruit or vegetable juices per week, 33% ≤1 weekly serving of fruits, 44% ≤1 weekly serving of whole grain breads, and 21% ≤1 weekly serving of any vegetable. In this study, women had higher intakes of fruits, vegetables, and whole grains than did men (Liebman et al., 2003). It remains difficult to address these complex nutritional problems—very high nutritional risk, high prevalence of overweight and obesity, low intakes in key food groups and individual and multiple nutrients, and altered meal patterns—in older populations, and much more difficult in older persons who reside in rural environments.

SELF-MANAGEMENT OF NUTRITIONAL HEALTH

Self-management of nutrition in order to achieve and maintain good nutritional health relies on choosing healthful foods and consuming a higher quality diet. Making poor food choices and consuming a low-quality diet results in nutritional deficiencies, nutritional excesses, and overall poor nutritional health. The process of food choice is influenced by the adequacy of personal and community resources, the level of food security or food sufficiency, and health factors and involves decisions made on convenience and quality (Furst, Connors, Bisogni, Sobal, & Falk, 1996). Research shows that the adequacy of local food resources is associated with diet and that rural, poor, and minority communities have less access to supermarkets and face higher prices for food. However, this knowledge has not translated to improve access to healthy food choices, especially among older adults in rural areas, many of whom rely on formal and informal food assistance programs to help meet basic dietary needs (Blanchard & Lyson, 2002; Morland, Wing, Roux, & Poole, 2002; Rose & Richards, 2004; Yadrick et al., 2001).

Other key factors that influence food choice and diet quality include competing financial demands for limited resources (e.g., health care, transportation, heating and cooling, and increased food costs), functional impairments (e.g., inability to acquire, prepare, and eat food that is available), social and geographic isolation, household environment (e.g., food preparation and storage facilities), frequency of grocery shopping, knowledge of healthful foods, oral problems, and depression (Anderson, 1990; Morton, Bitto, Oakland, & Sand, 2005; Radimer, Olson, Greene, Campbell, & Habicht, 1992).

Substantial proportions of rural elders report not having enough food to eat (Food Security Institute, 2003; Nord, 2002; Quandt & Rao, 1999; Sharkey & Schoenberg, 2005) not having enough money to purchase needed food (Sharkey, 2004; Sharkey & Haines, 2001; Sharkey & Schoenberg, 2005), and experiencing times when there is no food in the house and no money or food stamps to purchase food (Sharkey, 2003; Sharkey & Schoenberg, 2005). According to the 2003 Current Population Survey and using the 18-item U.S. Department of Agriculture Food

Security Survey Module, 11.6% of rural adults age 60 years or older reported food insecurity in the last 12 months. Other studies reported that 57% of rural elders in the Texas Rio Grande Valley and 26% of rural elders in North Carolina reported food insecurity—not having enough money to purchase needed food (Sharkey, 2004; Sharkey & Haines, 2001). In both of these studies, rural minority elders, Mexican Americans in one study and African Americans in the other, were at greater risk for food insecurity than comparable non-Hispanic White elders. It is problematic that there is a dearth of information on the extent to which food insecurity or food insufficiency persists over time, especially in rural areas. In a sample of 268 rural and urban older adults, Sharkey and Schoenberg (2005) found that the prevalence of individual food insufficiency increased from 12% at baseline to 15% 1 year later, with 7% reporting food insufficiency at both time points.

Food security and food sufficiency (i.e., having enough food to eat) in rural areas is dependent on the adequacy of personal and community resources and the quality of the food environment, including accessibility, availability, and affordability of healthful foods (Anderson, 1990; Wolfe, Olson, Kendall, & Frongillo, 1996). Personal resources such as available money and family and friends, the ability to maintain gardens, community resources such as transportation, formal and informal food assistance programs, and alternate food sources may dictate the distance one can travel to shop for groceries or the frequency of grocery shopping, and as a result, selection and price. Concomitantly, retail food prices using the Consumer Price Index indicated that since 2002, the percentage increase was greatest in nonmetropolitan areas and the annual average Consumer Price Index was greatest in nonmetropolitan areas in each year since 1999 (Bureau of Labor Statistics, 2005). This presents a great challenge for rural older adults, many of whom are poor and more likely to be women and live alone (U.S. Department of Agriculture, 2002).

Among older women, insufficient funds are known to make transportation difficult and constrain purchase of more foods and better quality foods (Molnar, Duffy, Claxton, & Bailey, 2001; Sharpe et al., 2003). In addition, personal resources are called upon to respond to expected and unexpected expenses, including transportation, utilities, home repair, and out-of-pocket medical expenses, including medications. As such, food choice is not simply the result of individual characteristics but also reflects the environment in which rural elders live. Family and friends can play a key role in an older person remaining food secure and food sufficient. They can provide direct sources of food, some from home production, as well as money and transportation to obtain food

(Morton et al., 2005; Olson, Rauschenbach, Frongillo, & Kendall, 1997; Quandt, Arcury, Bell, McDonald, & Vitolins, 2001). However, the increased distance in rural areas makes it difficult for family and friends to provide transportation (Souter & Keller, 2002).

Federal nutrition programs are a mainstay for community nutrition resources and include two major programs—Food Stamp Program and Elderly Nutrition Program. According to the 2003 Current Population Survey, a smaller percentage of rural elders participate in the Food Stamp Program than urban elders (7.9% versus 9.4%). Since 1999, average participation rates for older adults continue to fall to approximately 27% of eligible older adults who participated in 2002. In addition, disproportionately high numbers of older adult households (44%) received the minimum monthly food stamp benefit of $10 (U.S. Department of Agriculture, 2002a). In a study of 345 rural and urban homebound older adults, Food Stamp Program participation was low (<38%) among those with the lowest monthly income (<$750); almost 96% of participants received benefits of $10; the trend for participation declined with increasing age; and participation, independent of other factors, was associated with lower nutrient intakes (Sharkey et al., 2002). Furthermore, Food Stamp Program participation and the regular receipt of home-delivered meals were not enough to prevent older adults from being food insufficient (Sharkey, 2003). In addition to limited benefits, rural elders also face the problem that transportation, required by many to travel the distance to grocery stores, is not an allowable food stamp expenditure.

Older adult nutrition programs such as home-delivered and congregate meals reach only a fraction of the older population, and even fewer in rural areas (Ponza, Ohls, & Millen, 1996). A critical challenge to meeting nutritional needs in rural areas through the Elderly Nutrition Program is a limited understanding of the scope of the problem. Reporting requirements and limitations in prior evaluations provide limited or no information on the extent of Elderly Nutrition Program coverage in rural areas (Administration on Aging, 2000; Ponza et al., 1996). At present, for most providers of nutrition services for older adults, the only available information on nutritional risk is a product of routinely collected data on program participants. As a result, there is a void in information on nutrition needs for older adults who do not already participate in the Elderly Nutrition Program, especially in rural areas (Sharkey & Haines, 2002). One exception was a study to test the feasibility of a telephone-administered nutrition risk survey in a rural North Carolina county among 152 community-living older adults who were not Elderly Nutrition Program participants. In this study, Sharkey and Haines (2002) found 20% experienced difficulty chewing or swallowing, 20% usually ate alone, and over 70% consumed few servings of fruits, vegetables, or dairy products. Over half of the participants who were identified as being at high nutritional risk lived in areas of the rural county not receiving any nutritional services. Lacking this information, it becomes difficult for rural service programs to make long-range plans that include modified or new programs. Additional challenges to meeting nutrition needs through nutrition service programs include the following: limited funding targeted to rural areas, program reporting requirements that favor larger programs and staff, low population density, lack of infrastructure, adequacy of service variable from community to community, perceptions of service providers, limited pool of volunteers, time in which meals must be delivered in order to maintain safe temperatures, and distance too far to be reached by programs (Arcury, Quandt, Bell, McDonald, & Vitolins, 1998; Ralston & Cohen, 1994).

CHALLENGES TO NUTRITION AND HEALTH ISSUES

The community challenge to meeting nutritional and health needs in rural areas is enormous. Underlying planning and allocation of limited resources is a dramatic growth in the oldest old population in rural areas. This subgroup is characterized as having declining health and possible loss of independence, greater poverty, living alone, preponderance of economically vulnerable women, and less access to support services, housing, adequate nutrition, and transportation (Rogers, 1999). Yet community resources in many rural areas may be so severely depleted that safety nets are nonexistent or easily consumed by more pressing problems such as changes in the rural economy or natural disasters. Research suggests that rural areas face significant difficulty in developing sustainable and effective home- and community-based programs, as defined by *Healthy People, 2010*. Health care providers and community-based nutrition programs frequently lack sufficient know-how and resources to support disease prevention programs for chronic disease and risky behaviors. In addition, rural elders report barriers that diminish their use of home- and community-based services, which include lack of awareness of services, inadequate transportation, rigid program requirements, and limited service areas (Schoenberg & Coward, 1998; Sharkey et al., 2002). This will present rural areas with greater need and demand for services, rural areas that are already facing limitations in transportation, availability of facilities and resources, and delivery of services to a geographically disperse and isolated older population (Rogers, 1999).

BEST PRACTICES OR MODEL PROGRAMS

Despite the barriers and challenges, many provider-led and community partnership sponsored interventions are underway in rural communities to address such disparities (Gamm et al., 2003). Research on chronic disease management programs within six health systems serving rural patient populations has shown that disease management can be effectively implemented in rural populations without significant differences in important outcomes, such as hemoglobin A1c (Bolin, Gamm, Kash, & Peck, 2005). Additionally, in a recent pilot study to determine the impact of implementing elements of the chronic care model in a rural practice setting, the results demonstrated that this model has a positive influence on practices and patient outcomes in outlying rural areas (Siminerio, Piatt, & Zgibor, 2005).

The Administration on Aging, with the assistance of national partners, promotes and funds evidence-based demonstration programs to deliver best practices through the Aging Services Network. The National Council on Aging serves as a resource center for local and non-rural programs that target chronic disease management, healthy eating, self-management for depression, physical activity, medication management, and falls prevention. The next step should include the tools for expanding these programs to service providers in rural and remote areas. The Administration on Aging recognized the importance of a breakfast meal and funded a Morning Meals on Wheels Pilot Program, which confirmed the effects of a morning home-delivered meal on the improvement in dietary intake, food security, and health status among rural and urban elders (Weddle, Gollub, Stacy, & Wellman, 1998).

CONCLUSIONS

Rural older adults are disproportionately at risk for and experience numerous health problems, many of which are nutrition-related and often a consequence of inappropriate food choice. Healthful nutrition is critical for the prevention and day-to-day management of health conditions, such as diabetes, hypertension, and heart disease, and prevention of disease-related complications in older populations. For more rural older adults, dietary adherence may be particularly difficult. In trying to make good food choices and consume a healthful diet, rural older adults simultaneously face the complex demands of managing their health conditions while dealing with food insecurity and food insufficiency, inadequacy of personal and community resources, and the accessibility, availability, and affordability of healthful food. This topic is particularly important because without consistent availability of affordable healthy foods, programs for the prevention or management of disease or those that support nutritional needs of rural older adults may not be enough to ensure a healthy diet and prevent disease-related problems.

When designing and implementing programs to help rural elders, it is essential to have knowledge of where people live and where they shop for food. Information must also be available on the contributions of policy, community, and institutional levels of the environment to the enhancement or impedance of nutritional health (Gesler et al., 2004). As this chapter suggests, the factors that affect food choice for rural older adults are complex and relate to resources, lack of certain transportation, and changes that occur in food source (Souter & Keller, 2002). It is clear that rural older adults are already at great risk for food insecurity and food insufficiency. As the rural environment continues to change, limited access to supermarkets means that low-income rural older adults are at an increased risk of losing easy access to affordable food supplies, decreased availability of fresh foods, higher costs of food, increased risk for food insecurity, inappropriate food choice, and poor nutritional health (Morton et al., 2002; Olson et al., 1997). Knowing more about the rural environment and how it is changing is essential for combining environmental approaches with traditional health interventions to make it easier for individuals to make healthier food choices (Seymour, Yaroch, Serdula, Blanck, & Khan, 2004).

In order to respond to the nutritional and health needs of rural older adults, innovation will be required on the part of service providers in reviewing and restructuring existing programs (Schoenberg, Coward, Gilbert, & Mullens, 1997). It will also require the design and implementation of new programs, involving coordination among government, voluntary organizations, private businesses, and individuals to:

1. Develop community linkages and strategies that integrate chronic disease management and nutrition with other services;
2. Identify current transportation needs and cooperative strategies for increasing access to health resources, grocery stores and other food sources;
3. Develop appropriate Medicare payment incentives for rural health care providers to provide chronic disease management in their care of older rural patients;
4. View nutrition program activities as part of a chronic care model that supports improved disease management and helps older individuals remain independent and in their own homes;
5. Incorporate multiple food insufficiency items in assessments and reassessments that recognize issues related to absence of food,

forced scarce-resource decisions, access and availability of food (e.g., transportation, grocery shopping, and meal preparation), and food choice (Wolfe, Frongillo, & Valois, 2003);

6. Form connections with other willing agencies and communities to target activities that seek to ameliorate difficulty with continually securing healthy foods;

7. Provide nutrition education that teaches low-cost dietary alternatives and provides assistance in developing strategies for controlling food costs within a healthy diet (Hunt, Pugh, & Valenzuela, 1998); and

8. Encourage policy makers of health and social service programs servicing rural older adults to recognize the challenge to individual, family, and community resources for nutrition support among particularly vulnerable groups. Such efforts should include consideration of food sufficiency and food environment data as decisions are made regarding funding for home- and community-based services and food and nutrition programs.

In addition, it will be important to determine unmet need by region, which will enable service providers not only to target their programs to specific risk but also to tailor them to the values and needs of communities (Sharkey et al., 2002).

REFERENCES

Administration on Aging. (2000). *National Aging Program Information System (NAPIS)*. Retrieved August 31, 2000, from http://www.aoa.dhhs.gov/napis/default.htm

Agency for Healthcare Research and Quality & Centers for Disease Control and Prevention (AHRQ & CDC). (2001). Major cardiovascular disease (CVD) during 1997–1999 and major CVD hospital discharge rates in 1997 among women with diabetes—United States. *Morbidity and Mortality Weekly Report, 50*, 943–954.

American Diabetes Association. (2003). Economic costs of diabetes in the U.S. in 2002. *Diabetes Care, 26*, 917–932.

Anderson, S. A. (1990). Core indicators of nutritional state for difficult-to-sample populations. *Journal of Nutrition, 120*, 1559–1600.

Arcury, T. A., Quandt, S. A., Bell, R. A., McDonald, J., & Vitolins, M. Z. (1998). Barriers to nutritional well-being for rural elders: Community experts' perceptions. *The Gerontologist, 38*, 490–498.

Auchincloss, A. H., Van Nostrand, J. F., & Ronsaville, D. (2001). Access to health care for older persons in the United States: Personal, structural, and neighborhood characteristics. *Journal of Aging and Health, 13*, 329–354.

Blanchard, T. C., & Lyson, T. A. (2002). *Retail concentration, food deserts, and food disadvantaged communities in rural America.* Retrieved April 28, 2005, from http://srdc.msstate.edu/focusareas/health/fa/blanchard02_final. htm

Bolin, J. N., Gamm, L. D., Kash, B. A., & Peck, B. M. (2005). *Chronic disease management in rural areas. 2003–2004 Report: Rural urban differences in managed Medicare and Medicaid programs.* College Station, TX: Texas A&M University System Health Science Center, School of Rural Public Health, Southwest Rural Health Research Center.

Bolin, J. N., Gamm, L. D., Zuniga, M. A., Berger, E. M., & Kash, B. A. (2003a). *Survey results of physicians, nurses, and leaders providing disease management to rural populations.* College Station, TX: Texas A&M University System Health Science Center, School of Rural Public Health, Southwest Rural Health Research Center.

Bolin, J. N., Gamm, L. D., Zuniga, M. A., Berger, E. M., & Kash, B. A. (2003b). *Chronic disease management in rural areas: Patient Responses and Outcomes.* College Station, TX: Texas A&M University System Health Science Center, School of Rural Public Health, Southwest Rural Health Research Center.

Booth, S. L., Sallis, J. F., Ritenbaugh, C., Hill, J. O., Birch, L. L., Frank, L. D., et al. (2001). Environmental and societal factors affect food choice and physical activity: Rationale, influences, and leverage points. *Nutrition Reviews, 59*(3), S21–S39.

Bureau of Labor Statistics, Department of Labor. (2005). *Archived CPI detailed report tables.* Retrieved May 26, 2005, from http://www.bls.gov/cpi/cpi_dr.htm

Centers for Disease Control and Prevention (CDC). (2004). *The burden of chronic diseases and their risk factors.* Retrieved May 6, 2005, from http://www.cdc.gov/nccdphp/burdenbook2004/preface.htm

Congressional Budget Office. (2005). High-cost Medicare Beneficiaries. Retrieved May 6, 2005, from http://www.cbo.gov/showdoc.cfm?index=6332&sequence=0

Crippen, D. L. (2002). Congressional Budget Office testimony before the United States Special Committee on Aging: *Disease management in Medicare: Data analysis and benefit design issues.* Retrieved March 28, 2005, from http://www.cbo.gov/showdoc.cfm?index=3299&sequence=0

Disease Management Association of America. (2005). *Definition of disease management.* Retrieved February 10, 2005, from http://www.dmaa.org/definition.html

Eberhardt, M. S., Ingram, D. D., Makuc, D. M., et al. (2001). *Urban and rural health chartbook: Health, United States, 2001.* Hyattsville, MD: National Center for Health Statistics.

Food Security Institute. (2003). *Hunger and food insecurity among the elderly.* Retrieved April 17, 2003, from http://www.centeronhunger.org/pdf/Elderly.pdf

Furst, T., Connors, M., Bisogni, C. A., Sobal, J., & Falk, L. W. (1996). Food choice: A conceptual model of the process. *Appetite, 26*, 247–266.

Gamm, L. D., Hutchison, L., Dabney, B., & Dorsey, A. (2003). *Rural Healthy People 2010: A companion guide to Healthy People 2010*. College Station, TX: Texas A&M University System Health Science Center, School of Rural Public Health, Southwest Rural Health Research Center.

Ganguli, M., Dodge, H. H., Chen, P., Belle, S., & DeKosky, S. T. (2000). Ten-year incidence of dementia in a rural elderly U.S. community population: The MoVIES Project. *Neurology, 54*, 1109–1116.

Gesler, W. M., Hayes, M., Arcury, T. A., Skelly, A. H., Nash, S., & Soward, A. C. (2004). Use of mapping technology in health intervention research. *Nursing Outlook, 52*, 42–146.

Gesler, W. M., Savitz, L. A., & Wittie, P. S. (1998). Methods for assessing geographic aspects of health care for older adults in rural areas. In W. M. Gesler, D. J. Rabiner, & G. H. DeFriese (Eds.). *Rural health and aging research: Theory, methods and practical Applications* (pp. 43–66). Amityville, NY: Baywood.

Guralnik, J. M., Alecxih, L., Branch, L. G., & Wiener, J. M. (2002). Medical and long-term care costs when older persons become more dependent. *American Journal of Public Health, 92*, 1244–1245.

Halverson, J., Ma, L., Harner, E., & Hanham, R. B .V. (2004). *Adult obesity in Appalachia: An atlas of geographic disparities*. Morgantown, WV: West Virginia University.

Hauenstein, E. J., & Boyd, M. (1994). Depressive symptoms in young women of the Piedmont: Prevalence in rural women. *Women & Health, 21*, 105–123.

Hogan, P., Dall, T., & Nikolov, P. (2003). Economic costs of diabetes in the U.S. in 2002. *Diabetes Care, 26*, 917–932.

Hunt, L. M., Pugh, J., & Valenzuela, M. (1998). How patients adapt diabetes self-care recommendations in everyday life. *Journal of Family Practice, 46*, 207–215.

Institute of Medicine. (2000). *The role of nutrition in maintaining health in the nation's elderly*. Washington, DC: National Academy.

Jensen, G. L., & Friedmann, J. M. (2002). Obesity is associated with functional decline in community-dwelling rural older persons. *Journal of the American Geriatrics Society, 50*, 918–923.

Jensen, G. L., Friedmann, J. M., Coleman, C. D., & Smiciklas-Wright, H. (2001). Screening for hospitalization and nutritional risks among community-dwelling older persons. *American Journal of Clinical Nutrition, 74*, 201–205.

Jensen, G. L., Kita, K., Fish, J., & Heydt, D. F. C. (1997). Nutrition risk screening characteristics of rural older persons: Relation to functional limitations and health care charges. *American Journal of Clinical Nutrition, 66*, 819–828.

Kaufman, P. R. (1998). Rural poor have less access to supermarkets, large grocery stores. *Rural Development Perspectives, 13*(3), 19–26.

Larson, S. L., Machlin, S. R., Nixon, A., & Zodet, M. (2005). *Chartbook #13: Health care in urban and rural areas, combined year 1998–2000*. Rockville, MD:Agency for Healthcare Research and Quality. Retrieved May 31, 2005, from http://www.meps.ahrq.gov/Papers/CB13_04-0050/CB13.htm

Lassila, H. C., Stoehr, G. P., Ganguli, M., Seaberg, E. C., Gilby, J. E., Belle, S. H., et al. (1996). Use of prescription medications in an elderly rural population: The MoVIES Project. *Annals of Pharmacotherapy, 30,* 589–595.

Ledikwe, J. H., Smiciklas-Wright, H., Mitchell, D. C., Miller, C. K., & Jensen, G. L. (2004). Dietary patterns of rural older adults are associated with weight and nutritional status. *Journal of the American Geriatrics Society, 52,* 589–595.

Lethbridge-Cejku, M., Schiller J. S., & Bernadel, L. (2004). *Summary health statistics for U.S. adults: National Health Interview Survey, 2002.* Hyattsville, MD: National Center for Health Statistics.

Lewin, M. E., & Altman, S. (Eds.). (2000). *America's health care safety net: Intact but endangered.* Washington, DC: Institute of Medicine, National Academy.

Liebman, M., Propst, K., Moore, S. A., Pelican, S., Holmes, B., Wardlaw, M. K., et al. (2003). Gender differences in selected dietary intakes and eating behaviors in rural communities in Wyoming, Montana, and Idaho. *Nutrition Research, 23,* 991–1002.

The Lower Mississippi Delta Nutrition Intervention Research Consortium (Delta NIRI). (2004). Self-reported health status of residents of the Lower Mississippi Delta of Arkansas, Louisiana, and Mississippi. *Journal of Health Care for the Poor and Underserved, 15,* 645–662.

Marshall, J. A., Lopez, T. K., Shetterly, S. M., Morgenstern, N. E., Baer, K., Swenson, C., et al. (1999). Indicators of nutritional risk in a rural elderly Hispanic and non-Hispanic white population: San Luis Valley Health and Aging Study. *Journal of the American Dietetic Association, 99,* 315–322.

McGrath, E., Keita, G. P., Strickland, B. R., & Russo, N. (1990). *Women and depression: Risk factors and treatment issues.* Washington, DC: American Psychological Association.

Molnar, J. J., Duffy, P. A., Claxton, L., & Bailey, C. (2001). Private food assistance in a small metropolitan area: Urban resources and rural needs. *Journal of Sociology and Social Welfare, 28,* 187–209.

Morland, K., Wing, S., Roux, A. D., & Poole, C. (2002). Neighborhood characteristics associated with the location of food stores and food service places. *American Journal of Preventive Medicine, 22*(1), 23–29.

Morton, L. W., Bitto, E. A., Oakland, M. J., & Sand, M. (2005). Solving problems of Iowa food deserts: Food insecurity and civic structure. *Rural Sociology, 70*(1), 94–112.

Morton, L. W., Oakland, M. J., Bitto, E. A, Sand, M., & Michaels, B. (2002). *Iowa Community Food Assessment Project report 2001–02: Iowa State University Family Nutrition Program.* Retrieved May 20, 2005, from http://www.soc.iastate.edu/extension/publications/Iowa%20Community%20Food%20Assessment%20Report.pdf

National Rural Health Association. (2005). *What's different about rural health care?* Retrieved May 26, 2005, from http://www.nrharural.org/pagefile/different.html

Nord, M. (2002). Rates of food insecurity and hunger unchanged in rural households. *Rural America, 16*(4), 42–47.

Nutrition Screening Initiative. (1996). *Keeping older Americans healthy at home.* Washington, DC: Nutrition Screening Initiative.

Olson, C., Rauschenbach, B., Frongillo, E., & Kendall, A. (1997). Factors contributing to household food insecurity in a rural upstate New York county. *Family Economics and Nutrition Review, 10,* 2–17.

Place, J. L. (2004). Workforce development and competency enhancement. In *Bridging the health divide: The rural public health research agenda.* Pittsburgh, PA: University of Pittsburgh Center for Rural Health Practice.

Ponza, M., Ohls, J. C., & Millen, B. E. (1996). *Serving elders at risk: The Older Americans Act nutrition programs, National evaluation of the Elderly Nutrition Program, 1993–1995.* Princeton, NJ: Mathematica Policy Research.

Quandt, S. A., Arcury, T. A., Bell, R. A., McDonald, J. V., & Vitolins, M. Z. (2001). The social and nutritional meaning of food sharing among older rural adults. *Journal of Aging Studies, 15,* 145–162.

Quandt, S. A., & Rao, P. (1999). Hunger and food security among older adults in a rural community. *Human Organization, 58*(1), 28–35.

Quandt, S. A., Vitolins, M. Z., DeWalt, K. M., & Roos, G. M. (1997). Meal patterns of older adults in rural communities: Life course analysis and implications for undernutrition. *Journal of Applied Gerontology, 16,* 152–171.

Radimer, K., Olson, C., Greene, J., Campbell, C., & Habicht, J. (1992). Understanding hunger and developing indicators to assess it in women and children. *Journal of Nutrition Education, 24*(Supp.), 36S–45S.

Ralston, P. A., & Cohen, N. L. (1994). Nutrition and the rural elderly. In J. A. Krout (Ed.), *Providing community-based services to the rural elderly* (pp. 202–220). Thousand Oaks, CA: Sage.

Richardson, D. R., Hicks, M. J., & Walker, R. B. (2002). Falls in rural elders: An empirical study of risk factors. *Journal of the American Board of Family Practice, 15,* 178–182.

Rogers, C. C. (1999). Growth of the oldest old population and future implications for rural areas. *Rural Development Perspectives, 14*(3), 22–26.

Rose, D., & Richards, R. (2004). Food store access and household fruit and vegetable use among participants in the U.S. Food Stamp Program. *Public Health Nutrition, 7,* 1081–1088.

Saelens, B. E., Sallis, J. F., Black, J. B., & Chen, D. (2003). Neighborhood-based differences in physical activity: An environment scale evaluation. *American Journal of Public Health, 93,* 1552–1558.

Schoenberg, N. E., & Coward, R. T. (1998). Residential differences in attitudes about barriers to using community-based services among older adults. *Journal of Rural Health, 14,* 295–304.

Schoenberg, N. E., Coward, R. T., Gilbert, G. H., & Mullens, R. A. (1997). Screening community-dwelling elders for nutritional risk: Determining the influence of race and residence. *Journal of Applied Gerontology, 16,* 172–189.

Seymour, J. D., Yaroch, A. L., Serdula, M., Blanck, H. M., & Khan, L. K. (2004). Impact of nutrition environmental interventions on point-of-purchase behavior in adults: A review. *Preventive Medicine, 39,* S108–S136.

Sharkey, J. R. (2003). Risk and presence of food insufficiency are associated with low nutrient intakes and multimorbidity among homebound older women who receive home-delivered meals. *Journal of Nutrition, 133*, 3485–3491.

Sharkey, J. R. (2004). Variations in nutritional risk among Mexican American and Non-Mexican American homebound elders who receive home-delivered meals. *Journal of Nutrition for the Elderly, 23*(4), 1–19.

Sharkey, J. R., Branch, L. G., Giuliani, C., Haines, P. S., & Zohoori, N. (2004). Nutrient intake and BMI as predictors of severity of ADL disability over 1 year in homebound elders. *Journal of Nutrition, Health & Aging, 8*(3), 131–139.

Sharkey, J. R., Branch, L. G., Zohoori, N., Giuliani, C., Busby-Whitehead, J., & Haines, P. S. (2002). Inadequate nutrient intake among homebound older persons in the community and its correlation with individual characteristics and health-related factors. *American Journal of Clinical Nutrition, 76*, 1435–45.

Sharkey, J. R., Ory, M. G., & Browne, B. A. (2005). Determinants of self-management strategies to reduce out-of-pocket prescription medication expense in homebound elders. *Journal of the American Geriatrics Society, 53*, 666–674.

Sharkey, J. R., & Haines, P. S. (2001). Black/White differences in nutritional risk among rural older adults: The home-delivered meals program. *Journal of Nutrition for the Elderly, 20*(3), 13–27.

Sharkey, J. R., & Haines, P. S. (2002). Use of telephone-administered survey for identifying nutritional risk indicators among community-living older adults in rural areas. *Journal of Applied Gerontology, 21*(3), 385–403.

Sharkey, J. R., & Schoenberg, N. E. (in press). Prospective study of Black-White differences in food insufficiency among homebound elders. *Journal of Aging and Health, 17*(4), 507–527.

Sharpe, D. L., Huston, S. J., & Finke, M. S. (2003). Factors affecting nutritional adequacy among single elderly women. *Family Economics and Nutrition Review, 15*(1), 74–82.

Siminerio, L. M., Piatt, G., & Zgibor, J. C. (2005). Implementing the Chronic Care Model for improvements in diabetes care and education in a rural primary care practice. *Diabetes Educator, 31*, 225–234.

Souter, S., & Keller, C. S. (2002). *Food choice in the rural dwelling older adults.* Retrieved December 15, 2002, from http://www.snrs.org

Substance Abuse and Mental Health Services Administration. (2001). *2001 National household survey on drug abuse, mental health tables.* Retrieved October 14, 2002, from http://www.samhsa.gov/oas/NHSDA/2k1NHSDA/vol2/appendixh_6.htm

Swenson, C. J., Baxter, J., Shetterly, S. M., Scarbro, S. L., & Hamman, R. F. (2000). Depressive symptoms in Hispanic and non-Hispanic White rural elderly: The San Luis Valley Health and Aging Study. *American Journal of Epidemiology, 152*, 1048–1055.

U.S. Department of Agriculture. (2002a). *Elderly participation and the minimum benefit.* Retrieved May 25, 2005, from http://www.fns.usda.gov/oane/MENU/Published/FSP/FILES/Participation/ ElderlyPartRates.pdf2005

U.S. Department of Agriculture. Economic Research Service. (2002). *Rural population and migration: Rural elderly*. Retrieved May 26, 2005, from http://www.ers.usda.gov/Briefing/Population/elderly/

U.S. Department of Agriculture. (2002b). *USDA community food security assessment*. Retrieved January 10, 2005, from http://www.ers.usda.gov/publications/efan02013

Verbrugge, L. M., & Jette, A. M. (1994). The disablement process. *Social Science & Medicine, 38*(1), 1–14.

Wagner, E. H., Glasgow, R. E., Davis, C., Bonomi, A. E., Provost, L., McCulloch, D., et al. (2001). Quality improvement in chronic illness care: A collaborative approach. *Joint Commission Journal of Quality Improvement, 27*(2), 63–80.

Weddle, D. O., Gollub, E., Stacey, S. S., & Wellman, N. S. (1998). *The Morning Meals on Wheels Pilot Program: The benefits to elderly nutrition program participants and nutrition projects*. Miami, FL: National Policy and Resource Center on Nutrition and Aging.

Wheatley, B. (2001). Medicaid disease management: Seeking to reduce spending by promoting health. *State Coverage Initiated Issue Brief, 2*(4), 1–6.

Wolfe, W. S., Frongillo, E. A., & Valois, P. (2003). Understanding the experience of food insecurity by elders suggests ways to improve its measurement. *Journal of Nutrition, 133*, 2762–2769.

Wolfe, W., Olson, C., Kendall, A., & Frongillo, E. (1996). Understanding food insecurity in the elderly: A conceptual framework. *Journal of Nutrition Education, 28*, 92–100.

Yadrick, K., Horton, J., Stuff, J., McGee, B., Bogle, M., Davis, L., et al. (2001). Perceptions of community nutrition and health needs in the Lower Mississippi Delta: A key informant approach. *Journal of Nutrition Education, 33*, 266–277.

CHAPTER SIX

Rural Hospitals and Long-Term Care

The Challenges of Diversification and Integration Strategies

Andrew F. Coburn, Stephenie L. Loux, and Elise J. Bolda

The implications of caring for a growing aging population are especially apparent in rural communities where a limited infrastructure for providing long-term care services is likely to strain the capacities of families and communities to care for those needing such services. One fifth of those potentially needing or using long-term care services reside in rural places, accounting for approximately 10 million people in 2001 (Rogers, 2002). Changes in federal and state policies, consumer preferences, and other economic and demographic factors are transforming the landscape of our long-term care system. These changes are reflected in an increased reliance on private funding for services, an expansion of non-medical residential care alternatives, increasing in-home care options, and attempts to integrate and manage services across the primary, acute, and long-term care systems.

Rural hospitals play an important role in many rural communities in offering post-acute and long-term care services. In the 1980s and 1990s, the implementation of the Medicare Prospective Payment System (PPS) and the anticipated expansion of managed care prompted many hospitals, including many rural facilities, to diversify into a variety of post-acute care services, principally home health (Shah, Fennell, &

Mor, 2001). Some hospitals went beyond post-acute care to develop additional long-term care services, including assisted living and adult day care, among others (Davidson & Moscovice, 2003). The scope and nature of these service expansions varied considerably depending on many factors, including the financial condition for the hospital, state policies encouraging bed conversion, and community interests.

The implementation of more recent Medicare policy changes, including the Balanced Budget Act of 1997 (BBA), resulted in decreased payments to rural hospitals for skilled nursing and home health services, which may have reversed trends toward greater diversification (Mueller & McBride, 1999). In particular, BBA reductions in the rate of growth in hospital, physician, and other provider payments, together with decreases in Medicare payments for home health and skilled nursing facility services, may have been especially challenging for both rural hospitals and freestanding providers of these services and may have further undermined stressed rural health and long-term care delivery systems. Early studies have shown that some of these changes have already had a significant impact on rural hospitals' approach to the delivery of long-term care (Angelelli, Fennell, Hyatt, & McKenney, 2003; Stensland & Moscovice, 2001). Since the BBA, there have been numerous Medicare policy changes culminating in the passage of the Medicare Modernization Act that have increased payments to rural hospitals. Whether recent increases in Medicare payments to hospitals has slowed the reported decline in rural hospitals' diversification into long-term care remains unknown.

This chapter discusses the changing roles of rural hospitals in the delivery of long-term care services and the dilemmas inherent in rural hospital-led long-term care system development. The chapter focuses on four questions: (1) What roles are rural hospitals playing in post-acute and long-term care services? (2) What strategies have rural hospitals used for developing post-acute and long-term care services and how might these different strategies affect efforts to build long-term care system capacity as well as integration or coordination of services between the acute, post-acute, and long-term care service sectors? (3) How have recent changes in Medicare skilled nursing facility and home health payment systems affected the strategies of rural hospitals and impacted their ability to build long-term care system capacity? and (4) What are the future prospects for hospital leadership in the development of rural long-term care systems?

RURAL LONG-TERM CARE AND THE ROLE OF RURAL HOSPITALS

The rural and urban long-term care systems differ significantly in the types and mix of services they offer. Compared to the urban long-term care system, the rural system relies more on nursing home services, especially custodial level care, and less on formal community-based services, such as home health and assisted living, to provide care for their older population (Coburn & Bolda, 1999; Coward & Cutler, 1989; Coward, Horne, & Peek, 1995; Coward, Netzer, & Mullens, 1996; Kenney, 1993; Schlenker, Powell, & Goodrich, 2002; Shaughnessey, 1994).

Nursing Homes

Differences found in the usage patterns among the rural and urban older adults are likely caused by the greater availability of nursing homes in rural areas and the types of services offered by these facilities. In addition to having nearly 40% of the nation's nursing homes, rural areas have a higher number of nursing home beds. As shown in Figure 6.1, the number of nursing home beds in rural areas range from 116 to 146 per 1,000 residents age 75 years or older, compared to only 96 beds in urban areas (Phillips, Hawes, & Williams, 2003). However, rural nursing homes are smaller than urban facilities, averaging only 78 beds per facility compared to 102 beds in urban facilities (Dalton, Van Houtven, Slifkin, Poley, & Howard, 2002). In rural areas, certified skilled nursing beds and special care units are less common with only 53% of rural nursing homes having certified skilled nursing beds compared with 58% of urban facilities.

FIGURE 6.1   Nursing home beds per 1,000 older adult residents by rurality, 2000.
Source: Phillips et al., Nursing Homes in Rural and Urban Areas, 2003.

Home Health Care

Rural Medicare beneficiaries have poorer access to home health care services than urban beneficiaries. In addition to using fewer home health services, rural beneficiaries are less likely to obtain specialty services, such as therapy services or medical social services, and more likely to use nursing or home health aide services (Kenney, 1993). These differences are likely caused by the more limited supply of home- and community-based services in rural areas and by geographic, transportation, and financial factors that limit rural beneficiaries' ability to access these services. Recent studies show that differences in usage were further exacerbated by the implementation of the BBA. Between 1997 and 1999, home health care use among rural residents dropped 26%, whereas use by urban residents only dropped 19% (Komisar, 2002). Since 1999, this trend has continued with use among rural beneficiaries being 11% less than among urban beneficiaries in 2001 (64.2 versus 71.9 users per 1,000 beneficiaries, respectively; Murtaugh, McCall, Moore, & Meadow, 2003).

Recent research on rural home health care suggests that the role played by rural home health care agencies in providing care to rural beneficiaries differs based on beneficiary age and frailty (Franco, 2004; Coward, Lee, Dwyer, & Seccombe, 1993). Rural beneficiaries in the most need of these services, the oldest and frailest, have higher utilization rates (Coward et al., 1993). On the other hand, nearly 24% of rural residents received home health care services from an urban agency or a branch office of an urban agency. These home health care users tended to be younger (65–74 years old) than those receiving care from rural home health agencies (Franco, 2004). Together, these findings suggest that the limited supply of home- and community-based services in rural areas are targeted to those most in need, while urban agencies and their branch offices play a significant role in providing home health services to the younger and less frail rural elders.

Assisted Living

As with other long-term care services, rural residents have more limited access to assisted living facilities than their urban counterparts. In 1998, approximately 23% of the nation's assisted living facilities were located in rural areas. Compared to urban facilities, these rural facilities were smaller and offered their residents less privacy and fewer services. On average, rural facilities had only 34 beds per facility compared to 59 beds per facility in urban areas. Three quarters of urban assisted living units were classified as having mostly private units, whereas only 62% of rural units had this same classification. Instead, rural units were more likely to be classified as semi-private or shared by two or more unrelated individuals. Also, rural facilities were more likely to provide a low level of service, defined as offering help with at least two activities of daily living, 24-hour staff, housekeeping, and at least two meals a day, but not offering nursing care or having a registered nurse on staff. Consistent with rural long-term care being more likely to offer a custodial level of care, less than half of rural facilities would admit or retain patients with moderate or severe cognitive impairment. Only one third would accept patients who needed more than temporary nursing care, and only one quarter accepted patients with any type of behavioral problems (Hawes, Phillips, Holan, & Sherman, 2003).

Although more recent studies have provided rural health researchers and policy makers with a better understanding of the number and types of services offered to rural residents, we still have a limited knowledge about home- and community-based services. We still know little about whether and to what degree the more limited supply of specialized therapists or other health personnel in rural areas may restrict the availability and use of in-home services. It is unknown whether the higher cost of providing services in rural areas may affect the ability of agencies to provide care to rural elders in their homes (Coburn, 2001).

THE EVOLVING ROLE OF RURAL HOSPITALS IN LONG-TERM CARE

Policy and market trends have significantly influenced rural hospital strategies regarding network development and, specifically, diversification into post-acute and long-term care services. During the 1980s, following the implementation of the Medicare PPS, rural hospitals faced significant financial problems, which led many to develop new services, including skilled nursing facilities and home health services. A substantial number of rural hospitals also took advantage of the Medicare swing-bed program. According to the 2003 American Hospital Association (AHA) Annual Survey of Hospitals, 59% of all rural hospitals have swing beds (AHA, 2003). The theory behind these long-term care diversification strategies was that hospitals would be able to capture additional revenue across a broader continuum of services, thereby potentially mitigating financial strains in their inpatient care business. With Medicare skilled nursing and home health services still reimbursed on a cost-basis, there was also a greater likelihood of being able to distribute fixed costs and control profit margins for these services.

During the early 1990s, the expansion of managed care, together with more competitive purchasing behavior on the part of public and private purchasers, spawned the rapid development of health care networks and other organizational and health service delivery arrangements. Rural hospitals responded to market trends by developing formal and informal network relationships, which have taken many different forms, reflecting diverse institutional and community goals (Wellever, Wholey, & Radcliff, 2000). In some cases, acquisition or development of post-acute or long-term care services was an integral part of the network development strategy. With the passage of the BBA, however, the economic and financial environment changed dramatically for rural hospitals, skilled nursing facilities, and home health agencies. Not only did the BBA change Medicare hospital PPS payments in ways that would create problems for many rural hospitals (Mueller & McBride, 1999), it also mandated the implementation of prospective payment systems for Medicare skilled nursing facility and home health services.

Early studies have shown that the BBA has at least had short-term effects on how rural hospitals deliver long-term care (Angelelli, Fennell, Hyatt, & McKenney, 2003; Stensland & Moscovice, 2001). Since the BBA, PPS payments have been increased through the Balanced Budget Refinement Act in 1999, the Medicare, Medicaid, and State Children's Health Insurance Program Benefits Improvement and Protection Act in 2000, and most recently, the Medicare Prescription Drug, Improvement, and Modernization Act of 2003. However, we still lack information on the effects of these recent payment changes and whether the BBA has had any lasting effects on rural hospitals' abilities to provide long-term care.

Recent analyses of the 2003 AHA Annual Hospital Survey demonstrate that a significant proportion of rural hospitals still offer a variety of post-acute and long-term care services (AHA, 2003; Davidson & Moscovice, 2003). However, the proportion of hospitals offering these services began to level out in 2000 and 2003. As shown in Figure 6.2, between 1987 and 2000, there was significant growth in the proportion of hospitals having skilled nursing facilities, swing beds, and inpatient hospice care, with a slight decline in the proportion offering hospice care in 2000. However, in 2003, the percentage of hospitals instituting swing beds and offering inpatient hospice care remained unchanged, while having a skilled nursing facility declined from 45% to 43%.

We also examined the proportion of hospitals providing home health services over time (see Figure 6.3). The provision of these services by rural hospitals peaked in 1996, with 61% of rural hospitals offering these services and 18% offering them through a hospital affiliate. However, since 1996, the proportion of rural hospitals offering home health care services has steadily declined. In 2003, only 50% of rural hospitals had home health services and 15% offered them through a hospital affiliate.

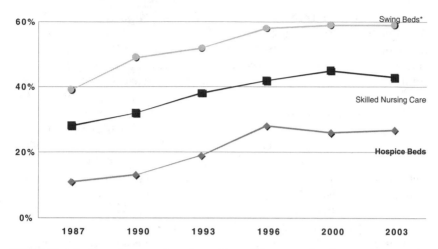

FIGURE 6.2   Inpatient services for older adults provided by rural hospitals, 1987–2003.

*Data on swing beds was unavailable for 2000. The percentage shown in the graph represents 1999 data.

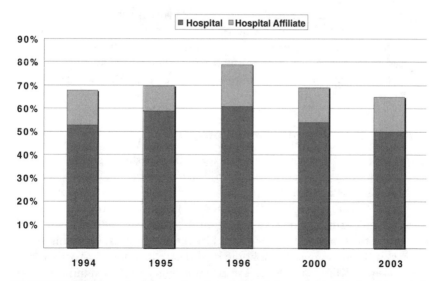

FIGURE 6.3   Home health services for older adults provided by rural hospitals or by a hospital affiliate, 1994–2003.

As shown in Figures 6.2 and 6.3, the proportion of hospitals offering formal post-acute and long-term care services has either remained relatively unchanged or declined since 1996. These findings suggest that the BBA may have had a significant impact on rural hospitals' ability or willingness to provide these services. In fact, in a recent survey of rural hospitals that had skilled nursing facilities and home health care services in 1997, Stensland and Moscovice (2001) found that some rural hospitals were facing difficulties in providing these services under PPS. Of the 401 rural hospitals sampled for the 2000 survey, 28% stated that their skilled nursing facilities were losing money, 14% had closed their skilled nursing facilities, and 30% had delayed hospital discharges due to a lack of available skilled nursing facility beds. On the other hand, a much higher proportion of hospitals were finding it difficult to provide long-term care services. Approximately 52% reported that their home health agency was operating at a loss while 13% had closed their home health agency. Therefore, the decline in rural hospitals offering home health services, shown in Figure 6.3, is likely a reflection on the changing financial circumstances of the home health and nursing home sectors following the implementation of the BBA.

As shown in Figure 6.4, a smaller percentage of rural hospitals offer non-Medicare covered long-term care services, such as assisted living, retirement housing, adult day care, and transportation. Until 2003, these services, with the exception of adult day care, had shown significant growth. For example, the percentage of rural hospitals offering assisted living has more than doubled from 3% in 1987 to nearly 7% in 2000. However, since 2000, the provision of each of these services has leveled off.

Critical Access Hospitals and Long-Term Care

Given that Critical Access Hospitals are typically the largest provider in their community and represent the hub of the local health care system, they play a significant role in providing services to rural elders. As a part of the 2004 evaluation of the Rural Hospital Flexibility Program, the Flex Monitoring Team conducted a survey of 474 Critical Access Hospitals to determine the types of services offered by these hospitals, including swing beds, skilled nursing facilities, home health care, hospice, and assisted living (Casey & Klingner, 2004). As shown in Figure 6.5, a significant proportion of these hospitals currently offer post-acute and long-term care services. Compared to other rural hospitals, Critical Access Hospitals tend to be more likely to provide these types of services, with a greater

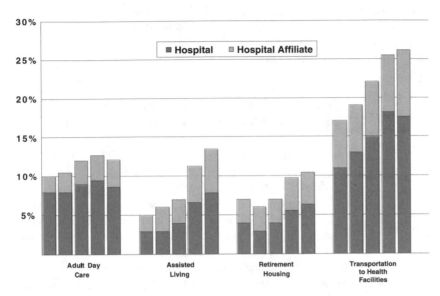

FIGURE 6.4 Services for older adults provided by rural hospitals or by a hospital affiliate, 1994–2003.

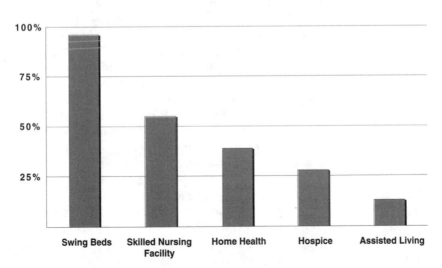

FIGURE 6.5 Long-term care services offered by critical access hospitals, 2004.
Source: Casey & Klingner, CAH National Survey, 2004.

percentage using swing beds, having skilled nursing facilities, and offering hospice and assisted living services. However, only 39% of Critical Access Hospitals provide home health care services, whereas 50% of all rural hospitals offer these services.

HOSPITAL STRATEGIES: DIVERSIFICATION, NETWORKING, AND SERVICE INTEGRATION

It is often said that if you have seen one rural community, you have seen one rural community. This aphorism certainly holds true with respect to rural hospital diversification strategies and rural long-term care delivery systems. The organizational, economic and financial, and community contexts differ among rural hospitals and are important factors in influencing whether and how hospitals have pursued the development of post-acute and long-term care services. In this section, we explore how these and other factors have shaped rural hospital diversification strategies and examine how differing motivations and objectives of rural hospitals may affect the capacity of rural health systems in meeting the growing demand for long-term care services.

Forces Shaping Diversification Strategies

Rural hospitals are shaped by both internal circumstances and community characteristics that influence their strategic options and choices. There are, however, a set of circumstances that make rural hospitals distinctly different from their urban counterparts. Rural hospitals tend to be smaller institutions with less financial and organizational capacity, they are usually located in regions and communities that have fewer providers and services, and they serve populations that tend to be older and poorer (Beaulieu, 1992; Bowlyow, 1989; Ricketts & Heaphy, 1999). Together, these circumstances create both the need for and the challenge in expanding long-term care services in rural areas.

In a study of pre-BBA hospital diversification strategies, Shah, Fennell, and Mor (2001) examined the role of organizational, market, and community factors in the diversification strategies of rural and urban hospitals in the 1990s. Among the organizational factors they studied, multi-hospital system membership was positively related to the likelihood of a hospital offering both a skilled long-term care unit (nursing facility) and home health services. Shah et al. (2001) also observed that rural hospitals were more likely to be located in concentrated markets and were more likely to offer both of these services. They further noted that hospitals located in counties with a higher proportion of persons age 85 years or older were more likely to have pursued a diversification strategy. Together, these findings suggest that market forces and community need appear to influence diversification choices made by rural hospitals. There is evidence that post-acute care and long-term care diversification of rural hospitals in the 1980s through development of swing beds, skilled nursing facility services, and home health services may have been part of a competition and survival strategy (Bowlyow, 1989). These strategies were likely adopted to manage inpatient usage and costs through earlier discharge of hospital patients to long-term care and to capture additional cost-based revenues from these services to subsidize their inpatient operations. Community need for long-term care may also have been a significant force in pushing hospitals to develop long-term care services. Rural hospitals are often looked to for leadership and capital for the development of services as the sole provider of hospital and health services in many rural communities.

INTEGRATING ACUTE AND LONG-TERM CARE IN RURAL AREAS

Beyond diversification, there has been growing interest in developing better integrated systems of care that span the acute, post-acute, and long-term care sectors (Coburn, 2001). There are many challenges to efforts by rural communities and hospitals to maintain or expand the scope of long-term care services and to build better integrated acute and long-term care delivery systems. These include fear that hospital dominance will lead to the over-medicalization of integrated acute and long-term care services (Stone & Katz, 1996), the substantial capital and other cost involved in service expansions, the problems of achieving critical mass and economies of scale in rural health systems, and perhaps most importantly, the countervailing financial incentives (Shah et al., 2001). What is this concept of integration and how might it be applied in the rural context?

In its simplest definition, the term "integration" means the bringing together into a more unified structure, previously independent administrative and service functions, services, organizations, or a combination of these (Bird, Lambert, Hartley, Beeson, & Coburn, 1995; Leutz, 1999; Morris & Lescohier, 1978). Integration can occur at different levels of both the organization and service system: policy, financing, organization, structure, administrative, and clinical. There are a number of vehicles that promote integration, including organizational and service system planning, the development of integrated information systems that support administrative and clinical integration, integrated care planning and management, and staff training (Coburn, 2001; Leutz, 1999).

The pursuit of integration has been premised on the assumption of both economic and clinical benefits. In theory, integrated models of financing and service delivery produce greater efficiency and cost savings (Shortell & Hull, 1996). By bringing the various components of the health and long-term care services together, it is presumed that integrated systems can achieve cost reductions through economies of scale and reductions in inappropriate care and, at the same time, improvements in the quality of care and outcomes (Gilles, Shortell, Anderson, Mitchell, & Morgan, 1993). For purchasers, including state Medicaid programs, integration of financing (Medicare and Medicaid) and service delivery (primary, acute, and long-term care) has been seen as a way of aligning parts of the health system that, under fee-for-service payment arrangements, have tended to be cost-shifted from one payer to another. For consumers, integration is assumed to produce more convenient, accessible, and clinically effective systems by reducing the degree of service and system fragmentation that characterize much of the medical and long-term care financing and delivery systems.

Integration Strategies

Organizations may engage in a combination of strategies to integrate medical and long-term care services. There is no clear continuum or hierarchy that can easily classify approaches to integration. As applied to primary, acute, and long-term care, it is important to distinguish between *what is being integrated* (the target population and scope of services), *how functional and clinical integration occur* (types of integration), and the *level of financial integration and strategic management that is being achieved* (degree of integration).

Population Served and Scope of Services

Depending on the policy or management objectives, there may be differences in the target population(s) as well as the types of services that need to be integrated. For instance, integration models targeting older adults who are well are most likely to encompass the full range of primary and acute care services and limited Medicare reimbursable post-acute care services, including short-term home health skilled services, rehabilitation care, skilled nursing facility services, and hospice care. If the frail elders are the target population, then the scope of services must be broadened to include Medicaid reimbursable institutional and home- or community-based long-term care services, including personal care, transportation, assisted living, adult day care, and respite services.

Which of these long-term care services are included in an integrated system will largely depend on:

- purchasers' demands, including federal and state policy objectives and financial incentives;
- existing service capacity relative to demand; and
- community development objectives for long-term care.

Types and Degree of Integration

Among the different types of integration, two are most relevant: clinical integration and functional integration (Gillies, Shortell, Anderson, Mitchell, & Morgan, 1993). Clinical integration is generally defined as the extent to which patient care services are coordinated within and across organizational units. Functional integration refers to the extent to which administrative and other support functions and activities are coordinated within and across organizational units.

There is no commonly accepted continuum or hierarchy defining or measuring degrees of integration. Various forms of integration are emerging that suggest a continuum (Conrad & Shortell, 1996). Two are most relevant to this chapter. The first is the classic form of vertical integration through common ownership such as a hospital purchasing a nursing home. The second form involves binding but changeable contractual relationships, where a hospital and long-term care provider may have contractual agreements but maintain separate ownership and governance. Such contractual arrangements may be accompanied by formal affiliation agreements laying out areas of cooperation but maintaining separate ownership and governance. Varying degrees of integration may be represented in these different forms—the proof is in the specific arrangement and agreements. In general, however, the degree of integration defined by mutual financial incentives and strategic management is greatest where organizations have common ownership. Affiliations may approximate common ownership, depending upon the tightness of the affiliation arrangement.

With regard to long-term care, clinical integration is especially important as a means for achieving greater access to the full range of long-term care services through "downward" substitution of home- and community-based services for more expensive nursing home and other institutionally-based care. At the organizational level, clinical integration may involve horizontal or vertical linkages or both among different types of service providers. There might be use of common patient assessment tools, a common or shared medical record, quality assurance protocols, the sharing of other clinical procedures or standards, or a combination of these. Clinical teams, the use of care coordinators, or both are also common strategies for achieving clinical integration.

Functional integration involves the sharing or coordination of support services across organizational units. Common financial management, human resource management, marketing, strategic planning, information systems, and quality improvement are often vehicles for functional integration. Functional and clinical integration strategies may be pursued independently of each other.

Within the long-term care literature, there are two models or types of integration posited by Weiner and Skaggs (1995). The first is most closely aligned with clinical integration and is referred to as "hands-off" integration. "Hands-off" integration relies on care coordination for integration of client services across the separate systems of acute and long-term care, as typified by the development of social health maintenance organizations. The second integration, "geriatrics model," calls for the elimination of boundaries between acute and long-term care as typified by the Programs for All-inclusive Care for the Elderly (PACE) approach to integration.

Rural Challenges to Integration: Resources

Service expansions and the development of integrated acute and long-term care programs are expensive, requiring a significant investment of capital and organizational leadership often lacking in rural areas (Kane, Illston, & Miller, 1992). For example, it has been estimated that PACE programs require between $1–1.5 million in start-up capital to cover the fixed costs of facility renovations and the initial operating losses that occur as the program moves to full enrollment (State Workgroup on PACE, 1999).

Rural hospitals have often been the financial engine for health system development in rural communities. Although the hospital's financial and administrative clout is needed to support the development of these new systems, they may not be the most appropriate provider base for the development of an acute long-term care network, given their predominantly medical orientation (i.e., hospitals). Nor can hospitals be expected to take the lead in initiatives that will target them for cost reductions under current prospective payment systems.

The financial pressures on small rural hospitals and other health care providers restrict access to the financial resources needed to develop the critical administrative and clinical systems that are central to an integration strategy. Many rural hospitals fared very well in the early years under the Medicare PPS system and invested heavily in the development of expanded rural health networks as a strategy for survival in the increasingly competitive world of managed care. The uncertainties created by repeated cuts in hospital payments and payments to other providers make it difficult for rural hospitals to invest in strategies and programs for achieving greater integration across the primary, acute, and long-term care sectors (Mueller & McBride, 1999).

Limited Services and Service Delivery Mechanisms in Rural Areas

To adequately address the complex health care and social support needs of frail older persons, programs that seek to integrate acute and long-term care services in rural areas must deal with the common service limitations that exist in many rural areas. Access to specialty services, such as physical therapy and psychiatry, and workforce recruitment and retention problems are fundamental to these service capacity challenges. In addition, programs must recognize that transportation and other costs are often higher in rural areas, making financing arrangements more complicated. It is unclear whether and to what extent networks and partnerships among rural and urban-based health and long-term care providers might facilitate the development of rural service capacity and integration.

Rural Means Small

What are the advantages and disadvantages of the small population base of most rural areas? On the one hand, a small population base of most rural areas makes it difficult to achieve economies of scale. There is a demographic reality that requires creativity and recognition that rural communities cannot be viewed through the same lens as urban communities. For instance, in April 2002, the U.S. Department of Health and Human Services called for development of rural PACE programs. This is unlikely to occur within current PACE guidelines largely due to population dispersion and the relatively small number of nursing home eligible persons living in rural communities. With estimates that mature PACE site membership must be from 250–300 members, and that fewer than 5% of eligible Medicare beneficiaries are likely to enroll in PACE, there simply are not enough frail older people to sustain a PACE program in most rural areas.

There may also be benefits of small population size that can be an advantage for rural communities and providers. In smaller communities where medical and long-term care service providers are likely to better know their clients and provider colleagues, care management across systems may be easier to achieve than in urban settings. Moreover, in smaller communities, health and long-term care providers must work together on a regular basis, which may make it possible to achieve cooperation more easily than in more complex organizational environments in urban areas.

Aligning the Incentives

Communities, medical and long-term care providers, and health plans have few incentives to develop programs that integrate acute and long-term care into the continuum of services. Historically, the incentives under the Medicare hospital PPS and home health and nursing home cost based payment systems propelled hospitals to add home health care and skilled nursing facility services. With the current uncertainties created by rapidly changing Medicare payment policies for hospital and post-acute care services, maintaining these services will be a challenge for many rural hospitals.

It is also hard to overestimate the importance of state policy in shaping the strategies that hospitals and other rural providers may adopt in the future. In some states like Minnesota, Wisconsin, and elsewhere, where the Medicaid and state long-term care program(s) have been active in developing new financing and managed care arrangements for the chronic care population, there is a far greater likelihood of rural participation and experimentation with different program models. Contrary to common perceptions, the experience of Minnesota, Wisconsin, and other states indicates that some rural communities are not only prepared to respond to these challenges but also represents valuable testing grounds for learning what works and what does not in this very new arena of integrated acute and long-term care services. Notwithstanding these successes, however, the fact that comparatively few rural hospitals have ventured into the arena of non-medical residential care, home care, and other long-term care services most likely reflects the absence of large enough financial or other incentives for doing so. Access to capital markets alone does not appear to hold sufficient incentives for rural hospitals as evidenced by the finding that fewer than 25% of eligible rural hospitals have taken advantage of two federal programs designed to improve rural hospital access to capital markets: the Housing and Urban Development 242 Hospital Mortgage Insurance Program and the U.S. Department of Agriculture Community Facilities Programs (Gregg, Knott, & Moscovice, 2002).

CONCLUSIONS

As suggested throughout this chapter, there is little room for optimism when it comes to speculating about the future role of rural hospitals as leaders in promoting the expansion and integration of acute and long-term care services in rural communities. With a limited capacity to pay for long-term care services out of their own pockets, rural elders are dependent on Medicare, Medicaid, and other public programs for funding to meet their long-term care needs. Moreover, the smaller economies of scale, higher costs of developing and providing services, and lower supply of critical health personnel represent significant challenges to the development of adequate long-term care services in rural areas. If rural hospitals and communities are able to maintain what post-acute and long-term care infrastructure they have, the challenge will be to develop better models for delivering health and long-term care services in rural communities. This opportunity is especially important in light of the limited financing for long-term care and the competition for health personnel. Typically, integration strategies involve the creation of new programs or organizational units where financial, staff, and other resources from multiple systems are pooled. The PACE demonstrations are good examples of such integrated models. The expansion of these models in rural settings remains uncertain. States and providers may seek to develop rural PACE or PACE-like programs or sites now that the PACE program has been opened to further expansion. But do these models conform to the realities of most rural areas and of current payment incentives? Probably not. Yet, this does not necessarily mean that rural communities and health and long-term care providers cannot pursue efforts to improve the provision of primary, acute, and long-term care services.

Fully integrated programs may not be the gold standard for improving the care of older persons. Other strategies that involve "linkage" or "coordination" approaches may be just as effective and certainly more feasible in most rural areas (Bird et al., 1995; Leutz, 1999). Rural providers already engage in a great deal of "linking" behavior that connects rural consumers to medical and long-term care services to which they are entitled. One strategy for system improvement in rural areas is for rural health and long-term care providers to more systematically develop the support systems needed to expand and improve these linkage strategies.

In the final analysis, integration is not an end in and of itself. Rather, it is a means toward the goal of improving the care of older persons by enhancing timely access to appropriate and high quality health and long-term care services. In rural areas, where integration is a noble but difficult goal to achieve, incremental linkage and coordination approaches may be more appropriate and effective.

Incentives are needed in new and existing programs to encourage rural providers and communities to assure continued service availability and to develop new long-term care and support service delivery models. The development of partnerships in rural communities and investigation of the potential benefits of service networks among rural and urban health and long-term care providers are needed to achieve these objectives. Achieving this objective is critical for developing a more adequate long-term care service system to meet the needs of older people in rural communities.

REFERENCES

American Hospital Association. (2003). *Annual survey of hospitals.* Chicago: Author.

Angelelli, J., Fennell, M. L., Hyatt, R. R., & McKenney, J. (2003). Linkages in the rural continuum: The Balanced Budget Act and beyond. *The Gerontologist, 43,* 151–157.

Beaulieu, J. E. (1992). Small rural hospitals with long-term care: 1983–1987. *Journal of Rural Health, 8,* 121–127.

Bird, D., Lambert, D., Hartley, D., Beeson, P., & Coburn, A. F. (1995). *Integrating primary care and mental health services in rural America: A conceptual and policy review* (Working Paper #3). Portland, ME: University of Southern Maine, Muskie School of Public Service, Maine Rural Health Research Center.

Bowlyow, J. (1989). Long-term care in small rural hospitals. *The Gerontologist, 29*(1), 81–85.

Casey, M., & Klingner, J. (2004). *2004 CAH survey: National data.* Minneapolis, MN: University of Minnesota, School of Public Health, Division of Health Services Research and Policy, Minnesota Rural Health Research Center.

Coburn, A. F. (2001). Models for integrating and managing acute and long term care services in rural areas. *Journal of Applied Gerontology, 20,* 386–408.

Coburn, A. F., & Bolda, E. J. (1999). Rural elderly and long term care. In T. C. Ricketts (Ed.), *Rural health in the United States* (pp. 179–189). New York: Oxford University Press.

Conrad, D., & Shortell, S. (1996). Integrated health systems: Promise and performance. *Frontiers of Health Care Management, 13*(1), 3–40.

Coward, R. T., & Cutler, S. J. (1989, February). Informal and formal health care systems for the rural elderly. *Health Services Research, 23,* 785–806.

Coward, R. T., Lee, G. R., Dwyer, J. W., & Seccombe, K. (1993). *Old and alone in rural America.* Washington, DC: American Association of Retired Persons.

Coward, R. T., Horne, C., & Peek, C. W. (1995). Predicting nursing home admissions among incontinent older adults: A comparison of residential differences across six years. *The Gerontologist, 35,* 732–743.

Coward, R. T., Netzer, J. K., & Mullens, R. A. (1996). Residential differences in the incidence of nursing home admissions across a six-year period. *Journals of Gerontology, 51B*(5), S258–S267.

Dalton, K., Van Houtven, C. H., Slifkin, R., Poley, S., & Howard, A. (2002). *Background paper: Rural and urban differences in nursing home and skilled nursing supply* (Working paper #74). Chapel Hill, NC: University of North Carolina at Chapel Hill, Cecil G. Sheps Center for Health Services Research, Rural Health Research and Policy Analysis Center.

Davidson, G., & Moscovice, I. (2003). *Rural hospitals: New millennium and new challenges*. Minneapolis, MN: University of Minnesota, School of Public Health, Division of Health Services Research and Policy, Rural Health Research Center.

Franco, S. J. (2004). *Medicare home health care in rural America*. Bethesda, MD: NORC Walsh Center for Rural Health Analysis.

Gillies, R., Shortell, S., Anderson, D., Mitchell, J., & Morgan, K. (1993). Conceptualizing and measuring integration: Findings from the Health Systems Integration Study. *Hospitals and Health Services Administration, 38*, 467–489.

Gregg, W., Knott, A., & Moscovice, I. (2002). *Rural hospital access to capital: Issues and recommendations* (Working Paper #41). Minneapolis, MN: University of Minnesota, School of Public Health, Division of Health Services Research and Policy, Rural Health Research Center.

Hawes, C., Phillips, C. D., Holan, S., & Sherman, M. (2003). *Assisted living in rural America: Results from a national survey*. College Station, TX: Texas A&M University System Health Science Center, School of Rural Public Health, Southwest Rural Health Research Center.

Kane, R. L., Illston, L. H., & Miller, N. A. (1992). Qualitative analysis of the program for all-inclusive care for the elderly. *The Gerontologist, 32*, 771–780.

Kenney, G. M. (1993). Rural and urban differentials in Medicare home health use. *Health Care Financing Review, 14*(4), 39–57.

Komisar, H. L. (2002). Rolling back Medicare home health. *Health Care Financing Review, 24*(2), 33–55.

Leutz, W. (1999). Five laws for integrating medical and social services: Lessons from the United States and the United Kingdom. *Milbank Quarterly, 77*(1), 77–110.

Morris, R., & Lescohier, I. H. (1978). Service integration: Real versus illusory solutions to welfare dilemmas. In R. Sarri & Y. Hansenfeld (Eds.), *The management of human services* (pp. 21–50). New York: Columbia University Press.

Mueller, K. J., & McBride, T. (1999). *Taking Medicare into the 21st century: Realities of a post-BBA world and implications for rural health care* (P99-2). Columbia, MO: Rural Policy Research Institute.

Murtaugh, C. M., McCall, N., Moore, S., & Meadow, A. (2003). Trends in Medicare home health care use: 1997–2001. *Health Affairs, 22*, 146–156.

Phillips, C. D., Hawes, C., & Williams, L. M. (2003). *Nursing homes in rural and urban areas, 2000*. College Station, TX: Texas A&M University System Health Science Center, School of Rural Public Health, Southwest Rural Health Research Center.

Ricketts, T. C., & Heaphy, P. E. (1999). Hospitals in rural America. In T. C. Ricketts (Ed.), *Rural health in the United States* (pp. 101–112). New York: Oxford University.

Rogers, C. (2002). *Rural population and migration: Rural elderly*. Retrieved February 28, 2005, from the Economic Research Service, United States Department of Agriculture Web site: http://www.ers.usda.gov/briefing/Population/elderly/

Schlenker, R. E., Powell, M. C., & Goodrich, G. K. (2002). Rural-urban home health care differences before the Balanced Budget Act of 1997. *Journal of Rural Health, 18*, 359–372.

Shah, A., Fennell, M., & Mor, V. (2001). Hospital diversification into long-term care. *Health Care Management Review, 26*(3), 86–100.

Shaughnessy, P. W. (1994). Changing institutional long-term care to improve rural health care. In R. T. Coward, C. N. Bull, G. Kukulka, & J. M. Galliher (Eds.), *Health services for rural elders* (pp. 144–181). New York: Springer Publishing.

Shortell, S. M., & Hull, K. (1996). The new organization of the health care delivery system. In S. Altman & U. Reinhardt (Eds.), *Strategic choices for a changing health care system* (pp. 101–148). Chicago: Health Administration.

State Workgroup on PACE. (1999). *Site selection and application process for PACE* (Issue Brief #1). San Francisco, CA: National PACE Association.

Stensland, J., & Moscovice, I. (2001). *Rural hospitals' ability to finance inpatient, skilled nursing, and home health care.* (Working Paper #37). Minneapolis, MN: University of Minnesota, School of Public Health, Division of Health Services Research and Policy, Rural Health Research Center.

Stone, R. L., & Katz, R. E. (1996). Thoughts on the future of integrated acute and long-term care. In R. J. Newcomer, A. M. Wilkinson, & M. P. Lawton (Eds.), *Annual review of gerontology and geriatrics* (Vol. 16, pp. 217–245). New York: Springer Publishing.

Weiner, J. M., & Skaggs, J. (1995). *Current approaches to integrating acute and long-term care financing and services* (Policy Paper #9516). Washington, DC: American Association of Retired Persons.

Wellever, A., Wholey, D., & Radcliff, T. (2000). *Strategic choices of rural health networks: Implications for goals and performance measurement* (Working Paper #31). Minneapolis, MN: University of Minnesota, School of Public Health, Division of Health Services Research and Policy, Rural Health Research Center.

CHAPTER SEVEN

Changes in the Medicare Program

Meeting New Challenges in Rural Health Care Delivery

Keith J. Mueller and Timothy D. McBride

Significant changes to the Medicare program were signed into law in December 2003, with passage of the Medicare Prescription Drug, Improvement, and Modernization Act (MMA). The most notable addition to the program is an outpatient prescription drug benefit, fully effective after January 1, 2006. The new benefit is available only through private plans, and there are significant incentives to encourage more widespread use of private plans for all Medicare benefits. The legislation creates the potential for an increased array of choices among health plans for Medicare beneficiaries, along with greater beneficiary responsibility to choose wisely.

The MMA can be seen as a threat to long-standing behaviors of beneficiaries and providers, or it could be viewed as creating opportunities for constructive change. This chapter uses a set of principles developed by the Rural Policy Research Institute (RUPRI) Health Panel (2001) to assess the implications of the MMA's changes to the Medicare program. There are some best practices that can be used to help beneficiaries and providers transition to the new coverage and payment rules and procedures in the MMA. This chapter will discuss those practices after first applying the RUPRI principles to the MMA in a general analysis.

PRINCIPLES FOR ANALYZING CHANGES IN MEDICARE

The Panel, a group of rural health policy scholars that includes the authors, laid out a set of five principles to guide Medicare policy:

1. Medicare should maintain *equity* of benefits and costs among beneficiaries regardless of where they live.
2. Medicare should promote the highest attainable *quality* of care for all beneficiaries.
3. Medicare should ensure that all beneficiaries have comparable *choices* of providers and plans available to them.
4. Medicare should ensure that beneficiaries have reasonable *access* to all medical services, including having essential services within a reasonable time/distance of where they live.
5. Medicare should include mechanisms to make *costs* affordable, to beneficiaries and to the taxpayers financing the system (RUPRI Health Panel, 2001).

Equity

Equity is central to any discussion of Medicare policy. All Medicare beneficiaries should have the opportunity to use health care services as a means to achieving the quality of life they desire, regardless of where they live. The opportunity may not be exactly the same, but it will be comparable. Beneficiaries who live in remote rural areas will not have the same geographic access to physician services as those who live in urban areas near teaching hospitals. Persons in remote areas may have access to nonphysician primary care providers (e.g., physician assistants, nurse practitioners), and those in rural but not remote areas will have access to primary care physicians but not necessarily subspecialty physicians. Nevertheless, all rural residents will have access to specialists, either to a nearby specialist or to a specialist after a consultation is made, by transportation, or by telecommunications. If by telecommunications, Medicare policy that allows for reimbursement of telecommunications services may be enhancing equity across beneficiaries. A summary of equity in the Medicare program is "the degree to which Medicare is able to serve all populations fairly, including beneficiaries and future beneficiaries, regardless of age, health, gender, race, income, place of residence, or personal preference" (National Academy of Social Insurance, 1999, p. 14).

Prior to the MMA, Medicare policy addressed the equity principle by offering access to the same health insurance benefits to all beneficiaries regardless of income, personal characteristics, or location of residence. However, the principle of equity was achieved by guaranteeing payment for the receipt of any services included in Parts A or B. The opportunity to purchase services has been augmented by Medicare payment policies that favor providers practicing in otherwise underserved areas (Critical Access Hospital payment, bonus payment to physicians, payment to Sole Community Hospitals, additional payment to home health agencies in rural areas) and those serving the poor (disproportionate share payment to hospitals). Beyond Parts A and B of the Medicare program, not all beneficiaries have had access to the same additional benefits at the same price through supplemental insurance or Medicare + Choice plans. The latter is an especially dramatic case of inequity, with few plans available in rural counties, particularly in rural counties not adjacent to metropolitan areas (McBride, Andrews, Makarkin, & Mueller, 2002).

MMA AND EQUITY

The MMA will potentially improve equity for Medicare beneficiaries, through provisions that affect payment to rural providers and through enhanced benefits for all beneficiaries. Title IV of the legislation created payment enhancements for rural providers: a bonus payment of 5% for physicians practicing in scarcity areas, continuation of a 5% add-on payment for home health agencies in rural areas, extending a period of "hold harmless" in outpatient payment for rural hospitals under 100 beds, increasing payment for Critical Access Hospitals, changing the calculation of inpatient hospital payment to use the same basic payment for all hospitals (raising the rural rate to the large urban rate), and increasing payment for long-distance ambulance runs (Mueller, 2004). These changes improve the likelihood that services will be available to rural beneficiaries close to where they live. However, several of the provisions are scheduled to end, so additional actions may be needed to secure the financial health of those providers during the time the provisions are in effect. If the climate of fiscal vulnerability present in late 2003 is still prevailing as temporary provisions expire, we can expect efforts to continue those provisions or replace them with more permanent arrangements (such as a different method of calculating outpatient payments) that protect the solvency of rural providers.

The MMA includes new benefits as part of the basic Medicare program, including preventive services and payment for prescription drugs. The former are now available through Part B of the program, and the latter were instituted as a new Part D. The new Part D benefit will be available only through private health plans, with the federal government subsidizing the premiums of those plans. Thus, beneficiaries will need to enroll in a private plan, either one that offers drug benefits only, such as a Prescription Drug Plan, or a Medicare Advantage plan (new name for a program that includes what were Medicare + Choice plans) that includes a prescription drug benefit. The intent of the legislation is that in every region of the United States (there are 26 regions for Medicare Advantage plans and 34 for Prescription Drug Plans), at least two plans will be offered, at least one of which is a Prescription Drug Plan. Unlike the experience of the Medicare + Choice program, realizing this goal will mean that rural beneficiaries have access to the same basic benefits as do urban beneficiaries. There may, however, still be differences in the details of how those benefits are funded (cost to the beneficiary for monthly premiums), implemented (different formularies for the Prescription Drug Plan and potentially different additional benefits), and accessed (availability of services in geographic proximity to the beneficiary). After a March 2003 deadline to file initial intent to submit a formal plan by June 2003, there were six Prescription Drug Plans with declared intent to offer plans everywhere in all 34 Prescription Drug Plan regions. Challenges await everyone involved in implementation of the new benefit in 2006 to maximize the opportunities it creates for rural beneficiaries. In addition, there are still concerns about equity in payment to Medicare Advantage plans that were not addressed with the passage of the MMA, and in fact the inequity problems may increase because the MMA increases payments to Medicare Advantage plans, which are overwhelmingly found in urban areas (McBride, Andrews, Mueller, & Shambaugh-Miller, 2003) and which are paid an amount greater than that paid to Medicare fee-for-service providers (Medicare Payment Advisory Commission [MedPAC], 2004).

Quality

Quality is defined by the Institute of Medicine as "The degree to which health services for individuals and populations increase the likelihood of desired health care outcomes and are consistent with current professional knowledge" (Lohr, 1990, p. 21). The challenge for Medicare in a rural environment is to use the levers of financial incentives and conditions of participation to motivate providers to improve the quality of care that they offer to individual beneficiaries in a manner that achieves optimum outcomes in each case, as well as elevates the standard of care for all patients because of improvements in practice. Doing so is especially challenging in rural places that are served by only a few providers and where resources are scarce to support new information systems and other methods of adopting new strategies in quality improvement.

Medicare payment policies will influence quality in two ways. First, if payment to rural providers does not at least equal their costs, quality could be negatively affected if providers reduce the services they provide either by not seeing new Medicare patients or by offering fewer services to the ones they do see. Second, payment policies can be designed to reward quality and efficiency, which should improve the overall level of quality that is assured for all beneficiaries. Further, payment policies can be used as a means to provide the resources necessary for rural providers to purchase and operate systems to improve the use of information in monitoring and improving processes of care. Medicare policies can also require quality monitoring and can set forth standards of quality that must be met. Such policies must be crafted in a manner sensitive to the practice environments in rural areas.

THE MMA AND QUALITY

The MMA included several policy changes relative to the role of payment in quality improvement. The changes favoring rural providers described earlier enable those providers to continue seeing Medicare patients. Another payment change, a floor in the adjustment of physician payment for differences in the value of work, may also increase access to physician services for rural beneficiaries, as may the results of mandated studies of the adjustment for practice expenses in rural areas. The MMA mandated studies of the effect of including performance incentives in the traditional fee-for-service system for paying physicians, hospitals, and other providers. The policy implemented by the Centers for Medicare and Medicaid Services in 2004 to allow hospitals a full market-basket increase equivalent of increase in medical inflation if they report on 10 quality indicators has been a success, with 98% of hospitals reporting. The Centers for Medicare and Medicaid Services now has a special web site (www.hospitalcompare.hhs.gov) that allows beneficiaries and others to see the quality scores for the hospitals in their states.

The MMA created special demonstration programs to test new means of emphasizing quality improvement in Medicare policies. Four funded demonstrations of disease management programs may discover new methods of promoting higher quality care for persons with conditions of chronic illness that require constant management. An additional three demonstration projects, one of which must be in a rural area, will be designed to evaluate methods to improve the quality of care for persons with chronic conditions. A separate five-year program will examine factors that encourage the delivery of improved patient care quality. The legislation also mandated studies related to drug safety and quality improvement (Mueller, 2004). The Centers for Medicare and Medicaid Services is implementing these demonstration programs through a sequence of requests for proposals. As of May 2005, one cycle of issuing a request for proposals, reviewing applications, making awards, and beginning the projects had been completed. There are chronic care improvement demonstrations that include rural areas in the following states: Georgia, Pennsylvania, Florida, Oklahoma, Mississippi, and Tennessee (CMS, 2004b). These new programs will focus on disease management among beneficiaries with multiple chronic illnesses.

Choice

The principle of choice seeks to provide beneficiaries with freedom of choice in selecting primary care providers and other providers, and in selecting among alternative insurance options. For rural beneficiaries, choice of providers is an issue because of the limited number of providers in much of rural America. A wide choice of general managed care plans is not likely to be available in rural America.

MMA AND CHOICE

The MMA may increase choice among providers if the payment policies favoring rural providers improve the supply of those providers in rural areas. Whether or not this occurs will be in part a function of how communities and recruiters use the new payments to attract providers. The MMA emphasizes increasing choice among Prescription Drug Plans by requiring that all beneficiaries will have at least two plans from which to choose in adding a prescription drug benefit. The effect of the MMA on choice of pharmacists is difficult to predict. Medicare Advantage and Prescription Drug Plans may be selective in contracting with pharmacists, as long as access standards are met. Therefore, beneficiaries may not have equivalent financial access to all pharmacies in their area. While they can still patronize the pharmacy of their choice, their health plan may not pay all of the charges of that pharmacy if it is not part of the plan's preferred network.

Although historically there have been far fewer Medicare Advantage plans from which to choose in rural counties than in urban counties and access to supplemental plans has been limited, the MMA provides incentives to lure these plans into rural areas, including additional payment, lower risk, and a requirement of new Preferred Provider Organization plans to be available to all beneficiaries throughout any of the 26 regions in which they are offered. Initial applications from Medicare Advantage plans, submitted by the end of March 2005, included 55 new Health Maintenance Organizations, 73 new Preferred Provider Organizations, and 13 new Private Fee-For-Service plans, which would be added to 152 Health Maintenance Organizations, 26 Preferred Provider Organizations, and seven Private Fee-For-Service plans (CMS, 2005). However, given the history of Medicare + Choice, it seems likely that the provisions of the MMA will lead mostly to increases in Medicare Advantage enrollment in urban areas, with little increase in rural areas.

Costs

Containing costs is also central to any discussion of redesigning Medicare, especially because Medicare spending has grown rapidly in the last few decades, from $7.1 billion in 1970, to over $274 billion in 2003 (Congressional Budget Office, 2004). Within the objective of cost minimization, there are two separable but related cost goals that any Medicare policy should try to achieve: (1) contain the total budgetary costs of the Medicare program and (2) contain the beneficiary's out-of-pocket-costs for health care.

In pursuing these two goals, policy analysts and policy makers must recognize that the goals often conflict. For example, policies that lower the out-of-pocket costs for older adults shift those costs to the taxpayer, which does not achieve the first goal but does achieve the second. Another fundamental issue affecting Medicare policy change is that the goal of minimizing costs often conflicts with the goals of access, quality, equity, and choice. For instance, reforms that expand access to Medicare-covered services or expand the benefit package (e.g., to include prescription drugs) are likely to increase costs for either the taxpayer or the beneficiary.

Several factors could explain why out-of-pocket health spending is a greater burden on rural beneficiaries (Coburn & Ziller, 2000) than on their urban counterparts:

1. rural people have lower health status, which could lead to higher health costs;
2. rural people have less access to Medicare + Choice and supplemental insurance plans (Mueller & McBride, 1999), which have lower out-of-pocket costs;

3. rural people have lower incomes and higher poverty rates, raising their costs as a percentage of income;
4. rural people may face higher costs for the same types of services due to problems with economies of scale and limited competition in their health markets (Mueller et al., 1999).

THE MMA AND COSTS

The MMA seeks to make prescription drugs affordable to Medicare beneficiaries through two principle strategies. First, for beneficiaries whose income falls below 150% of the federal poverty guideline and who have limited assets, subsidies are provided. When income is below 135% of poverty and 2006 resources are less than $6,000 per individual or $9,000 per couple, the subsidy is 100% of the premium plus thresholds on cost sharing for prescriptions of $2 per generic drug and $5 per brand name drug (lower for persons in Medicaid and Medicare). Persons between 135% of poverty and 150% of poverty with assets below $10,000 per individual and $20,000 per couple would have costs limited to a $50 deductible, 15% cost sharing up to the out-of-pocket limit ($2,250 annually), and $5 per brand name drug and $2 per generic drug. For beneficiaries not receiving income- and asset-based subsidies, the costs of the new benefits in Medicare will be a function of what the plans in their area offer and what their previous prescription drug coverage was. Because rural older adults were less likely to have prescription drug coverage than were urban persons before passage of the MMA and because rural older adults have lower incomes than do urban elders, on balance, the prescription drug provisions may be slightly more beneficial to rural persons than to urban persons. However, the supposition implicit in the MMA is that competing plans in each region will offer plans that attract enrollment, which should include competition based on the out-of-pocket costs for beneficiaries, and there will be intense competition in rural areas.

The effect of the MMA on costs to Medicare is a matter of considerable controversy. All analyses conclude that the new benefits will increase the costs of the program, by over $400 billion over 10 years, and perhaps as high as $540 billion. In the long run, the costs are even greater, exceeding 4% of gross domestic product for just the Part D portion of Medicare (Social Security and Medicare Boards of Trustees, 2004). Several provisions in the MMA explicitly increase costs to the program for the purpose of attracting private plans into areas of the country previously not served by private plans. These include a stabilization fund, an immediate increase in payment to Medicare Advantage plans as a result of setting a minimum to be at least the equivalent of fee-for-service expenditures, and a fund to use for assuring network adequacy when providers need payment higher than costs to remain viable. If the long-term benefits of relying on competing private health plans to contain costs are valid, at some future time the cost curve would at least drop to lower annual increases and could even reverse.

Access

Access is usually defined as existing when services are available to beneficiaries when they need them and within a reasonable amount of time. Defining access is difficult and complex for several reasons. First, defining when beneficiaries actually "need" services is difficult. Second, it is difficult to agree upon the specific services to which beneficiaries should have access. Third, determining what is a "reasonable amount of time" for defining access is difficult and subjective.

Evidence shows that access is a problem for rural Medicare recipients, and that barriers to access exist for many rural residents (Coburn & Bolda, 1999; Stearns, Slifkin, & Edin, 2000). Hospital closures, fewer medical professionals, and a lack of specialty services (Conner, Kralewski, & Hillson, 1994; Knapp, Paavola, Maine, Sorofman, & Politzer, 1999; Rosenblatt & Hart, 1999) accentuate access problems. Medicare payment policies can contribute to access problems when those payments are less than actual costs (e.g., the reported negative Medicare margins in small rural hospitals).

The MMA and Access

The MMA contained provisions increasing payment to rural providers, as described earlier in this chapter in the discussion of equity. The legislation also mandated studies to help determine the validity of differential payment for rural providers. The studies included a U.S. Department of Health and Human Services (U.S. DHHS) study of the variation in prescription drug spending across regions to include recommendations regarding the appropriateness of adjusting the government subsidy to account for the variation; a MedPAC study of the basis for variation in costs between different areas, the appropriate geographic area for payment, and the accuracy of risk adjustment methods; a U.S. DHHS report to describe the impact of additional financing on the availability of Medicare Advantage plans in different areas; a MedPAC study of the impacts of changes in hospital payment policies; a U.S. DHHS study to determine if costs incurred by rural hospitals for outpatients exceed those incurred by urban hospitals; a Government Accounting Office study of access to physicians' services through an analysis of claims data; a MedPAC report on the effects of refinements to the practice expense component of payment for physician services; and a MedPAC study of payment margins of home health agencies paid under the Medicare prospective payment system. All studies will be completed by the end of 2007.

BEST PRACTICES TO OPTIMIZE GAINS FROM THE MMA

The MMA may benefit many of the nation's older adults and, potentially disproportionately, older adults in rural areas. Prior to 2003, rural elders were more likely than their urban counterparts to lack coverage for prescription drugs, have lower household income, lack Medigap coverage, have higher out-of-pocket expenses for prescription drugs, and be in poorer health (Caplan & Brangan, 2004; Coburn & Ziller, 2000). In an analysis prepared for AARP, PricewaterhouseCoopers estimated that following enactment of the MMA, the status of 28% of Medicare beneficiaries would change from having no drug coverage to being covered, and that an additional 17% would no longer lack protection against catastrophic coverage. They also estimated that $145 billion would be spent over a 10-year period to provide benefits to approximately 8.5 million people as of 2006 who meet the MMA requirements for low-income protections but were not eligible for Medicaid (Rodgers & Stell, 2004). Given that rural beneficiaries are more likely to have incomes making them eligible for these special provisions, and that they are more likely to have chronic illnesses that require medication, they are more likely to benefit from best practices that maximize enrollment into the drug plans created in response to the MMA. The MMA is not a final solution to the woes of the Medicare program, including providing adequate coverage for all beneficiaries for the indefinite future. As Marilyn Moon points out, even the prescription drug benefit for low-income beneficiaries may erode over time because of indexing the benefit structure. Enrollment into the prescription drug program by low-income beneficiaries may disappoint advocates of the benefit; Moon cites the Congressional Budget Office estimates that only 75% of those with incomes below 135% of poverty are expected to enroll, and only 35% of those with incomes between 135% and 150% of poverty are expected to participate in the low-income benefit (Moon, 2004).

Regardless of views of its strengths and weaknesses, the MMA has redefined the Medicare program, with major changes to occur starting January 1, 2006, and some important changes already in place (e.g., preventive health benefits and a prescription drug discount card). State governments and civic organizations can take actions to help Medicare beneficiaries take full advantage of the changes that the MMA brings to the program. Most of the actions should focus on the beneficiaries with the most to gain—low-income, disproportionately rural beneficiaries currently lacking adequate coverage. An important action will be to educate those beneficiaries about the new benefits and how they can use them appropriately by enrolling in the program. Another critical activity will be to coordinate state programs, both Medicaid and pharmacy assistance programs, with the new Medicare benefit. Finally, the MMA creates opportunities for innovative activities in care management that states and others can initiate. Some of this activity is already evident, with demonstration projects put in place by health plans in Florida, Pennsylvania, and other states. States could implement care management programs for dually eligible Medicare beneficiaries by creating state-funded benefits supplementing the improved set of Medicare benefits, including prescription drugs and preventive care services.

Beneficiary Education and Enrollment

As evident from the experiences of enrolling Medicare beneficiaries into the program that provides discount drug cards, much work will be needed to help low-income beneficiaries understand the new drug benefit and enroll in an appropriate plan. As of December 7, 2004, 1.5 million low-income beneficiaries had signed up for the discount drug card and the $600 credit, of approximately 7 million that are eligible (Sherman, 2004). The total enrollment into the discount drug card program was 5.8 million (CMS, 2004a), and many of these were enrolled automatically by their Medicare + Choice plans.

What can be done to provide complete, accurate information to seniors as the full benefits of the MMA become available? State governments can generate best practices through their State Health Insurance Assistance Programs. The U.S. DHHS has awarded $21 million to these programs in fiscal year 2005 and will award another $31.7 million in fiscal year 2006 (McClellan, 2004). These programs provide one-on-one advice and counseling and can work with local organizations to answer questions. Another state venue for beneficiary education is the state pharmacy assistance programs operating in 21 states in 2004. On October 28, 2004, U.S. DHHS announced awards totaling $62.5 million to those states for fiscal year 2005, to be repeated in fiscal year 2006. The Centers for Medicare and Medicaid Services has pledged to work with states to disseminate best practices in outreach and education (U.S. DHHS, 2004a).

Nongovernmental organizations will also be involved in beneficiary education. A Centers for Medicare and Medicaid Services initiative, Regional Education about Choices in Health, seeks "to cultivate

community-based partnerships with organizations that use existing out-
lets to conduct education activities for populations with barriers caused
by differences in language, literacy, location, low income, and/or culture" (McClellan, 2004, p. 47). The Centers for Medicare and Medicaid
Services, along with the Administration on Aging, is providing $3.95
million to more than 100 community-based organizations and coalitions
to help them enroll seniors into the prescription drug program (U.S.
DHHS, 2004b). Best practices should emerge from their experiences, as
well as from efforts of organizations not receiving federal government
grants. The latter might include, for example, state chapters of AARP.

Coordination with Medicaid and State
Pharmacy Assistance Programs

MEDICAID

A large portion of state Medicaid expenditures is for care received
by persons also eligible for Medicare—the "dual eligibles." Before
the MMA was enacted, a significant amount of spending for dual eligibles was for prescription drugs—$10.7 billion in fiscal year 2000.
However, that total represented only 15.2% of the total state spending for dual eligibles, compared to nursing facility payments which
represented 40.8% of the total (Tritz & Lindley, 2003). Although
MMA coverage of prescription drugs should result in state savings,
overall Medicaid spending will be affected only modestly. Some states
may not realize any savings, if increased enrollment in Medicaid (due
to the attractiveness of the Medicare drug benefit for low-income
seniors) increases expenditures more rapidly for all categories. This is
especially true in the early years, when the "clawback" state payment
to Medicare is 85% or more of total predicted drug expenditures. A
final variable that could increase Medicaid expenditures in at least
some states is the method of basing the clawback on national average increases in prescription drug expenditures, which could mean
that states with effective cost-control programs pay more into the national account than they would otherwise spend. Taking these factors
into account, plus the cost of enrolling beneficiaries, the Congressional Budget Office calculated that the program would cost the states
$1.2 billion between fiscal years 2004 and 2006, with 10-year relief
through 2013 to be $17.2 billion, most of which would occur in the
final four years (Guyer, 2003).

Two state activities will be important to monitor and identify
best practices. First, states will need to manage their budgets in light
of the new commitment to the Medicare program, inherent unless they
withdraw completely from the Medicaid program. Because dually eligible

beneficiaries will enroll in private plans through which they will receive their drug benefits, the various methods states have used to control those expenditures (prior authorization, use of lower cost drugs in formularies, copayments, negotiated price reductions) will not be used by the state and their use by private plans may not be as aggressive. Therefore, the states will need to focus even more on the costs of other services, such as skilled nursing care. Rapid dissemination of best practices from those experiences may help save the fiscal health of Medicaid programs.

States may wish to establish working relationships with the Prescription Drug Plans enrolling Medicare beneficiaries in their regions for the purpose of assuring appropriate medications are available to dual eligibles. This could be especially important for beneficiaries with disabilities and multiple chronic illnesses. Under the MMA, Prescription Drug Plans must operate a drug utilization management program that reduces costs when appropriate and includes a medication therapy management program for targeted beneficiaries. Prescription Drug Plan formularies could put certain beneficiaries at risk because they cannot access newly available medications or because they need access to more drugs within a therapeutic class than the plan allows (Crowley, 2004). States can be active partners for dual eligibles in two ways: by helping them select plans best suited for their particular needs, including plans that are approved to serve special needs populations, and by working with plans, especially those approved to serve special needs populations, to expand formularies to better serve dual eligibles. During 2005 and beyond, best practices in both types of activities should be described and disseminated.

STATE PHARMACY ASSISTANCE PROGRAMS

As discussed in an earlier section of this chapter, U.S. DHHS awarded state pharmacy assistance programs (SPAPs) $62.5 million in grants to assist them in transitioning to a new role of coordinating their programs with the new Part D Medicare benefit. States will be able to pay drug costs not covered by Medicare, supplement drug coverage with purchase of additional benefits for excluded drugs, provide a state supplemental benefit program, and contribute to the cost-sharing requirements of Part D. That is, beneficiaries must incur $2,250 in true out-of-pocket expenses before the catastrophic benefit is effective. As of August 2003, 38 states had programs to reduce the cost of prescription drugs for some portion of their residents, and 30 of these states had a direct benefit program (Trail, Fox, Cantor, Silberberg, & Crystal, 2004). In general, states have adopted one or more of three strategies—direct benefit or subsidy, price reduction, or tax credits (Fox, Trail, & Crystal, 2002). Most states target low-income seniors and disabled beneficiaries who do not qualify for Medicaid coverage, and the states receive rebates from manufacturers (GAO, 2000).

During 2004, 13 states made changes in laws or legislative resolutions to align their programs to MMA provisions. For example, many of those changes were to automatically enroll beneficiaries in a discount card program (National Conference of State Legislatures, 2004). The Web site of the National Conference of State Legislatures (www.ncsl.org) is a source of best practices in legislative action to align SPAPs with the MMA. As the time of the full benefit nears (January 1, 2006), states will need to determine the extent to which they will continue SPAPs, focusing on the gaps that remain in coverage and cost after beneficiaries enroll in Part D of Medicare. Some states may choose to discontinue their SPAPs as a means of budget savings, assuming beneficiaries will do at least as well with Part D. There may be reason to link activities related to Medicaid with this decision, such as working with Prescription Drug Plans focused on special populations to provide comprehensive drug benefits to the population who formerly used SPAP benefits.

Care Management

States and other organizations can learn from experiences in Medicaid to implement systems of care management that would improve the health of seniors while managing the costs of care. The MMA promotes the concept of disease management, including providing support for demonstration projects. A very direct approach is to work with pharmacists to implement a program of case management to ensure medication safety and monitor health care utilization. Iowa's Medicaid program conducted a demonstration of this approach between October 2000 and July 2002. Working with 2,211 Iowa Medicaid patients taking four or more medications and the 117 pharmacies they used, the project found that in the 28 pharmacies that used case management services most intensively, patients had a significant decrease in high-risk medication use and medication safety improved (Chrischilles, Carter, Lund, Rubenstein, Chen-Hardee, Voelker et al., 2004). Other states, such as Virginia and Mississippi, have similar programs (Wheatley, 2002). Pharmacy case management is a best practice worthy of replication. After 2006, doing so will require collaborating with the private plans that enroll Medicare beneficiaries.

Managing use of prescription medications is a critical element of disease management programs, which are designed to achieve cost savings and prevent worsening of chronic conditions. States have adopted disease management programs targeting the following conditions: diabetes, asthma, hyperlipidemia, hemophilia, congestive heart failure, hypertension, depression, and chronic obstructive pulmonary disease. Most have met with at least moderate success in improving the management of these diseases (Wheatley, 2002). States to learn from include Florida, Maryland, Mississippi, North Carolina, Texas, Utah, Virginia, and West Virginia (Wheatley, 2002).

CONCLUSIONS

Changes made to the Medicare program by the MMA may have profound impacts on the well-being, both economic and health, of rural Medicare beneficiaries. Some of the effects will be indirect because the payment provisions may increase payment to rural providers, which would in turn affect access for beneficiaries. Similarly, changes in how benefits are made available, such as offering the outpatient prescription drug benefit only through private health plans, may affect the ability of rural beneficiaries to participate in the new benefit. The changes affect beneficiaries directly through provisions regarding cost sharing and out-of-pocket expenses, which generally make the new benefits affordable for low-income beneficiaries but which may or may not do so for beneficiaries at other income levels. The impact of the Medicare prescription drug program on beneficiaries currently holding prescription drug coverage (through employer coverage, a Medicare Advantage plan, supplemental coverage, or Medicaid coverage) is more uncertain. Some of these beneficiaries will be unaffected by the new plan, but some may actually be made worse if they lose their current coverage.

State governments and other organizations have opportunities to coordinate their efforts on behalf of older adults with the changes in the Medicare program. State programs targeting low-income elders, such as prescription drug assistance programs, could be used to fill remaining gaps after the new MMA benefits are effective in 2006. States may have opportunities to use Medicaid resources more creatively since there will be a federally-funded benefit for prescription medications. On the other hand, some states may face new budget problems because they will have to pay more to the federal government under the clawback provisions of the MMA than they would otherwise have spent for Medicaid, primarily because the new drug benefit may result in higher drug expenditures than the state was experiencing.

All organizations, public and private, will have a great deal of work to do in educating beneficiaries about the new program and choices available to them. Beneficiaries will need to consider alternative plans on multiple dimensions, including out-of-pocket expenses, participating providers, drug formularies, and conditions at time of renewal. Although the Centers for Medicare and Medicaid Services will be heavily engaged in beneficiary education, local organizations and local pharmacies will be important to the seniors in their areas.

The MMA created new opportunities for rural older adult beneficiaries:

- all beneficiaries will have access to at least two (actually six, given the presence of national plans) plans offering a prescription drug benefit subsidized by the Medicare program;
- demonstrations programs designed to improve the management of chronic conditions include rural beneficiaries as enrollees into those plans, creating the possibility that approaches will be designed specifically for rural beneficiaries;
- payment systems were adjusted to improve payment to rural providers, helping to assure access to services for beneficiaries; and
- health plans offering benefits other than mandatory Medicare benefits, Medicare Advantage Plans, have additional incentives to enroll beneficiaries in rural areas.

The MMA also presents significant challenges to rural beneficiaries and the organizations that serve them:

- rural beneficiaries will initially be unfamiliar with choosing among health plans and will need assistance to make wise choices;
- Medicare Advantage plans may not engage in marketing activities that reach eligible rural beneficiaries because doing so is prohibitively expensive, given the small numbers of potential enrollees; and
- new changes in Medicare payment policies, including implementing a system of pay-for-performance that pays providers who achieve certain levels of quality as set by key indicators, require analysis for possible effects on rural providers who for reasons of limited resources may not be able to achieve the same results as urban counterparts.

Efforts to catalog best practices among state, federal, and private organizations should begin as soon as possible. This chapter has suggested several possibilities. There will also be opportunities to improve the program, including its implications for rural residents and providers, as implementation continues. We have suggested principles to use when examining the rural implications of the MMA, which should inform further legislative and regulatory policy choices.

REFERENCES

Caplan, C., & Brangan, N. (2004). *Prescription drug spending and coverage among rural Medicare beneficiaries in 2003* (Data Digest No.106). Washington, DC: AARP Public Policy Institute.

Centers for Medicare and Medicaid Services. (2004a). *Medicare modernization benefits in the first year* (Fact Sheet, December 8). Washington, DC: CMS Office of Public Affairs. Retrieved December 29, 2004, from http://www.cms.hhs.gov/media/press/release.asp?Counter=1276

Centers for Medicare and Medicaid Services, Medicaid Health Support. (2004b). *Medicare awards for programs to improve care of beneficiaries with chronic illnesses* (Fact Sheet, December 8). Washington, DC: CMS Office of Public Affairs. Retrieved May 14, 2005, from http://www.cms.hhs.gov/medicarereform/ccip/factsheet.pdf

Centers for Medicare and Medicaid Services. (2005). *Lower-cost health plan choices available to more beneficiaries in 2005* (Press Release). Washington, DC: CMS Office of Public Affairs. Retrieved February 18, 2005, from http://www.cms.hhs.gov/media/press/release.asp

Chrischilles, E. A., Carter, B. L., Lund, B. C., Rubenstein, L. M., Chen-Hardee, S. S., Voelker, M. D., et al. (2004). Evaluation of the Iowa Medicaid pharmaceutical case management program. *Journal of the American Pharmacy Association, 44*, 337–349.

Coburn, A., & Bolda, E. (1999). The rural elderly and long-term care. In T. C. Ricketts III (Ed.), *Rural health in the United States* (pp. 179–189). New York: Oxford University Press.

Coburn, A. F., & Ziller, E. C. (2000, August). *Designing a prescription drug benefit for rural Medicare beneficiaries: Principles, criteria, and assessment* (Policy Paper No. P2000-14). Omaha, NE: RUPRI Center for Rural Health Policy Analysis. Retrieved May 16, 2005, from http://www.rupri.org/publications/archive/reports/P2000-14/

Congressional Budget Office. (2004, January). *The budget and economic outlook: Fiscal years 2005 to 2014.* Washington, DC: Congress of the United States, Congressional Budget Office.

Connor, R. A., Kralewski, J. E., & Hillson, S. D. (1994). Measuring geographic access to health care in rural areas. *Medical Care Review, 51*, 337–377.

Crowley, J. S. (2004, July). *The new Medicare prescription drug law: Issues for dual eligibles with disabilities and serious conditions* (Issue Paper No. 7119). Washington, DC: The Henry J. Kaiser Family Foundation. The Kaiser Commission on Medicaid and the Uninsured. Retrieved June 6, 2005, from http://www.kff.org/medicaid/7119.cfm

Fox, K., Trail, T., & Crystal, S. (2002, May). *State pharmacy assistance programs: Approaches to program design* (Field Report). New York: The Commonwealth Fund. Retrieved June 7, 2005, from www.cmwf.org

General Accounting Office. (2000, September). *State pharmacy programs: Assistance designed to target coverage and stretch budgets* (Report to Congressional Requesters, GAO/HEHS-00–162). Washington, DC: GAO Health,

140   HEALTH SERVICES PROVISION AND POLICY ISSUES

Education and Human Services Division. Retrieved October 13, 2005,
from http://www.gao.gov/archive/2000/he00162.pdf

Guyer, J. (2003, December). *Implications of the new Medicare prescription drug
benefit for state Medicaid budgets* (Issue Paper No. 4162). Washington,
DC: The Henry J. Kaiser Family Foundation. The Kaiser Commission on
Medicaid and the Uninsured. Retrieved May 17, 2005, from http://www.
kff.org/medicaid/4162.cfm

Knapp, K. K., Paavola, F. G., Maine, L. L., Sorofman, B., & Politzer, M. (1999).
Availability of primary care providers and pharmacists in the United States.
Journal of the American Pharmaceutical Association, 39, 127–135.

Lohr, K. (Ed.). (1990). *Medicare: A strategy for quality assurance* (Vol. 1).
Washington, DC: National Academy Press.

McBride, T. D., Andrews, C., Makarkin, A., & Mueller, K. J. (2002, August).
*An update on Medicare + Choice: Rural Medicare beneficiaries enrolled
in Medicare + Choice plans through September 2001* (Rural Policy Brief
7, No. 4). Omaha, NE: RUPRI Center for Rural Health Policy Analysis.
Retrieved May 17, 2005, from www.rupri.org/healthpolicy

McBride, T. D., Andrews, C., Mueller, K., & Shambaugh-Miller, M. (2003,
March). *An analysis of availability of Medicare + Choice, Commercial
HMO, and FEHBP plans in rural areas: Implications for Medicare reform*
(PB2003–5). Omaha, NE: RUPRI Center for Rural Health Policy Analysis.
Retrieved October 14, 2005, from www.rupri.org/healthpolicy

McClellan, M. (2004, September 14). *Titles I and II: Features of the pro-
posed regulations.* Testimony before the Senate Committee on Finance,
Washington, DC.

Medicare Payment Advisory Commission. (2004, March). *Report to the Congress: Medicare payment policy.* Washington, DC: Author.

Moon, M. (2004, June). *How beneficiaries fare under the new Medicare drug bill* (Issue Brief). New York: Commonwealth Fund. Retrieved October 13, 2005, from http://www.cmwf.org/publications/
publications_show.htm?doc_id=227453

Mueller, K. J. (2004). *The Medicare Prescription Drug, Improvement, and Modernization Act of 2003: A summary of provisions important to rural health
care delivery* (Policy Paper No. P2004–1). Omaha, NE: RUPRI Center for
Rural Health Policy Analysis. Retrieved June 13, 2005, from www.rurpi.
org/healthpolicy

Mueller, K. J., & McBride, T. D. (1999). Tracking the response to the Balanced
Budget Act of 1997: Impact on Medicare managed care enrollment in rural
counties. *Journal of Rural Health, 15*(1), 67–77.

Mueller, K. J., Coburn, A., Cordes, S., Crittenden, R., Hart, J. P., McBride, T.,
et al. (1999). The changing landscape of health care financing and delivery:
How are rural communities and providers responding? *Milbank Quarterly,
77*, 485–510.

National Academy of Social Insurance. (1999, February). *Medicare and the
American social contract: Restructuring Medicare for the long term project* (Final report). Washington, DC: National Academy of Social Insurance

Study Panel on Medicare's Larger Social Role. Retrieved December 28, 2004, from www.nasi.org/usr_doc/med_report_soc_contract.pdf

National Conference of State Legislatures. (2004). *State pharmaceutical assistance programs.* Retrieved December 28, 2004, from http://www.ncsl.org/programs/health/drugaid.htm

Rodgers, J., & Stell, J. (2004). *The Medicare prescription drug benefit: Potential impact on beneficiaries* (Report No. 2004–13). Washington, DC: AARP Public Policy Institute. Retrieved May 18, 2005, from www.aarp.org/ppi

Rosenblatt, R. A., & Hart, L. G. (1999). Physicians and rural America. In T. C. Ricketts III (Ed.), *Rural health in the United States* (pp. 38–51). New York: Oxford University Press.

Rural Policy Research Institute Health Panel. (2001, May). *Redesigning Medicare: Considerations for rural beneficiaries and health systems* (Special Monograph). Columbia, MO: RUPRI. Retrieved June 8, 2005, from www.rupri.org

Sherman, M. (2004). *Medicare drug card enrollment falls short. Yahoo!News.* Retrieved December 8, 2004, from http://news.yahoo.com/news?tmpl=story&cid=537&u=/ap/20041207

Social Security and Medicare Boards of Trustees. (2004). *Status of the Social Security and Medicare programs: A summary of the 2004 annual reports.* Retrieved December 1, 2004, from http://www.ssa.gov/OACT/TRSUM/tr04summary.pdf

Stearns, S. C., Slifkin, R. T., & Edin, H. M. (2000). Access to care for rural Medicare beneficiaries. *Journal of Rural Health, 16*(1), 62–73.

Trail, T., Fox, K., Cantor, J., Silberberg, M., & Crystal, S. (2004, August). *State pharmacy assistance programs: A chartbook* (No. 758). New York: Commonwealth Fund. Retrieved May 17, 2005, from www.cmwf.org

Tritz, K., & Lindley, M. (2003). *Dual eligibles: Medicaid expenditures for prescription drugs and other services* (CRS Report for Congress, July 11). Washington, DC: Congressional Research Service, Library of Congress.

U.S. Department of Health and Human Services. (2004a). *HHS announces awards to states to tell low-income beneficiaries about 2006 drug benefit* (News Release). Washington, DC: CMS Public Affairs Office. Retrieved November 9, 2004, from http://www.hhs.gov/news/press/2004pres/20041028.html

U.S. Department of Health and Human Services. (2004b). *HHS works with grassroots to help millions of Medicare beneficiaries see savings with drug cards* (News Release). Washington, DC: CMS Media Affairs. Retrieved November 9, 2004, from http://www.hhs.gov/news/press/2004pres/20040930a.html

Wheatley, B. (2002, December). *Disease management: Findings from leading state programs* (State Coverage Initiatives Issue Brief Vol. III, No. 3). Washington, DC: Academy Health.

PART III

Selected Services

CHAPTER EIGHT

Caregiving in a Rural Context

Donna L. Wagner and Kelly J. Niles-Yokum

Ensuring that adequate support is available to older Americans with long-term care needs is a challenge nationwide. Although we have seen a decrease in the disability rates among older adults (Manton & Stallard, 1996), advanced age continues to be associated with a need for assistance and long-term services. For the vast majority of elders, family and friends provide the services they need to continue to live independently in the community. Recent estimates suggest that one out of four families is providing assistance to an older family member (National Alliance for Caregiving/AARP, 1997). In rural areas, the caregiving support provided by families and friends are of particular importance because of a lack of formal home- and community-based services commonly concentrated in more populated areas of the country (Dwyer, Lee, & Coward, 1990; Krout, 1998). Although informal sources of support can be a lifeline for rural elders, in many rural communities, the primary sources of support available to other elders—adult children—may also be absent.

This chapter will begin with an overview of caregiving in general. We will then review existing research on caregiving in a rural context and discuss the issues associated with caregiving that are unique to rural areas. The chapter ends with a discussion of practice concepts and principles that foster support for older adults in rural areas and research needs in order to improve our understanding of rural caregiving

tomorrow and in the future. Our analysis will be guided by the following questions:

- How does informal caregiving in the rural community differ
  from informal caregiving in the urban/suburban community?
- What factors are present in the rural community that influence
  informal caregiving now and are likely to influence it in the
  future?
- What do we know about the interface between informal and formal
  care and how it is different in the rural environment?
- What practice elements and models hold promise for strengthening
  caregiving by and for elders in the rural community?
- What research is needed to foster our understanding of the needs
  of rural elders and their caregivers for the future?

INFORMAL CAREGIVING AND WELL-BEING
OF OLDER PERSONS

The literature on caregiving by and for older persons is extensive and
consistent in one important finding—the majority of assistance and support for older persons is provided by an informal source. In 1987, the
U.S. Select Committee on Aging reported that 80% of all services received
by older adults were provided by family or friends. In the nearly two
decades since that report was issued, this estimate has remained constant.
Help and support for an older family member is imminent regardless
of the distance between caregiver and care recipient, the employment
status of the care provider, or the presence of other competing demands
on the caregiver's time. The estimates of the number of caregivers for
older adults range between a low of 5.9 million caregivers to more than
22 million households (Family Caregiver Alliance, 2001).

Regardless of the number of caregivers, it is well accepted that informal caregiving is the primary source of long-term care in this country.
A recent estimate of the cost of replacing formal paid care for the informal
care provided by families for persons with disabilities is between $45
and $94 billion (Spillman, Black, & Mayes, 2004). Arno (2002) estimates
the value of this unpaid care as high as $257 billion a year. To the elder
who needs help, the support and care given them by their family and
friends not only is of instrumental importance but is an emotional anchor
for their well-being.

Recognition of the importance of family caregiving to the long-term
care system has resulted in the passage of the National Family Caregivers

Support Act by Congress (2000) and the development of a national initiative by the National Governor's Association (NGA). The NGA has developed a set of recommendations for the nation's governors regarding family caregiving in order to foster and support family care while managing the rising cost of long-term care services (NGA, 2004). Changing demographics add urgency to the development of policy to support family caregivers. These demographic changes include increasing numbers of older adults, smaller families, more women in the workforce, among others, and are well recognized by policy makers and planners nationwide.

Spouses and adult children make up the majority of informal care networks of older adults (Brody, 1985; Cantor, 1979; Stone, Cafferata, & Sangl, 1987). Because older women have higher life expectancies and therefore are less likely than older men to be married, they are more likely to have provided care (to a husband or other relative) than men and are also more likely to be helped by their adult children than by their husbands. A national survey of family caregivers (National Alliance for Caregiving/AARP, 2004) found that the average older person receiving help was a 75-year-old widow who lives alone and is being helped by a daughter who lives nearby. Her daughter is employed and in her late 40s and she spends an average of 20 hours a week providing care and support. Informal caregiving for older persons primarily involves adult children caring for older parents. However, just as there is heterogeneity among the older population, there is also a wide range of caregiving situations for older adults. Because the aging population is growing and living longer, it is not unusual to see a 70-year-old daughter caring for her 90-year-old mother. Older spouses are providing care and grandchildren in their 20s and 30s are caring for grandparents. Although it is commonly assumed that family caregiving is a woman's obligation, males are also frequently involved in providing care to aging parents or spouses (Thompson, 2002).

Among working caregivers, surveys have found that almost as many men in a workforce report care responsibilities as women (Bond, Galinsky, & Swanberg, 1998). With nearly 80% of the women between the ages of 25 and 44 involved in the workforce, traditional gender roles are being renegotiated (Barnett, 1998). Contrary to expectations, working caregivers do not seem to provide less care and support than nonworking caregivers (Brody & Schoonover, 1986; Matthews, Werkner, & Delaney, 1989; Stoller, 1983). In a recent survey of working caregivers, we found that 80% of the respondents were involved in at least one instrumental support activity and more than half were providing multiple instrumental supports (transportation, grocery shopping, helping with housework, preparing meals, managing finances, arranging needed services, and managing medication) (Wagner, DeViney, & Hunt, 2003).

In addition to providing instrumental assistance, some family care-givers are providing personal care assistance. Personal care, or help with activities of daily living (ADLs), is less common for the family provider. In comparing the results of the 1987 AARP national survey of family caregivers with those of the 1997 National Alliance for Caregiving/AARP national survey, fewer caregivers reported involvement in helping with ADLs. Those caregivers reporting that they did not help with ADLs rose from 33% in 1987 to 48% in 1997 (Wagner, 1997a).

Wolf (1999) has described family care as an efficient mechanism for long-term care services to older adults because of the knowledge of the care recipient's needs, preferences, and desires which a family mem-ber brings to the care situation. Family caregivers and care recipients can derive pleasure from the caregiving situation that would not necessarily be present in a formal care situation. Finally, family care affords the older person a sense of autonomy and control that may not be present in formal care situations. Baker and Palletthehn (1995), for example, found that el-ders were resistant to formal care options even when the need was acute because of a perceived lack of control over these options or the implica-tions for their own lives and the lives of their family members. Although the caregiving literature is replete with a range of studies that focus on the importance of family care to the long-term care system and the well-being of elders, the burden and benefits of the care situation, and conceptual and theoretical approaches to understanding informal care, research and knowledge about specific subpopulations such as within rural areas or among ethnic and racial groups is sparse in comparison.

IS CAREGIVING DIFFERENT IN A RURAL AREA?

The rural environment is changing and, although the myths of isola-tion and homogeneity persist, rural communities are very different today from the past (Flora, Flora, & Fey, 2004). Technology has brought the world into the living rooms of rural families and recent immigrants from around the world have altered the culture and social structure of many rural communities. However, there continue to be many differences be-tween the rural America and the urban and suburban America of today. We will begin with the demographics of the rural community.

Demographic Factors of Importance

There are proportionately more elders living in rural areas than in other types of communities. Smith and Longino (1994) point out that 25% of all older adults in the country live in rural areas and their numbers are increasing. Glasgow (2000) also documents the demographic differences using U.S. Census data and finds that while 12% of the metropolitan population is age 65 years or older, nearly 15% of the rural population is age 65 years or older. The accepted explanation for this proportionate difference is the outmigration of younger people, the immigration of retired people to rural areas, and the aging-in-place of older people (Buckwalter & Davis, 2002; Glasgow, 2000; Longino, 2003). With a proportionately smaller number of young and middle-age adults (Krout, 1988), the demographic picture of rural America may suggest that fewer potential caregivers are present and available when needed for rural elders. On the positive side, however, Glasgow (2000) points out that the rates of married elders are slightly higher in rural areas. Spouses, as the most likely care provider, may be more available as a result of this rate differential but are also more likely than adult children to have adverse health effects as a result of caregiving activities. This good news/ bad news scenario permeates our discussion about rural caregiving in part because of the lack of in-depth understanding based upon objective research.

Health characteristics and poverty levels of rural older adults also are predictive of higher levels of need than in the urban population. Rural elders have higher rates of disability and morbidity than their urban peers and higher rates of poverty as well (Glasgow, 2000; McAuley, Spector, Van Nostrand, & Shaffer, 2004). While these demographic facts may be indicative of a sub-population in need and lacking the familial support available to elders living in more urban areas, this interpretation is premature and based primarily upon conjecture and "conventional wisdom."

Distance and Proximate Caregiving

Caregiving is an intimate and personal activity that, for the most part, is based on face-to-face contact between the caregiver and the care recipient. The estimated 7 million Americans providing long-distance care to older adults in the United States usually rely on the help and support of a family member who lives near the care recipient (Wagner, 1997b). For caregivers who are caring at a distance, the distance itself is often cited as the biggest problem they face in their caregiving responsibilities. Rural communities are, by definition, distant from their urban counterparts, and often within rural communities, distance is a factor in accessing neighbors as well as services (Krout, 1998).

Geographic proximity plays an important role in identifying a designated caregiver and the ways in which the caregiver can manage their caregiving responsibilities. Distance can influence the type of family support that is available to an older person as well as the designation of the family caregiver. Typically, there is a primary caregiver who is responsible for care decisions and care arrangements. Stern (1996) found that the family member who lived closest to the older person in need of help was most likely to be the designated caregiver regardless of their gender, personal situation, or employment status. Research that has examined residential proximity of adult children to their aging parents suggests that urban elders are more likely than rural elders to live close to an adult child (Krout, 1988; Lee & Cassidy, 1985). An exception to this was found among rural farm families; however, these families represent the minority within a rural community (Glasgow, 2000). Finally, Buckwalter and Davis (2002), in their review of rural care issues, remind us that limited access to adult children by rural elders is experienced even within the Hispanic community. They also suggest that as a result of this distance, cultural norms are changing and barriers to care are imminent. These studies and others suggest that distance may put the rural elder at a disadvantage when it comes to informal caregiving. Not only are the adult children likely to be distant to the rural elder, but any existing services or neighbors are also frequently distant.

Care Norms and Patterns

Although research specifically on rural caregiving patterns and expectations is somewhat limited, existing literature provides us with some understanding of care norms and patterns that may differ between urban and rural elders. Glasgow (2000) found support for the idea that rural elders had higher expectations regarding assistance from adult children than urban elders. In their review of the literature, Buckwalter and Davis (2002) report differences between common assumptions about rural caregiving and the reality. Among these differences is the assumption that rural elders are embedded in extended family systems that provide care when, in reality, their caregivers are likely to be a combination of spouses, adult children who may care from a distance, and neighbors or friends.

The use of fictive kin as surrogate informal care providers for rural elders seems, on the surface, another likely difference between urban and rural elders. Fictive kin are those individuals who, while not related, are imbued with the same rights and responsibilities as kin (Mac Rae, 1992). Since rural elders may have less access to their adult children and lack the time and opportunity to create strong ties with friends and neighbors, the notion of instrumental social networks of fictive kin is appealing. An estimated 5-10% of community elders receive informal assistance from a friend or neighbor (Barker, 2002). Little research exists on this element of the care system, however, and the extent of the importance of friends and neighbors in rural caregiving and the relationship between care-providing friends and neighbors are matters of conjecture at this time. Shenk (1998) identifies three factors that influence the effectiveness of an older woman's support system; her social interaction patterns developed over a lifetime, the length of time she has lived in the community, and her family configuration, including marital status and geographic location of adult children. Longevity in residence may be related to deeper relationships and therefore more opportunities for fictive kin relations. In Barker's (2002) work on caregiving by friends and neighbors, she found that more than half of the care situations (58%) were actually started as a result of caregiving rather than as a result of a long-standing relationship between caregiver and care recipient. She was not, however, limiting her study to care by someone with the status of fictive kin. Nonetheless, there is much we do not know about caregiving dyads and their development over time in rural, as well as urban, areas.

There are also likely differences between rural and urban communities related to the family care provider and the costs they incur as a result of caregiving. Nationally, 40% of the family caregivers are spouses (Center on an Aging Society, 2005). Spouses report spending more time in caregiving activities and in the case of older spouses, are more likely to report adverse health effects of caregiving than adult children. There are also, as reported earlier, more men who are involved in caregiving today than in the past. Based on data from the Informal Caregiver Supplement to the 1999 National Long Term Care Survey, reported by the Center on an Aging Society, 26% of the caregivers were men in 1989 and 36% were men in 1999.

The recent National Alliance for Caregiving/AARP survey of caregivers (2004) found that nearly 60% of the respondents were working. This contrasts with the data collected and reported above, which found that approximately one-third were working. Findings regarding work and caregiving are mixed as to the effect on the caregiver. In one recent Canadian survey of 55 rural caregiving women, those who were employed were more likely to report good health than those caregivers who were not employed (Blakely & Jaffe, 2000). The women reported, as do most caregivers, that caregiving limited their leisure time activities and interfered with their work. However, those women who were working and who had other family help with the caregiving were the most likely to say that their health had not been affected by their caregiving.

In the rural area with slightly more married couples and higher numbers of men than in the urban areas (Dwyer, Lee, & Coward, 1990; Glasgow, 2000), we might expect to see a higher level of spousal care and a lower level of adult children as primary caregivers than in urban areas. As outlined above, we might also see a preponderance of fictive kin support when compared with urban areas. Finally, the demographics suggest that there may be more peer caregiving in rural areas due to a relative lack of middle-aged adults. These care patterns, if in fact they are in place, are not necessarily less supportive or less effective at maintaining the elder in his or her community than other care patterns. However, likely to be absent is the occasional support that is reassuringly available to a caregiver when the Meals-on-Wheels is delivered on a routine basis and the professional home health aid arrives to assist with bathing or personal care.

INTERFACE BETWEEN FORMAL AND INFORMAL CARE

In the literature about rural older adults there is a presumption that limited access to formal care in rural areas increases the importance of informal care. Shenk's (1998) assertion that rural elders may be more independent than other elders and may also be hesitant to seek help from formal services when it is needed is confounded by the idea put forth by Buckwalter and Davis (2002) that rural elders may not only lack information about available services but hesitate to use them because of a welfare stigma associated with the use of the service.

The discussion of substitution between formal and informal care has been ongoing for more than 20 years now. The focus of this discussion, however, has changed over time from the idea that formal services were necessary to "shore up" lagging family care (Doty, 1986), to concerns about the meaning of formal care in the context of the family— does it foster or preclude informal services (e.g., Penrod, Harris, & Kane, 1994). More currently, formal services are seen as a problem for family caregivers in that the service professionals do not recognize the work of the informal caregiver nor provide adequate support to care providers on whom they are depending to carry out health care tasks in the absence of the professional care worker (Levine, 2004). It is unclear exactly how formal and informal services interface in the case of rural elders. Although we assume that individual family norms and preferences play a role in the selection of formal services or in the decision to forego them altogether, little is known about the extent to which community context, accessibility of services, or community norms influence this decision.

Glasgow (2000) points out that the research that compares urban and rural service availability has consistently found that the rural areas have fewer home- and community-based services and a lack of health care options. Rural elders also experience higher rates of institutionalization than is found among urban elders, perhaps as a result of a lack of community-based options, available informal care options, or both (McAuley, Spector, Van Nostrand, & Shaffer, 2004). McAuley and colleagues suggest that, in rural areas, the use of professional home care services may substitute for the lack of informal care or home- and community-based options that are widely available in urban areas.

Nonetheless, the interface between formal and informal services in rural America is not well understood. Nationwide, the use of formal services by elders is low, with a reliance on informal care. In an analysis of national data, the Center on an Aging Society (2005) found that the majority of older adults with limitations (67%) relied solely on informal sources for needed assistance. While an increasing number supplemented the informal support with paid services—a third, up from 24%—fewer elders relied solely on formal care, less than 8%. In the rural communities, the choice to supplement informal care with formal care may be affected by a variety of factors, including the lack of appropriate formal services.

Buckwalter and Davis (2002) point out that many of the service options available to rural elders are merely modified versions of services designed for urban areas. These options may not be acceptable to elders in need, and thus, the design of the service, coupled with a reticence to use formal services as discussed in Shenk (1998) and Glasgow (2000), suggests that there are few options available for many rural elders. It is also essential that we increase our understanding of the interface between formal and informal services. Conventional wisdom regarding rural elders or ethnic elders suggests that there is a preference for independence and self-reliance and that these groups would not choose formal options for assistance. However, research suggests that these assumptions may be nothing more than assumptions. A recent meta-analysis found that the assumption that ethnic minority caregivers were resistant to formal services and used them less often than White caregivers was not supported by existing research (Pinquart & Sorensen, 2005). Similarly, Buckwalter and Davis (2002) suggest that the design of the service programs in rural areas and their relative inaccessibility may be more of a barrier to their use than individual attitudes or preferences.

Another important factor in the formal versus informal interface among rural elders and their caregivers is the use of nursing home care as a surrogate for home care. Advocates of home- and community-based long-term care often address the institutional bias of care in the United States but, applied to the rural context, home- and community-based services may be lacking and the only option is an institutional provider of service. The question then becomes, how do rural communities establish systems that are person-centered and address the needs of caregivers and care recipients without taking home and community out of the equation? The next section will explore practice elements of importance to rural caregivers and care recipients and discuss some promising practice models.

CREATING A SUPPORTIVE CONTEXT FOR RURAL CAREGIVING

One place to begin the discussion about the development of a supportive context for rural caregiving is the seven principles developed by researchers at rural long-term care conferences held in 1994 and 1999. The principles, according to Beaulieu, Rowles, and Kuder (2001), include the following:

- community locus of control;
- nonlinear models of care;
- client-centered philosophy of care;
- family-centered decision-making;
- access to information;
- cooperation among providers; and
- redefinition of health professional roles.

If formal long-term care services are to be acceptable and accepted by rural older adults, their needs, preferences, and characteristics need to be considered in the design. Although we have some idea of factors that may influence the design of rural services based on the literature of rural researchers, there is general agreement that more research is needed.

Design Factors of Importance

As discussed by Ritchie et al. (2002), rural elders are at special risk due to a lack of coordinated service systems that meet their needs. Researchers and practitioners who focus on the rural caregiver and rural communities have identified a number of design factors of importance for new or modified service initiatives. These factors include the following:

- recognition that rural communities are diverse in population characteristics, values, and culture;
- initiatives that involve local residents during the design, planning, and implementation stages;

- recognition that geographic distance is not only a geographic barrier but a psychological barrier as well;
- initiatives that recognize the importance of fictive kin, neighbors, and friends in rural support systems that may contain few close relatives because of out-migration;
- service and access hours that reflect the needs of working caregivers—on a variety of work shifts;
- outreach and service design factors that do not stigmatize the caregiver or the care recipient; and
- mobile options that bring assessment, services, and support to the caregivers and their care recipients.

Community planners for rural services must also be sensitive to the balance between informal and formal care and the extent to which informal care is supported and not pushed aside in favor of bureaucratic models. A number of rural caregiving initiatives have been started that hold promise for enhancing the support for caregiving in rural communities and a discussion of selected initiatives follows.

RURAL CAREGIVING INITIATIVES

Recently, a number of caregiving initiatives have emerged that hold promise for increasing the support to rural older adults and their caregivers. In part these new initiatives have been spurred on by the passage of the National Family Caregivers Support Act. This Act, passed by Congress in 2000, recognizes the importance of family caregivers in the long-term care system and mandates services to support, educate, and serve family caregivers. Efforts to reach rural elders have historically been supported by the development and work of the Extension Service Centers and university-based centers for rural life and the scholars who are affiliated with these centers. Additionally, organizations such as the Robert Wood Johnson Foundation have identified rural issues as priority areas in their funding.

The development of information technology has also opened up new avenues for service for rural communities—coordinated planning and sharing of information, interdisciplinary research in distant rural communities, telemedicine, and educational services, for example. This new technology has provided a pathway for rural community leaders and planners to educate policy makers and others about the unique characteristics of rural communities, their strengths and needs, and the preferred manner for support and assistance. The models described below were selected as illustrative examples of initiatives that support rural caregiving.

Educational Services

Educational services are of critical importance to informal caregivers and the professionals who serve them. A number of initiatives designed to educate families and professionals have been operating nationwide, and, more recently, under the National Family Caregivers Support Act, new and expanded programs have been developed. On a national level, the U.S. Department of Agriculture directs the AgrAbility Project. The program brings together cooperative extension services at land-grant universities with nonprofit disability service organizations in an effort to provide education and support to individuals and their families. Also, on the national level, the American Psychological Association's Committee on Rural Health publishes articles and provides resources through the Resource Center for Rural Behavioral Health in an effort to ameliorate the paucity of trained mental health professionals in rural communities, a problem for many caregiving families.

On a state level, the University of Maine Center on Aging convenes an Annual Rural Geriatric Conference for Professionals who work with rural elders and their families. The Administration on Aging is also funding a collaborative demonstration project in Maine to examine whether and how a combination of information, support, and training can reduce risks associated with caregiving in rural areas. In Oklahoma, a state in which nine of the 11 Area Agencies on Aging are considered rural agencies, developed a "Caregivers Connection" 14 years ago in order to provide training about caregiver issues to area agency staff. Single access to respite care was developed and, based upon funding from the National Family Caregivers Support Program, a series of workshops with caregivers were conducted to examine need.

Consumer-Directed Models

Consumer-directed models of service and support offer potential for rural communities. The national cash and counseling demonstration evaluation (CCDE) was funded through a public-private partnership between the U.S. Department of Health and Human Services, Assistant Secretary for Planning and Evaluation, and the Robert Wood Johnson Foundation. Arkansas was the first state to implement the cash and counseling model and currently offers residents services through the Independence Choices Program. The original demonstration consisted of three states—Arkasas, New Jersey, and Florida. Since the original CCDE, 13 additional states have adopted the cash and counseling model.

Currently, the Centers for Medicare and Medicaid are offering states funds through Real Choice System Change Grants. These grants to states are in response to the 1999 Olmstead Decision, which requires states to provide services to persons with disabilities in the most independent setting possible. For most, and particularly for those in rural communities, this means that service provision should be available in the home- and community-based settings and not in institutional settings.

The consumer-directed model provides recipients with a monthly cash allowance and support to develop a care plan to meet their long-term care needs. Individuals can use their funds to pay family members or an unrelated personal assistant. The consumer-directed or cash and counseling model is ideally suited to rural areas in that it is not dependent on traditional services provided through formal home health agencies, nor does it prescribe a certain family member as a caregiver; rather it allows the individual with long-term support needs to determine his or her own care plan and strategy. Additionally, consumer-directed models may be a successful strategy for communities to address current or expected shortages in the formal caregiver workforce.

Outreach and Respite Models

Respite is an important element of any support program for family caregivers. In rural areas, respite can be problematic because of the distance between a facility offering respite and the caregiver who needs it. Mobile adult day services are offered in Georgia by the Central Savannah River Area Rural Day Care Program. The Administration on Aging provided funds for the program through the Alzheimer's Demonstration Grants to the States program. The program offers adult day services and respite services to low-income elders on a schedule that takes the program as far as 50 miles away several times weekly. In South Carolina, the Project Care Option and Public Education (COPE) provides respite care and information and assistance to low-income and minority families who are providing care for elders with dementia. The respite is provided in-home and the information and assistance is provided by telephone by ElderLink, Inc.

The Veterans Health Administration has also experimented with outreach efforts to serve rural veterans. The Coordination and Advocacy for Rural Elders program was designed to provide case management services to rural veterans who were at risk due to fragmented services and a lack of coordinated efforts (Ritchie et al., 2002). One of the important factors of this program is that it is providing important insight to the Veterans Health Administration about the unmet needs of older rural veterans and could, in the future, foster better support for rural veterans.

Although rural communities lack the deep infrastructure of professionals and formal services found in urban communities, they are rich in their tradition and their residents who value independence and communal support. As rural America ages, each community must seek its own solution to the problems associated with long-term support needs and chronic illness. The models of support we have described in this chapter are merely a small sampling of initiatives currently being developed, demonstrated, and refined for and by rural America. Technology, respect for local traditions and values, and creative partnerships will ensure that rural America continues to be a supportive environment for persons of all ages and abilities. Future developments to support the aging populations in the rural communities must be based on sound research. The final section will discuss the research needs for rural caregiving concerns and considerations.

CONCLUSIONS

More research on rural elders, their caregivers, and their ability to manage over time in the rural environment is needed. Although research is abundant, if not redundant, on caregivers for older adults and the range of care situations and outcomes, it is lacking in specific analyses regarding rural communities and caregiving. As the rural areas change and become more diverse and linked by communication networks to the larger culture in the United States, baseline measures of the state of rural care become more urgent. Not only are rural communities excellent laboratories in which to study family caregiving and the resilience of the family support systems, these communities present opportunities to explore ways in which diverse families are integrated into small communities or affect these communities when they migrate into a rural area. Some research questions follow that relate specifically to the rural context and hold promise for understanding service needs and program design to better serve rural elders and their caregivers.

In addition to research that would increase our understanding of family caregiving differences by community type, more research on the specific aspects of rural caregiving is needed. Research areas of central importance include:

- strategies employed by rural elders who are distant from adult children to maintain a supportive network to meet their needs;
- coping strategies and styles of caregiving by adult children who have migrated from the rural area and are caring from a distance;
- ways in which rural older adult couples manage self-care and factors that influence them to be successful in remaining independent over time;

- the role of fictive kin in rural communities as caregivers and the ways in which care is begun and managed over time;
- social exchange patterns between new immigrants of diverse backgrounds and rural elders;
- care trajectories over time in rural areas compared to environments with a broader complement of formal services; and
- ways in which rural elders incorporate available formal services into their care system and their preferences and choices when care is needed.

Other questions of interest include a focus on the exchange of money either directly or through subsidy of needed personal care services between rural elders and adult children who are living outside the community and rural elders and adult children living in the same community, as well as use of neighbors and others as liaisons with distant relatives or formal services. Kuder, Beaulieu, and Rowles (2001) also suggest that research is needed on effective family caregiving, the outcomes of family empowerment, the needs of special populations in rural areas, and the effectiveness of case management in the rural environment among others. Finally, more research is needed on the design of formal services, the service needs of rural elders, and ways in which the specific community norms and values can be addressed in the development of formal services.

As our population ages and increasing numbers of families are faced with the difficult challenges associated with caregiving, we will, as a society, be required to develop new strategies for ensuring the well-being of our elders and their families. Demographic changes related to population aging such as smaller family size and improvements in life expectancy have important personal and family implications. Family caregiving is one important implication of these demographic changes, and it brings with it the rewards associated with helping those you love as well as challenges. Supporting family caregivers and fostering the ability of older individuals to remain in the community is of central importance to the family and the elder. It is also of central importance to public policy makers, employers, service providers, and community planners. The more we learn about how families manage caregiving and their strategies for effective caregiving, the better able we will be to support their efforts—an essential ingredient to a healthy future for us all. Rural elders may be particularly well served by an increased understanding and support of informal caregiving. With fewer alternatives for care and diverse family situations, these rural families are challenged in a way that urban and metropolitan elders may not experience.

The rural elder managing his or her advancing age and possibly declining health deserves more than responses that are based upon conventional wisdom or stereotypes about life in a rural community. While we have begun to examine life in this setting, more research is needed in order to design appropriate responses for the one-fourth of older Americans who live in rural areas. In focusing our attention on this understudied and underserved population, we are also likely to learn something important about the aging process and the aging family.

REFERENCES

Arno, P. S. (2002, February). *The economic value of informal caregiving, U.S. 2000*. Paper and updated figures presented at the American Association for Geriatric Psychiatry meeting, Orlando, FL.

Baker, D. I., & Palletthehn, P. (1995). Care or control: Barriers to service use by elderly people. *Journal of Applied Gerontology, 14*(3), 261–274.

Barker, J. C. (2002). Neighbors, friends, and other nonkin caregivers of community-living dependent elders. *Journal of Gerontology: Social Sciences, 57B* (3), S158–S167.

Barnett, R. C. (1998). Toward a review and reconceptualization of the work/family literature. *Genetic, Social and General Psychology Monographs, 124*, 125–183.

Beaulieu, J., Rowles, G. D., & Kuder, L. (2001). Current research in rural models of integrated long-term care. *Journal of Applied Gerontology, 20*, 379–385.

Blakley, B., & Jaffe, J. (2000). Coping as a rural caregiver: The impact of health care reforms on rural women informal caregivers. *Centres of Excellence for Women's Health Research Bulletin, 1*(1), 12–13.

Bond, J. T., Galinsky, E., & Swanberg, J. E. (1998). *The 1997 national study of the changing workforce*. New York: Families and Work Institute.

Brody, E. (1985). Parent care as a normative family stress. *The Gerontologist, 25*(1), 19–30.

Brody, E. M., & Schoonover, C. B. (1986). Patterns of parent-care when adult daughters work and when they do not. *The Gerontologist, 26*(4), 372–381.

Buckwalter, K. C., & Davis, L. L. (2002). *Elder caregiving in rural communities*. Retrieved September 7, 2005, from the National Family Caregiver Support Program Resource Room: http://www.aoa.gov/prof/aoaprog/caregiver/care-prof/progguidance/background/program_issues/special_caregiver_pop.asp

Cantor, M. (1979). Neighbors and friends: An overlooked resource in the informal support system. *Research on Aging, 1*, 434–463.

Center on an Aging Society. (2005, February). *A decade of informal caregiving: Family caregivers of older persons*. Data Profile No. 1. Washington, DC: Georgetown University.

Doty, P. (1986). Family care of the elderly: The role of public policy. *Milbank Quarterly, 62*(1), 34–75.

Dwyer, J., Lee, G., & Coward, R. (1990). The health status, health services utilization, and support networks of the rural elderly: A decade review. *Journal of Rural Health, 6*(4), 378–398.

Family Caregiver Alliance. (2001). *Selected caregiver statistics.* Retrieved September 7, 2005, from http://www.caregiver.org/caregiver/jsp/content_node.jsp?nodeid=439

Flora, C. B., Flora J. L., & Fey, S. (2004). *Rural communities: Legacy and change.* Boulder, CO: Westview.

Glasgow, N. (2000). Rural/urban patterns of aging and caregiving in the United States. *Journal of Family Issues, 21,* 611–631.

Krout, J. A. (1988). Rural versus urban differences in elderly parents' contact with their children. *The Gerontologist, 28,* 198–203.

Krout, J. A. (1998). Services and service delivery in rural environments. In R. T. Coward & J. A. Krout (Eds.), *Aging in rural settings* (pp. 247–266). New York: Springer Publishing.

Kuder, L., Beaulieu, J., & Rowles, G. (2001). State and local initiatives and research questions for rural long-term care models. *Journal of Applied Gerontology, 20,* 471–479.

Lee, G., & Cassidy, M. (1985). Family and kin relations of the rural elderly. In R. T. Coward & G. R. Lee (Eds.), *The elderly in rural society* (pp. 151–192). New York: Springer Publishing.

Levine, C. (2004). *Always on call: When illness turns families into caregivers.* Nashville, TN: Vanderbilt University Press.

Longino, C. F. (2003). Demographic and resettlement impacts on rural services. In R. J. Ham, R. T. Goins, & D. K. Brown (Eds.), *Best practices in service delivery to the rural elderly: A report to the Administration on Aging* (pp. 151–192). Morgantown, WV: West Virginia University Center on Aging.

Mac Rae, H. (1992). Fictive kin as a component of the social networks of older people. *Research on Aging, 14,* 226–247.

Manton, K. G., & Stallard, E. (1996). Changes in health, mortality, and disability and their impact on long-term care needs. *Journal of Aging & Social Policy, 7*(3–4), 25–52.

Matthews, S. H., Werkner, J. E., & Delaney, P. J. (1989). Relative contributions of help by employed and nonemployed sisters to their elderly parents. *Journal of Gerontology: Social Sciences, 44*(1), S36–S44.

McAuley, W. J., Spector, W. D., Van Nostrand, J., & Shaffer T. (2004). The influence of rural location on utilization of formal health care: the role of Medicaid. *The Gerontologist, 44*(5), 655–664.

National Alliance for Caregiving/AARP. (1997). *Family caregiving in the US: Findings from a national study.* Bethesda, MD: Author.

National Alliance for Caregiving/AARP. (2004). *Caregiving in the U.S.* Bethesda, MD: Author.

National Governors Association. (2004). *State support for family caregivers and paid homecare workers: Issue Brief.* Retrieved December 15, 2004, from http://preview.nga.org/Files/pdf/0406AgingCaregivers.pdf

Penrod, J. D., Harris, K. M., & Kane, R. L. (1994). Informal care substitution: What we don't know can hurt us. *Journal of Aging and Social Policy, 6*(4), 21–31.

Pinquart, M., & Sorensen, S. (2005). Ethnic differences in stressors, resources, and psychological outcomes of family caregiving: A meta-analysis. *The Gerontologist, 45*(1), 90–106.

Ritchie, C., Wieland, D., Tully, C., Rowe, J., Sims, R., & Bodner, E. (2002). Coordination and advocacy for rural elders (CARE): A model of rural case management with veterans. *The Gerontologist, 42,* 399–405.

Shenk, D. (1998). *Someone to lend a helping hand: Women growing old in rural America.* Amsterdam, The Netherlands: Gordon and Breach.

Smith, M. H., & Longino, C. F. (1994). Demography of caregiving. *Educational Gerontology, 20,* 633–644.

Spillman, B., Black, K., & Mayes, D. (2004). *Analyses of informal caregiving: Evidence from the informal caregiving supplement to the 1999 National Long-Term Care Survey. Background Paper for The National Long Term Care Survey and Informal Care Supplement: Purpose, Design, and Contents.* Washington, DC: US Department of Health and Human Services, Office of the Assistant Secretary for Planning and Evaluation.

Stern, S. (1996). Measuring child work and residence adjustments to parent's long-term care needs. *The Gerontologist, 36*(1), 76–87.

Stoller, E. P. (1983). Parental caregiving by adult children. *Journal of Marriage and the Family, 45,* 851–858.

Stone, R., Cafferata, G., & Sangl, J. (1987). Caregivers of the frail elderly: A national profile. *The Gerontologist, 27,* 616–626.

Thompson, E. (2002). What's unique about men's caregiving? In B. J. Kramer & E. H. Thompson (Eds.), *Men as caregivers: Theory, research, and service implications* (pp. 20–47). New York: Springer Publishing.

Wagner, D. L. (1997a). *Comparative analysis of caregiver data for caregivers to the elderly: 1987 and 1997.* Retrieved September 7, 2005, from the National Alliance for Caregiving: http://www.caregiving.org/data/analysis.pdf

Wagner, D. L. (1997b). *Caring across the miles: Findings of a survey of long-distance caregivers.* Washington, DC: National Council on the Aging.

Wagner, D. L., DeViney, S., & Hunt, G. G. (2003, November). *Sons at work: Managing work and eldercare.* Paper presented at 56th Annual Scientific Meeting, Gerontological Society, San Diego, CA.

Wolf, D. (1999). The family as provider of long-term care: Efficiency, equity, and externalities. *Journal of Aging and Health, 11,* 360–382.

CHAPTER NINE

Housing for Rural Elders

Policies, Practices, and Prospects

W. Edward Folts, Kenneth B. Muir, James R. Peacock,
Bradley Nash, Jr., and Katherine L. Jones

Adequate shelter is an obvious and fundamental need for all human beings. However, the significance of housing goes well beyond mere bricks and mortar designed to fend off environmental threats. A house not only provides a "sense of security, privacy, comfort and independence" (Wacker, Roberto, & Piper, 1998, p. 278), it can also serve as a component of one's self-identity. Furthermore, it can function to integrate individuals into their neighborhoods and communities and facilitate access to employment and a wide range of social services (Koff & Park, 1999; Pynoos, Schafer, & Hartman, 1973; Wacker, Roberto, & Piper, 1998).

Housing adequacy can become increasingly important as people age. As age-based needs emerge, the living environment takes on a more significant role with respect to adaptive behaviors and quality of life (Hooyman & Kiyak, 2002; Lawton & Nahemow, 1973). Because of the variability of environmental press, which "refers to the demands that social and physical environments make on the individual to adapt, respond, and change" (Hooyman & Kiyak, 2002, p. 7), a continuum of housing options would appear to be beneficial. As typically envisioned, a continuum of housing encompasses a wide range of household types meeting the diverse service needs and financial capabilities of independent, semi-dependent, and dependent older adults (Newcomer & Weeden, 1986). However, despite the obvious advantages of a full array of housing types with multiple levels of services and amenities, such a continuum has never really existed—at least in the United States This is due, in part, to federal housing policies that lack coherence and adequate funding. Moreover, because of what Noll (1981) has called the urban bias inherent in government programs, the lack of a functional housing continuum is especially evident in rural areas. This is a particularly significant issue because not only are older Americans disproportionately concentrated in rural areas; rural older adult households have a higher poverty rate as well.

DEMOGRAPHY OF RURAL AGING

Despite the fact that rural housing has always been a low-priority public policy issue, demographic trends among the older rural population are likely to make this a compelling issue in the first half of the 21st century. The 2003 American Housing Survey found that households headed by individuals age 65 years or older made up about 20% of the total number of United States households, whereas almost 29% of rural households were headed by adults age 65 years or older. Further, the poverty rate for rural older households (19.1%) is higher than that of all older households (17.8%) (U.S. Department of Housing and Urban Development, 2004). Table 9.1 presents the geographic and age characteristics of households based on data from this survey. Because almost a third of all households headed by an older adult are in rural areas, age-specific housing issues in these areas should be taken more seriously than they are at present.

There are several important factors that tend to obscure the reality of living in rural areas and prevent the objective living conditions of rural older adults from gaining widespread notice. In the U.S., about

TABLE 9.1   Geographic and Age Characteristics of U.S. Households: 2003

Households	Number[a]	Percentage
Total households	**105,842,000**	
Urban population	78,369,000	74
Rural population	27,474,000	26
65+ households	**21,627,000**	
Urban population	15,349,000	71
Rural population	6,278,000	29

[a]Numbers do not sum to total due to rounding.
Source: American Housing Survey, 2003.

80% of the older adult population own their homes compared to about 90% of rural older adults, and about 28% of all homeowners have a mortgage compared to 24% of homeowners in rural areas (U.S. Department of Housing and Urban Development, 2004). Absent further comparative data, it would not seem unreasonable to conclude that older rural residents are either collectively better off, or at least no worse off than the population as a whole. What needs greater consideration, however, is the specific nature of the homes that rural elders typically own. For instance, often overlooked is the fact that older rural residents (14.4%) are more likely to live in mobile homes or manufactured housing than their urban counterparts (3.8%) (U.S. Department of Housing and Urban Development, 2004).

Perhaps a more significant issue pertains to the age of the structures that rural older adult homeowners occupy. As noted by the Housing Assistance Council (2003, p. 13), "[n]early half (46%) of rural elder households, compared to just over one-third of nonmetro households under the age of 65, live in homes that are more than 40 years old." Indeed, approximately 10% of rural older adult households, compared to 7% of urban older adult householders, occupy structures that were built in 1919 or earlier (U.S. Department of Housing and Urban Development, 2004). An obvious implication of this is that the older housing stock would have a greater likelihood of physical and structural problems. In fact, 5.4% of homes owned by rural elders have moderate to severe physical problems relating to plumbing, heating, electrical wiring, and the like. This is slightly higher than the 5.2% of all rural households and the 5.1% of urban elder households that face moderate and severe physical and structural problems. In addition, whereas only 7% of urban elder households experience outside leakage problems, 9.4% of rural elder households have water leakage from roofs, basements, or other exterior sources in need of repair (U.S. Department of Housing and Urban Development, 2004).

The available housing options are also limited by a lack of mobility among the older population. It has long been known that older adults are less likely to move than other age groups. From 1995 to 2000, only 22.8% of individuals age 65 years or older moved in comparison to 47.7% of individuals younger than age 65 (Administration on Aging, 2004). Less appreciated is the idea that older people who do move are more likely to stay within the same geographic area. *A Profile of Older Americans: 2003* reports, for example, that among older movers, 59.7% moved within the same county and only 18.8% moved out of state (Administration on Aging, 2004). One practical consequence of this tendency to remain in place is that older people are less likely to move to areas offering better housing or better access to services.

FEDERAL HOUSING POLICIES AND RURAL ELDERS

Although demographic trends suggest that the housing needs of a rapidly expanding older population should be a public priority, the United States has never had a comprehensive policy related to housing for older adults. Indeed, Wilma Donahue (1954, p. 21) wrote a half century ago that while "significant progress has been made in housing younger families especially since the Second World War . . . what has been done to house the aging during this and earlier periods has been *negligible in comparison to the need*" [emphasis added]. A fuller understanding of why there is no comprehensive federal housing policy for older adults requires that one look at the underlying principles of the policies and programs that do exist (Liebig, 1998). As noted by Liebig (1998, p. 56), housing policies that are in place have "been guided by a supplementary, rather than a comprehensive approach, with a focus on those groups unable to secure housing in the private market." The result has been a somewhat jumbled mixture of state initiated tax abatement programs combined with federal mortgage legislation designed to promote individual homeownership. For those who cannot afford ownership, what remains is "a relatively modest subsidy program of federally assisted housing production and rental assistance" (Liebig, 1998, p. 56).

Within this context, several of the housing programs administered by the U.S. Department of Housing and Urban Development (HUD) are especially relevant (Koff & Park, 1999; Wacker, Roberto, & Piper, 1998). Section 8 programs, whether in the form of rental subsidies to landlords or rental vouchers to tenants, are intended to assist low-income individuals regardless of age. Similarly, although nearly half of all public housing occupants are older adults, the program is intended to serve all low-income individuals. Other federal programs, such as Section 202 housing and Section 255 home equity conversion plans, however, specifically target older adults. Section 202 is a housing construction program that uses federally guaranteed loans to encourage nonprofit sponsors to develop congregate rental housing for those age 62 years or older. Linked directly to Section 8 subsidies, Section 202 housing complexes usually offer additional supportive services, such as transportation and meals (Wacker, Roberto, & Piper, 1998). For individuals who own their own homes, Section 255 is a federal mortgage insurance program that allows "older homeowners to convert their home equity into spendable [sic] dollars" (Koff & Park, 1999, p. 309). Often used for home repairs and improvements, the income from these reverse mortgages can be used for any type of living expenses—including supportive services (Wacker, Roberto, & Piper, 1998).

Though intended to meet the housing needs of poor people, the residents in Section 8 and Public Housing programs are disproportionately older adults. This, and the long waiting lists associated with subsidized housing (Koff & Park, 1999) promote the misconception that much is being done to meet the housing needs of older people and that older people are characteristically poor. One unfortunate result of this is that the argument for developing a more comprehensive housing policy for the aged is further eroded (Pynoos, 1987). The real problem is, of course, that these programs are inadequately funded and cannot meet even the most basic housing needs of those they are designed to serve. This allocation problem impacts Section 202 and congregate housing as well (Wacker, Roberto, & Piper, 1998).

A much less discussed problem related to federal housing programs is that they tend to reflect an urban perspective that puts rural residents in an especially disadvantaged position (Noll, 1981). As Lawton (1980, p. 58) bluntly noted: "[Housing for older adults is] most adequate in urban metropolitan areas, less adequate in towns outside metropolitan areas, and *least adequate in rural areas*" [emphasis added]. Although this is likely due to a complex set of circumstances, Koff and Park (1999) have identified several key factors that make federal housing programs difficult to implement in non-urban locations. First, rural housing typically necessitates smaller-scale projects, which raises the cost per unit to a level that may exceed government guidelines and is likely to be less attractive to potential developers. Second, rural areas often lack the necessary personnel to develop and implement federal housing programs. Third, higher levels of rural poverty increase risks and make it more difficult to construct new housing or convert existing facilities. Finally, the general lack of transportation and access to services in rural areas adversely impacts the overall efficacy of federal housing programs.

To be fair, for several decades now, the federal government has attempted various strategies intended to more adequately address the housing needs of rural older adults (Collings, 1999). For example, as noted by the Housing Assistance Council (2003, p. 23) "[a]pproximately 25 percent of Section 202 funding must be set aside for use in rural areas." However, demand has consistently outstripped supply, with the ratio at best being two older adult applicants for every Section 202 vacancy in the most rural locales. More significantly, overall funding for Section 202 has been cut by over one-third over the last decade or so, which has further reduced the supply of rural housing for low-income older adults (Housing Assistance Council, 2003).

There are several other federal programs that target rural housing needs in general and those of older adults in particular. Since 1950 the Farmers Home Administration provided direct low-interest loans to assist low-income farm families in constructing and purchasing housing. Though the Farmers Home Administration was formally eliminated in 1995, these Section 502 loans are now administered by the recently created Rural Housing Service (RHS). As noted by Collings (1999, p. 101) RHS "evolved from the failure of HUD predecessor agencies and states to provide housing finance in small and remote rural areas."

Along with Section 502 loans for individuals, RHS also administers Section 515 loans to fund rental and congregate housing construction for low income rural individuals (Wacker, Roberto, & Piper, 1998). RHS also administers a rental assistance program through Section 521 for those rural residents who cannot afford Section 515 housing on their own. Overall, about one-third of all Section 515 occupants are older adults, thus exemplifying its significance as a rural housing option. In fact, some Section 515 congregate housing is specifically funded for older residents. Unfortunately, however, Section 515 does not "provide for the funding of services, an integral aspect of housing for seniors" (Housing Assistance Council, 2003, p. 24). Perhaps even more disconcerting, federal funding for the program has been reduced by over 75% since 1994 (Housing Assistance Council, 2003).

In addition, RHS is also responsible for Section 504, a federal rehabilitation program for the repair and improvement of existing rural housing. Section 504 loans are available to any low-income homeowners who wish to make major repairs or renovations, remove electrical and structural hazards, or weatherize a home by installing better heating systems or insulation. The loans are capped at $20,000 at 1% interest over 20 years, and a large number of older adult homeowners do take advantage of them. Additionally, Section 504 grants, which do not have to be paid back, are reserved specifically for very low-income rural homeowners age 62 years or older. The grants can be worth up to $7,500 and can be used for a wide array of home repairs or improvements similar to those covered by Section 504 loans (Housing Assistance Council, 2003; Wacker, Roberto, & Piper, 1998). Overall, given the age of many homes owned by rural elders, Section 504 is a valuable resource for improving living conditions. Nevertheless, as might be expected, this and other RHS services are characterized by the same lack of adequate funding that mark many other federal housing programs.

However one perceives the relative adequacy of existing housing policies, renewed massive federal budget deficits, state budget shortfalls and rescissions, and the tax policies of the last few years have combined with the decades-long emphasis on less government to adversely impact those programs that are in place. In fact, it is not unreasonable to suggest that these elements have had an overall chilling effect and required researchers, advocates, policy makers, developers, and others to direct their energies away from the development of more adequate and comprehensive housing programs for older rural adults and toward defending existing fragmented policies from retrenchment efforts at all levels. The end result is that the housing situation for rural elders has become quite pressing.

Exacerbating this is an unusual paradox. Despite the objective deficiencies found in housing occupied by older adults in rural areas, there is also a pervasive subjective housing satisfaction among this population (Lee, 1986). High levels of housing satisfaction, irrespective of the objective condition of that housing, leaves the impression that existing programs and personal preferences are fully capable of meeting the housing needs of rural older adults. An equally plausible explanation is that this situation is, at least in part, the result of a lack of alternatives.

Because most existing intervention modalities are based on economies of scale that involve relatively large numbers of people concentrated in well-defined and easily accessible geographic areas, it has typically been assumed that the needs of rural older populations could not be addressed in an economically efficient manner. Thus, the needs of older rural residents have received little serious attention.

As it relates to housing, there is another important but somewhat contradictory reason that rural populations are generally underserved, and it has to do with the perceived need. Although the label did not come into use until much later, geographic concentrations of older people began to emerge in the early 1900s as prototypical retirement communities (Folts & Streib, 1994). Typically, these large communities were constructed in rural areas where land costs were negligible and construction materials were abundant. It was not until the early 1960s, however, that the modern retirement community took its present form (Folts & Streib, 1994). Basically, there are three types of modern retirement communities: naturally occurring retirement communities (NORCs) (Hunt, Merrill, & Gilker, 1994); leisure oriented retirement communities (LORCs) (Folts & Muir, 2002; Folts & Streib, 1994); and care oriented retirement communities (CORCs) (Brecht, 1994).

NORCs

A NORC can be described as a process rather than a physical location, as it is basically any area that develops a substantially large elder population without conscious planning (Hunt et al., 1994). Specifically, NORCs have been described as the "phenomenon of a location attracting and retaining older residents, even though that location was not originally intended to do so" (Hunt et al., 1994, p. 107). NORCs may also occur when older residents age-in-place, when younger residents move out leaving older people behind, or when older residents move into a location (Marshall & Hunt, 1999). Two types of NORCs are especially relevant to rural areas: Amenity NORCs, which may be viewed as the result of wealthy and healthy older people being drawn to a particular location because of its perceived advantages and natural amenities; and Convenience NORCs, which may be viewed as the result of older people, usually lower income, being pushed out of their present location because of its isolation or perceived inadequacy in access to services, shopping, and health care.

LORCs

LORCs provide residents with housing options that include access to organized leisure activities and the facilities in which to perform those activities. Most commonly, LORCs cater to the desires of wealthier older adults, although more affordable LORCs are emerging (Folts & Streib, 1994). Despite the early developers' intent to provide less expensive housing options, LORCs quickly evolved into service-rich living environments for affluent older adults. Contributing to this were a demand for additional services, better quality housing, more amenities, and, perhaps most importantly, an emerging older population with the financial resources to afford the improved lifestyle (Folts & Streib, 1994).

CORCs

CORCs include what have typically been referred to as continuing care retirement communities and life-care retirement communities (Brecht, 1994). Although funding schemes, statutory regulations, and even the variety of services offered vary widely, the defining characteristics of CORCs include multiple levels of personal care in a service-rich living environment and an assurance that residents will have services in place and available when they need them. In general, CORCs require a substantial payment up front usually derived from the sale of the resident's private home, as well as a monthly fee determined in the contractual arrangement negotiated between the resident and the facility. These funds, and the interest gained from investing them, are then used to cover the costs associated with the operation of the CORC and the provision of services.

Despite their popularity among a segment of the older population, all of these modern retirement community arrangements have contributed to the incorrect assumption that older rural populations are adequately housed in a wide variety of housing choices, obviating the need for other further interventions. The problem is that while CORCs, as well as LORCs and NORCs, have been extensively studied and documented in the gerontological literature (Brecht, 1994; Folts & Muir, 2002; Golant, 1992; Mangum, 1994; Streib, LaGreca, & Folts, 1986; Winklevoss & Powell, 1984), it is rarely mentioned that living in a typical retirement community, wherever it is located, is prohibitively expensive and far beyond the means of all but the wealthiest of potential residents. Moreover, obscured by the rapid development and relative luxury of modern retirement communities is the fact that the residents are almost exclusively wealthy in-migrants from more urban areas and the total number of housing units remains extraordinarily small.

Still, the development of this range of rural modern retirement communities promotes the incorrect impression that there is a wide array of housing options available to older rural adults from which they can choose the lifestyle they prefer. Although this may describe reality for an exceedingly small number of older adults with extraordinary financial resources, there is no housing continuum in any meaningful sense relevant to the vast majority of rural older adults. The housing continuum myth persists, however, because of two closely related misconceptions.

First, it is generally believed by the public that a wide range of specialized housing for older adults, unfortunately often described by professional gerontologists as a continuum, is available in *all* geographic areas and to *all* older adults who desire to live in them. The fact is that whether they choose the lifestyle or not, the only real choices available to most rural older adults are home ownership, rental housing—both of which are more likely to be substandard—or some form of care arrangement—typically institutionalization.

A second and perhaps more serious misconception is that the variety of retirement community housing types that are currently available imply a range of accompanying services that are available to the larger general population. While it is true that some retirement communities offer a wide range of services—including transportation on-demand, maintenance, security, and others—it is rare that these services are made available to the surrounding areas. Thus, because retirement community residents may be a substantial proportion of the population in some rural areas, what appears to be a service-rich area is, in reality, service-poor for a majority of the older residents.

BEST PRACTICES

It is not inconsequential that best practice is often inappropriately applied to housing arrangements designed to meet the needs of older people. The problem, of course, is one of perspective. Almost any organized housing arrangement can become a best practice by simply focusing organizational goals to make them achievable and modifying performance criteria to ensure success. The mere existence of a particular housing program for rural older adults and its survival beyond initial funding are obviously inadequate criteria for best practices. However, even HUD's definition of a best practice lacks sufficient definition to be useful. To become a HUD best practice award recipient, for example, all that is required is that a project "provide access to a significantly greater number of supportive and health services [and be] more adept at utilizing community resources" (Cox, 2001, p. 97). This suggests that to become a best practice using HUD definitions, housing programs should have access to supportive and health services and other community resources that are not typically available in rural areas.

Housing developments, even those in rural areas, are established with clear and distinct business goals in mind. The difficulty is that those goals often have little to do with the adequacy of the services offered or the potential for improved living conditions of the residents. Lacking objective measures of the value of assistance to an individual, programs designed to meet the needs of older populations have typically relied on units of service-based outcome measures that assume the more units delivered the better the service. As a result, in judging the efficacy of a particular housing model, urban populations and the age-segregated and self-contained populations of NORCs, LORCs, and CORCs are at a distinct advantage over the more widely dispersed rural populations of older adults.

Not unexpectedly, identifying best practices in housing for rural older populations is not an easy task. Although there are many well designed and well managed proprietary models of housing that combine services, dwelling units, and lifestyles in a package that meet both the care needs and the housing preferences of their older residents, it is also the case that these housing models are available to a small fraction of those who would likely benefit from them and their costs are well beyond the means of most older rural residents. Similarly, there is ample evidence that all of the currently available Public Housing programs are meeting a real and extensive need. However, lack of coordination and preposterously low funding levels (or even the loss of funding) seriously compromise the efficacy of the effort. For instance, Section 515 loans, administered by Rural Housing Services, have experienced program funding cuts of 75% over the past decade, and Section 202 funding has been cut by more than a third in the same time period (Housing Assistance Council, 2003). Furthermore, given the current economic and political environments we have created for ourselves, it unlikely that substantial improvements will be made in the near future.

Any program targeting housing for rural elders faces significant obstacles due to the demography of the target population and compounded by issues with the geographic locale. Developers face low population density, geographic isolation, small actual and potential markets, as well as a shortage of qualified and experienced service providers (e.g., caregivers, service workers, and other program and residential developers) with whom to combine efforts (Housing Assistance Council, 2003).

Within this context, there are three need-driven and locally organized models of housing that are especially worthy of note. Each of these types can be thought of as a best practice within the context of the needs, abilities, and personal preferences of those who choose to live in them. None of these is exclusively a rural housing alternative, but all of them offer some measure of hope for the less wealthy rural aging population. Home sharing, Share-A-Home, and cooperative living have all been successful at meeting a variety of needs for a specific, albeit small, population of older adults. Often located in rural areas, the flexibility of these housing types allows them to be responsive to a wide variety of needs but it also interferes with attempts to classify the underlying models. Although making it difficult to fully understand them, it is this inherent flexibility that holds the most promise for older adults in rural areas.

Home Sharing

Home sharing is not a new phenomenon. It is known, for example, that a type of home sharing was widely practiced in the earliest periods of human history (Rogers, 1994). Not only that, but there are tantalizing, though fragmentary, references to even more ancient but highly organized attempts to find living arrangements for "worthy" but infirm members of particular communities (Rogers, 1994). The basic home-sharing model, unchanged from ancient times, involves an attempt to identify and match homeowners who have vacant space with those who need shelter in a cooperative arrangement that has the potential to benefit both. The only modern addition to this basic model is the scope of the effort and the formality of the matching process. Despite many locally specific details, in its basic form, home sharing still involves unrelated adults sharing a home that one of them owns (Jaffe, Pawasarat, & Howe, 1994). This type of arrangement appears to work best when the two parties are similar in age, of the same sex, and can both make a meaningful contribution to the success of the match.

Although it is obvious that this type of arrangement does nothing to directly address the larger issue of structural deficiencies in rural housing, home sharing can have an indirect impact in two areas. First, the additional, though modest, income that is typically generated by a successful match can be used to improve the objective housing conditions thus benefiting both parties. Second, and more important, home sharing involves combining households such that it is likely that the objective conditions of the person seeking housing are greatly improved. A further, yet largely unrecognized benefit involves subjective feelings of security and belonging that can develop from this arrangement and that can benefit both renter and homeowner. Despite these benefits, home sharing, can never meet the housing needs of any but a small fraction of rural older adults because it is critically dependent on the availability of older homeowners who consider themselves to be over-housed and the availability of older renters who have the required financial resources and, more importantly, who are acceptable to the homeowner. Still, for like-minded and compatible individuals who can overcome the territorial issues implied by home ownership, home sharing can be a particularly positive experience.

Share-A-Home

Although only two parties participate in home sharing, Share-A-Home involves a group of unrelated older adults who contribute to the rental or purchase of a large home and then hire a manager to provide a wide array of personal and domestic services (Streib, Folts, & Hilker, 1984). Share-A-Home, which began in Florida in the late 1960s, most closely resembles a group-living arrangement in that unrelated adults live as a self-contained and self-supporting household. It is this self-sufficiency and the fact that each home defines the level of service to be provided that holds promise for rural older adult populations.

As with other alternative living arrangements, however, Share-A-Home is not without serious impediments to large-scale adoption (Streib, Folts, & Hilker, 1984). For one thing, it is unclear which, if any, regulatory categories the model fits. In some states Share-A-Home facilities have been defined as group-homes while in others they are assisted living facilities. In still others, they operate outside the state regulatory mechanism altogether. This is not an easily resolved issue. The underlying problem is that the model lacks a clear and concise definition that establishes the legal relationship of the residents to each other and to the manager.

In Florida, Streib et al. (1984) reported that one of 16 Share-A-Home facilities in operation at the time was simultaneously defined as a boarding-home by the state, a group-home by the county, and a multi-family residence by the municipal zoning board. After a lengthy and contentious legal proceeding, a circuit court ruled that this particular

Share-A-Home facility was neither a boarding-home nor a group-home under then existing state definitions. The language of the court made it clear that this Share-A-Home was sufficiently similar to a traditional family that it could escape regulation by the state and county. Although not contested for this particular facility, left unresolved was the zoning issue and whether other facilities could be included in the ruling. For privately funded Share-A-Home facilities, regulatory confusion requires substantial attention to issues of liability and legal standing. It also makes it unlikely that public funds could ever be used for the establishment of Share-A-Home facilities (Streib, Folts, & Hilker, 1984).

Cooperative Living Arrangements

Unlike the two previously discussed options, cooperative living arrangements hold the promise of providing housing for relatively large numbers of older adults in rural areas. As the name suggests, cooperative housing involves the cooperation of a number of older consumers to design a service package reflective of their means and needs. Most of the existing cooperatives have involved altruistic organizations including churches and philanthropic fraternal groups that have provided organizational expertise and a non-profit legal entity through which cooperatives might be established. The fact that sponsoring organizations have also typically provided substantial subsidies in no way precludes individuals from accomplishing the same goal although at a higher personal cost.

Basically, cooperative living arrangements involve any number of individuals who are willing to jointly purchase and own dwelling units and whatever amenities or services they need and can afford. One particular model of cooperative housing, called co-housing in the United States (McCamant & Durrett, 1988), resembles a modified commune in that the day-to-day responsibilities of care and maintenance are equally shared among the residents. Although not specifically targeted to older adults, the underlying principle that each resident has a joint responsibility for the well-being of each other resident makes co-housing a particularly promising model for rural older adults.

Cooperative housing is not a new concept. In fact, the first large LORCs, including the original Leisure World and early phases of other similar retirement communities, were organized as cooperatives. In its simplest form, the primary difference between cooperatives and condominiums is that cooperatives involve individual ownership of a corporation that owns the property and facilities while condominium owners individually own their dwelling units and jointly own the common facilities. Although popular for several decades, changes in federal policy related to guaranteed loans for cooperatives in the late 1960s had the effect of making this type of living arrangement less financially feasible than condominiums (Folts & Streib, 1994). However, development within this housing model does continue. For example, the Homestead Housing Center, a Midwestern cooperative housing development organization, provides "development, design, and organizational services to localities planning to build senior co-ops" (Housing Assistance Council, 2003, p. 16). After the co-op is built and operating, Homestead is replaced by older adult owners who then oversee the operations, policy, and improvements of the co-op (Housing Assistance Council, 2003). Current low interest rates and the availability of land in rural areas may provide renewed interest in cooperative housing and may draw other development organizations to this model of rural housing for older adults.

The three models discussed here have the potential of addressing the objective adequacy issues of rural housing for substantial numbers of older adults. However, since home sharing, Share-A-Home, and cooperatives are neither widely available nor well known suggests a problem beyond the mere logistics of providing housing-related services in rural areas. It is useful, at least for analytical purposes, to consider three types of barriers: personal, political, and social.

BARRIERS TO RURAL HOUSING

Personal Barriers

The most important personal barrier is the fact that, like younger people, older adults overwhelmingly prefer single-family owner-occupied homes. So ingrained a part of the American Dream is homeownership that any other type arrangement implies a level of financial or personal dependency that is typically unacceptable. An additional personal barrier is rooted in cultural meanings of home and land ownership. For many rural elders, land may have been owned by a single family for generations. In such cases, not only does home and land ownership ascribe a sense of responsibility and even self-identity within a community, it may also signify regional heritage and familial identity. Thus, moving from the homestead and giving up the land may be culturally unthinkable, regardless of whatever supportive housing programs are available. As long as the objective condition of a dwelling unit is qualitatively less important than the fact that it is owner-occupied, little progress in improving the objective living conditions of rural older people can be expected.

Political Barriers

The most salient of the political barriers is the fact that rural populations have never been a particularly powerful political group. In fact, our system ensures that rural populations will be, in a political sense at least, almost invisible. As long as it is politically expedient to focus on more concentrated populations, the needs of rural older adult homeowners and renters will continue to be largely ignored. This situation has produced an interesting contradiction. The relatively low housing costs and tax rates that characterize rural areas and make them economically attractive to older adults cannot sustain the types services needed to meet their needs. Unless and until the needs of the older rural population become important to the service delivery system, little is likely to change and rural residents of all ages are likely to remain underserved.

Social Barriers

Finally, there are social barriers that serve to perpetuate "things as they are" in rural areas. Rural areas typically involve low tax rates and, consequently, few tax-based services. This is a dangerous combination that almost dictates rural populations will be of lower income and more likely to need a wide array of unavailable services. At the same time, there is evidence to suggest that the widely held stereotype of rural populations as being less well educated and of generally lower economic means is not entirely false (U.S. Census Bureau, 2002). Thus, it is unlikely that those in other areas will willingly embrace public policies that require sharing scarce resources with a population that is believed to be unable or unwilling to address its own problems.

CONCLUSIONS

It is recognized that the significance of housing goes well beyond providing a safe structure in which to reside. One's own home implies independence, self-identity, and integration into neighborhoods and communities. For rural elders, it is especially evident that the ideal of a continuum of a full array of housing types with multiple levels of services and amenities has never really existed due, in part, to government programs focusing efforts toward higher density regions.

Almost 25% of rural households are headed by older adults, and the poverty rate for rural older households is higher than that of all older households. Older rural homeowners tend to face higher rates of problems with their housing structures compared to their urban

counterparts. They are more likely to live in mobile homes, manufactured housing, or in aging structures that are more likely to have
moderate to severe physical problems relating to plumbing, heating,
electrical wiring, and water leakage.

Although housing assistance programs have been designed and implemented, they tend to be inadequately funded and cannot usually meet
even the most basic housing needs of those they are designed to serve.
This is especially evident with programs designed to meet the housing
needs of rural elders. In fact, there is little to attract a potential devel-
oper to this target population. Due to the rural locale, developers face:
smaller-scale projects due to a smaller market and low population density; higher levels of rural poverty, which increases investment risks; limited experienced and qualified service providers and developers to design
and implement housing programs; and a general lack of transportation
and easy access to services in rural areas, which would adversely impact
the overall efficacy of housing programs should they even be developed.

Although a variety of housing models (e.g., NORCs, LORCs, and
CORCs), which combine services, dwelling units, and lifestyles have
emerged, it remains true that living in a typical retirement community,
wherever it is located, is prohibitively expensive and far beyond the
means of most older adults. Because these models are often developed in
rural areas, this contributes to the incorrect assumption that older rural
populations are adequately housed in a wide variety of housing choices.
Furthermore, although it is true that retirement communities generally
offer a wide range of services, these services are seldom made available
to elders living outside the retirement community. Thus, because retirement community residents may be a substantial proportion of the population in some rural areas, what appears to be a service-rich area is, in
reality, service-poor for a majority of the older residents. In reality, there
is no housing continuum available to the vast majority of rural older
adults. The only real choices available to most rural older adults are
home ownership, rental housing, or institutionalization.

A more feasible housing arrangement might include home sharing, Share-A-Home, or some form of cooperative living. Developing
best practice models of any of these arrangements would necessitate
significant organizational and information sharing efforts. For home
sharing, such efforts should attempt to identify and match homeowners
who have vacant space with those who need housing in an arrangement
to potentially benefit both. For Share-A-Home models, efforts would
require finding and organizing a group of unrelated older adults who
contribute to the rental or purchase of a large home and then hire a
manager to provide personal and domestic services. For cooperative
living arrangements, efforts would focus on organizing an even larger

number of individuals who are willing to jointly purchase and own dwelling units and arrange for themselves whatever amenities or services they need and can afford.

The development of rural housing options for older adults also faces additional barriers. Because, especially in rural areas, home and land ownership can ascribe a sense of responsibility, community identity, regional heritage, and familial identity, leaving the familial homestead may be culturally unthinkable for some rural elders regardless of the structural conditions of the home. Also, because rural housing costs tend to be lower, the tax rates that characterize rural areas usually cannot sustain the necessary services to meet the needs of rural elders. Beyond this, due to the likelihood of rural populations being less educated and of lower income, it is unlikely that potential funding sources will embrace public policies that require sharing scarce resources with a population that is believed to be unable or unwilling to address their own problems.

With a public policy mechanism that is seriously fragmented and grossly underfunded and with a proprietary sector focused on the wealthiest of consumers, it is legitimate to ask the question: What then are we to do? The cold reality is that neither existing public policies nor private sector approaches are likely to meet the housing needs of rural older adults. It is also highly unlikely that some as yet undiscovered resource will suddenly appear and solve the complex and seemingly overwhelming problem of a large number of people spread out over a vast area who need specialized services and adequate housing but who, for a variety of reasons, cannot meet their own needs. It is not merely the lack of resources that is the problem. The problem is, as always, an allocation problem and that is a problem that is unlikely to be resolved in the near future.

REFERENCES

Administration on Aging. (2004). *A profile of older Americans: 2004*. Retrieved September 19, 2005, from the Administration on Aging Web site: http://assets.aarp.org/rgcenter/general/profile_2004.pdf

Brecht, S. B. (1994). Continuing care retirement communities. In W. E. Folts & D. E. Yeatts (Eds.), *Housing and the aging population: Options for the new century* (pp. 145–168). New York: Garland.

Collings, A. (1999). The role of the federal rural housing programs. In J. N. Belden & R. J. Wiener (Eds.), *Housing in rural America: Building affordable and inclusive communities* (pp. 101–107). Thousand Oaks, CA: Sage.

Cox, B. M. (2001). Linking housing and services for low-income elderly: Lessons from 1994 best practice award winners. *Journal of Housing for the Elderly, 15*(1–2), 97–110.

Donahue, W. (1954). Where and how older people wish to live. In W. Donahue (Ed.), *Housing the aging* (pp. 21–36). Ann Arbor, MI: University of Michigan.

Folts, W. E., & Muir, K. B. (2002). Housing for older adults: New lessons from the past. *Research on Aging, 24*(1), 10–28.

Folts, W. E., & Streib, G. F. (1994). Leisure oriented retirement communities. In W. E. Folts & D. E. Yeatts (Eds.), *Housing and the aging population: Options for the new century* (pp. 121–144). New York: Garland.

Golant, S. M. (1992). *Housing America's elderly: Many possibilities/few choices.* Newbury Park, CA: Sage.

Hooyman, N. R., & Kiyak, H. A. (2002). *Social gerontology: A multidisciplinary perspective* (6th ed.). Boston, MA: Allyn and Bacon.

Housing Assistance Council. (2003). *Rural seniors and their homes.* Washington, DC: Housing Assistance Council.

Hunt, M. E., Merrill, J. L., & Gilker, C. M. (1994). Naturally occurring retirement communities in urban and rural settings. In W. E. Folts & D. E Yeatts (Eds.), *Housing and the aging population: Options for the new century* (pp. 107–120). New York: Garland.

Jaffe, D. J., Pawasarat, P., & Howe, E. (1994). Homesharing for the elderly: An option for independent living. In W. E. Folts & D. E. Yeatts (Eds.), *Housing and the aging population: Options for the new century* (pp. 221–244). New York: Garland.

Koff, T. H., & Park, R. W. (1999). *Aging public policy: Bonding the generations* (2nd ed.). Amityville, NY: Baywood.

Lawton, M. P. (1980). Residential quality and residential satisfaction among the elderly. *Research on Aging, 2*, 309–328.

Lawton, M. P., & Nahemow, L. (1973). Ecology and the aging process. In C. Eisdorfer & M. P. Lawton (Eds.), *Psychology of adult development and aging* (pp. 619–674). Washington, DC: American Psychological Association.

Lee, G. R. (1986). Rural issues in elderly housing. In R. J. Newcomer, M. P. Lawton, & T. O. Byerts (Eds.), *Housing an aging society: Issues, alternatives, and policy* (pp. 33–41). New York: Van Nostrand Reinhold.

Liebig, P. S. (1998). Housing and supportive sources for the elderly: Intergenerational perspectives and options. In J. S. Steckenrider & T. M. Parrot (Eds.), *New directions in old-age policies* (pp. 51–74). Albany, NY: State University of New York.

Mangum, W. P. (1994). Planned housing for the elderly since 1950: History, policies, and practices. In W. E. Folts & D. E. Yeatts (Eds.), *Housing and the aging population: Options for the new century* (pp. 221–244). New York: Garland.

Marshall, L. J., & Hunt, M. E. (1999). Rural naturally occurring retirement communities: A community assessment procedure. *Journal of Housing for the Elderly, 13*(1/2), 19–34.

McCamant, K., & Durrett, C. (1988). *Co-Housing: A contemporary approach to housing ourselves.* Berkeley, CA: Ten Speed.

Newcomer, R. J., & Weeden, J. P. (1986). Perspectives on housing needs and the continuum of care. In R. J. Newcomer, M. P. Lawton, & T. O. Byerts (Eds.),

Housing an aging society: Issues, alternatives, and policy (pp. 3–9). New York: Van Nostrand Reinhold.

Noll, P. F. (1981). Federally assisted housing programs for the elderly in rural areas: Problems and prospects. In M. P. Lawton & S. L. Hoover (Eds.), *Community housing choices for older Americans* (pp. 90–108). New York: Springer Publishing.

Pynoos, J. (1987). Setting the elderly agenda. In J. A. Hancock (Ed.), *Housing the elderly* (pp. 209–223). New Brunswick, NJ: Center for Public Policy Research, Rutgers University.

Pynoos, J., Schafer, R., & Hartman, C. W. (1973). Introduction. In J. Pynoos, R. Schafer, & C. W. Hartman (Eds.), *Housing urban America* (pp. 1–12). Chicago: Aldine.

Rogers, W. W. (1994). The ancient foundations of institutional health care. In W. E. Folts & D. E. Yeatts (Eds.), *Housing and the aging population: Options for then new century* (pp. 393–411). New York: Garland.

Streib, G. F., Folts, W. E., & Hilker, M. A. (1984). *Old Homes—new families: Shared living for the elderly.* New York: Columbia University Press.

Streib, G. F., LaGreca, A. J., & Folts, W. E. (1986). Retirement communities: People, planning, and prospects. In R. J. Newcomer, M. P. Lawton, & T. O. Byerts (Eds.), *Housing an aging society: Issues, alternatives, and policy* (pp. 94–103). New York: Van Nostrand Reinhold.

U.S. Census Bureau. (2002). *Statistical abstract of the U.S. 2000.* Retrieved October 11, 2002, from http://www.census.gov/statab

U.S. Department of Housing and Urban Development. (2004). *American Housing Survey for the United States: 2003.* Retrieved December 5, 2004 from http://www.census.gov/prod/2004pubs/H150-03.pdf

Wacker, R. R., Roberto, K. A., & Piper, L. E. (1998). *Community resources for older adults: Programs and services in an era of change.* Thousand Oaks, CA: Pine Forge.

Winklevoss, H. E., & Powell, A. V. (1984). *Continuing care retirement communities: An empirical, financial, and legal analysis.* Homewood, IL: Richard D. Irwin.

CHAPTER TEN

Transportation and Aging

Challenges in Rural America

Helen Kerschner

Older adults often move to rural areas or remain there to avoid the complexities and costs of the urban environment. Unfortunately, when they no longer drive, they often face huge problems accessing life-sustaining as well as life-enhancing services. Today, with public policy focusing on enabling elders to stay in their homes as long as possible, transportation is increasingly identified as one of the major problems of older adults as expressed by policy makers, service professionals, caregivers, and older adults (Bernier & Seekins, 1999). In fact, ensuring transportation access for older adults to maintain independence was the third resolution from the 2005 White House Conference on Aging. This chapter addresses the challenges that seniors, family members, service agencies, and transportation providers face in meeting the transportation needs of older adults who no longer drive. It also describes the solutions that communities have developed for improving transportation access; solutions that, in turn, can improve the ability of seniors' access to basic essentials as well as quality-of-life activities.

TRANSPORTATION NEEDS

Professionals and service providers in transportation and aging, older adults and their families are very aware of the problems that may result from ceasing to drive—problems that can make accessing transportation

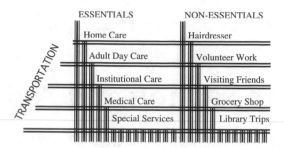

FIGURE 10.1   The tie that binds.

options difficult. They know that these problems do not occur just because a person is aged 60, 70, 80, or 90 years but rather are related to health and mobility. They know that when transportation becomes limited, life becomes limited. Being able to get where you need to go is a basic need of older adults. In that respect, transportation has been described as "the tie that binds" seniors to the essentials of life (doctor, pharmacy, social service program, grocery store) and to the fun things in life (movie theatre, hairdresser, home of a friend, volunteer activities, educational programs) (Kerschner, 2001). This concept is depicted in Figure 10.1. Those essential and nonessential trips are critical to ensuring that older adults are able to access and engage in both quantity and quality-of-life activities.

DESTINATION NEEDS

Older adults in rural communities need to access a variety of life-sustaining destinations. Nonemergency medical trips are an important aspect of senior mobility (U.S. DOT, 1997). Other life-sustaining destinations include trips to the grocery store, pharmacy, physician's office, and employment settings. Although these basic services often are the ones that receive the most attention and financial support, activities that sustain independence and enhance life may be just as important, as they are the things that affect quality of life. Quality-of-life destinations include the home of a friend or family member, recreational or volunteer activities, religious activities, a nursing home, senior center, the movies, community center, bank, lawyer's office, a funeral home, cemetery, library, local college, or restaurant.

SERVICE AVAILABILITY

Seniors living in rural areas tend to be older, have lower incomes, and be in poorer health than seniors in suburban and urban areas (Ricketts, Johnson-Webb, & Randolph, 1999; Rogers, 2002). Transportation can present a

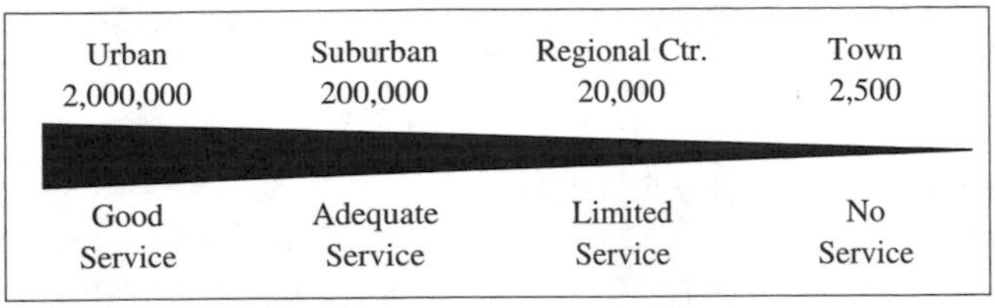

FIGURE 10.2   Community's size versus service availability.

problem to them because of distances that they may need to travel to get to health and social services and quality-of-life activities. This is illustrated in Figure 10.2. Many small towns in rural America do not have a local physician's office, shopping center, movie theatre, library, bank, or beauty shop. This means a person may need to travel up to 20 miles to a regional center or county seat to take care of personal needs. If the passenger has a health condition that requires dialysis or radiation therapy, for example, it may be necessary to go to a clinic or hospital in a distant suburban or urban community.

The lack of service availability in rural communities and the geographic distances between the people and their destinations can make access difficult when people do not drive—difficult for them and for a community transportation service that is trying to serve them. To illustrate, a rural transportation service may need to travel 5 or 10 miles to pick up a passenger, and then travel another 20 or 30 miles to the destination, and travel an equal distance on the return trip. Translated into hours, it can require the use of a vehicle and driver for up to 10 hours, sometimes three times a week. This means that the actual cost of a long-distance dialysis trip can be $100 or $150 three times a week. Such an amount could be prohibitive for many rural transportation services and their passengers. In summary, the geographic dispersion and isolation of the population, the narrow range of services and service providers, and the limited transit alternatives complicate the ability of seniors to access services, regardless of whether services are being transported to seniors or seniors are being transported to services.

TRANSPORTATION SERVICE CHALLENGE

For a glimpse at the challenges faced by seniors in getting to essential and quality-of-life activities, let us look at the activities, trips, and destinations of Mrs. Smith and Mr. Jones, both of whom live in rural communities, as shown in Table 10.1.

TABLE 10.1　Hypothetical Transportation Needs of Two Seniors

Service	Days per week	Location	Miles
Mrs. Smith's Transportation Schedule			
Dialysis	3	Dialysis center	40
Meal program	3	Senior center	8
Visit husband	3	Nursing home	4
Participate in church activities	2	Church	6
Total trips per week	11	Total miles per week	168
Mr. Jones's Transportation Schedule			
Radiation treatments	5	Hospital	20
Computer learning program	2	Oasis	10
Volunteer at school	2	RSVP* site	4
Grocery store and pharmacy	1	Store	6
Total trips per week	10	Total miles per week	134

*RSVP, Retired and Senior Volunteer Program

Obviously, transportation will be critical to the ability of Mrs. Smith and Mr. Jones to get to their destinations. If they do not drive, or transportation is not available, they may be unable to receive health care, get medications or groceries, or participate in the community. The result may be isolation and/or an inability to live independently.

The Driving Option

In 2000, almost 35 million Americans were age 65 years or older. According to the U.S. Department of Transportation (U.S. DOT), 95% of the men and 75% of the women age 65 years or older were licensed drivers. The study by Foley and colleagues suggests that limitations related to vision, activities of daily living, and mental health that occur as people age result in an age-related decline in the percentage of senior drivers in a community (Foley, Heimovcitz, Guralnik, & Brock, 2002). For example, although men and women age 74 years or older can expect to continue to drive for several years, many will live additional years when they can no longer drive (see Table 10.2). What this means is that the more than 4 million older Americans in the age 85 years

TABLE 10.2　Women and Men Driving After Age 74

Gender	Life expectancy	Driving expectancy	Years not driving
Men	18 years	11 years	7 years
Women	21 years	11 years	10 years

or older group are faced with the possibility of being transportation dependent for several years.

Public Transit Option

Paratransit transportation differs from the majority of public transportation options because it does not follow a fixed route or schedule. Unfortunately, neither public nor paratransit options are frequently available in rural America. Recent data indicate that 30% of the United States population lives in nonmetropolitan or rural areas; 40% of that population has no public transportation in the form of buses and paratransit, and 25% of the population has inadequate transportation. One reason for the problem is that only 6% of the federal transit funds are spent in rural or nonmetropolitan areas (Glasgow, 2000). This translates to 4.4 million people age 65 years or older with no public transportation and 500,000 with inadequate transportation.

Even if it is available, older adults may face difficulties accessing transportation services because of loss of mobility, failing health, or economic vulnerability; the same conditions that made it difficult or impossible for them to drive. For many elders, it can be difficult to walk to the curb, let alone to a bus stop a few blocks or a mile from home, or to climb the steps of a bus or van once they get there. Comments from seniors and caregivers participating in a national focus group project highlight the physical as well as the personal aspects of the problem (Kerschner & Aizenberg, 1999).

> I need something that goes to my house.
>
> Bus drivers have no compassion, especially for seniors.
>
> I couldn't step up on the bus. I would have to crawl.
>
> I have lots of problems carrying loads when I use public transportation.
>
> It takes three hours for what would be a ten minute drive with a car.
>
> I want to go places for recreation but don't find it easy at night.

Transportation access problems can be especially severe for those age 85 years or older. This age group is more at risk for chronic conditions and disability and has a greater need for medical care, rehabilitation, social services, and physical support (U.S. DOT, 1997). In other words, although some might believe that older adults do not use available community transportation options because they do not want to or because they are inconvenient, the real problem is that the transportation options do not accommodate their needs including their emotional concerns and physical needs.

FIVE TRANSPORTATION SOLUTIONS

The transportation challenges faced by both seniors and transportation providers in rural America are considerable. Five solutions discussed in this section are: create senior friendliness, adapt existing options, create new options, provide supportive transportation, and identify promising practices.

Solution I: Promote "Senior Friendliness"

Transportation providers often express their desire to be customer-friendly. Customer-friendliness can mean on-time performance, flexible service routes and schedules, courteous drivers, and comfortable vehicles. One of the results of the Kerschner and Aizenberg (1999) project was the 5 As of Senior Friendly Transportation which were developed by the Beverly Foundation in 2000. The components of the 5 As—availability, accessibility, acceptability, affordability, and adaptability—have been discussed in other literature on community-based services in rural areas (e.g., Krout, 1994). The 5 As, defined in Figure 10.3, were subsequently reinforced in a national survey of senior transportation programs (Kerschner & Aizenberg, 2001). Today, the 5 As are used by governmental and nongovernmental entities as a conceptual approach to assess the ability of public transportation, paratransit, and specialized transit services to meet the transportation needs of seniors (General Accounting Office, 2004).

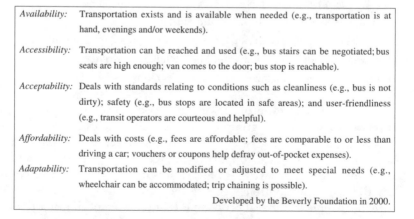

Availability:	Transportation exists and is available when needed (e.g., transportation is at hand, evenings and/or weekends).
Accessibility:	Transportation can be reached and used (e.g., bus stairs can be negotiated; bus seats are high enough; van comes to the door; bus stop is reachable).
Acceptability:	Deals with standards relating to conditions such as cleanliness (e.g., bus is not dirty); safety (e.g., bus stops are located in safe areas); and user-friendliness (e.g., transit operators are courteous and helpful).
Affordability:	Deals with costs (e.g., fees are affordable; fees are comparable to or less than driving a car; vouchers or coupons help defray out-of-pocket expenses).
Adaptability:	Transportation can be modified or adjusted to meet special needs (e.g., wheelchair can be accommodated; trip chaining is possible).

Developed by the Beverly Foundation in 2000.

FIGURE 10.3   The 5 A's of senior-friendly transportation.

Solution II: Adapt Existing Options

A number of adaptive solutions have been developed to improve transportation for seniors. In many instances they support existing public and paratransit options and accommodate the special circumstances of rural areas (Rosenbloom, 2002). Following are some options:

- vehicle-sharing programs by vehicle owners with nonowners;
- shared vehicle use among organizations in communities;
- group purchase partnership for vehicle(s) by two or more agencies;
- empty seat use by car pooling and car sharing;
- community fleet ownership, allowing residents to reserve, pay, and drive;
- vehicle renting by transit operators for rural residents;
- sale of unused capacity providing service to other users in down times;
- central maintenance facility for small programs offering economies of scale;
- service program offering group insurance, driver training, or driver sharing;
- limousine or personal auto business providing drivers for a fee.

Although such innovations can help solve many of the transportation difficulties that are faced by the general population, they may not meet the special needs of older adults. Additionally, not all communities are willing or able to make such adjustments and expenditures, and even when they do, older adults may still face many problems getting where they need to go. Finally, in many instances such adaptations will not make the vehicle or program "senior friendly."

In an attempt to meet the needs of seniors, services often modify existing transportation equipment and programs. Examples include: providing financial incentives, altering or modifying fixed-route services, linking with volunteer groups, providing financial supplements, making physical adaptations to vehicles, providing driver training, and changing pick-up and delivery locations. It is possible, for instance, for a public or paratransit service to purchase buses that kneel, provide door-to-door and door-through-door (in addition to curb-to-curb) service, or link with volunteer groups in order to provide transportation escorts, or supplement their driver pool. Other possibilities might include development of a driver sensitivity training program to improve the relationship between taxi drivers and older adults, or the expansion of a non-emergency medical care transportation program in order to provide quality of life in addition to quantity-of-life rides.

Solution III: Create New Options

During the course of the Kerschner and Aizenberg (1999) study, seniors and their caregivers discussed transportation problems as well as community-based solutions. Many of the solutions involved special transportation programs that had been developed "just for seniors." Subsequent surveys by the Beverly Foundation identified and indexed more than 400 supplemental transportation programs (STPs) for seniors in 50 states (Kerschner & Westphal, 2004). In the STPs study, 40% identified themselves as being located in rural areas. Table 10.3 provides a summary of the characteristics of these programs.

TABLE 10.3   Characteristics of STPs in Rural America

Characteristic	Percentage	Characteristic	Percentage
Organizational status		**Escorts**	
Non-profit	86%	Are provided	42%
Funding		Not provided	66%
Grants	71%	**Service hours**	
Tax revenue	20%	Daytime	61%
Rider fees	41%	Daytime and evenings	16%
Rider donations	15%	Weekdays	55%
Purpose of trip		7 days a week	20%
Medical	70%	Sundays	5%
Essential	18%	Anytime	4%
Religious	21%	**Reservation requirements**	
Social/recreational	44%	Same-day service	35%
Any	42%	24 hours in advance	35%
Other	11%	2 days in advance	20%
Vehicle used		2+days in advance	17%
Auto	36%	**Service type**	
Taxi	2%	Door-to-door	72%
Van	54%	Curb-to-curb	13%
Bus	35%	Fixed-route	6%
Drivers		Door-through-door	14%
Volunteer	32%	Other	3%
Paid	44%	**Rider fee**	
Mix	21%	Flat rate	19%
Riders targeted		Mileage rate	19%
Senior	64%	Sliding scale	9%
Seniors and ADA	40%	Rider donation	16%
Everyone	14%	None	54%

Note: Supplemental Transportation Programs (STPs), Americans with Disabilities Act (ADA).

The fact that STPs provide rides and supplement transportation is important. However, what sets them apart from most other transportation programs is that they reach what might be called a hidden population of older adults (those age 85 years or older) who have special mobility needs. They meet those needs through trip chaining, providing door-to-door service and transportation escorts, and numerous other methods of personal support. Because it is so difficult, if not impossible, for traditional systems to provide such personalized services, STPs often function as a critical element of a community's transportation service system. According to several service providers, in many instances, they are "the only game in town."

Solution IV: Provide Supportive Transportation

Needs for supportive transportation services are especially important to seniors who have physical or mental limitations that make it difficult to walk, lift, see, hear, climb, or, in general, do the activities necessary to independently access a transportation service. These are the same physical and mental limitations that make it difficult, if not impossible, for seniors to drive their cars. For instance, when a senior must stop driving because of macular degeneration, that same vision problem may make it difficult to get to or to use a traditional fixed-route transit without extra assistance. Alternately, when memory limitations associated with Alzheimer's disease force a senior to stop driving, those same memory problems may make it impossible to access a curb-to-curb paratransit or taxi service without extra assistance. In many communities, the person providing supportive transportation will take the elder to the door, help them on the vehicle and/or stay with them at the destination.

In rural communities it can be extremely expensive if the person providing the support is paid. The 10-hour trip three times a week is a good example. Transit providers are increasingly solving the problem by mobilizing family members, friends and neighbors, and paid drivers to provide supportive transportation assistance. The most common and low-cost method, however, is to recruit volunteer drivers who not only drive but also provide escort transportation assistance.

In the Kerschner and Westphal (2004) database of STPs, 53% of the transportation programs included some form of volunteer driver involvement, 72% provided door-to-door service, 44% provided escort service, and 14% said they provided door-through-door service. In a more recent Beverly Foundation survey of volunteer driver programs, 93% provided door-to-door service, 77% provided door-through-door service, and 77% provided escort services (Kerschner & Pang, 2005). It should be pointed out that door-through-door service may be available to a much greater extent than the data would suggest. Liability concerns and insurance requirements tend to put transit providers in a "don't ask, don't tell" situation in which they believe it is necessary and know it is being provided, but they do not talk about it and cannot report it.

Solution V: Promising Practices in Rural America and Beyond

Five innovative transportation services that serve older adults in rural areas are described below. Each represents a special type of service method, destination, or supportive service that makes it possible for senior riders to access activities and services. Also, each is a recipient of a Beverly Foundation STAR Award for Excellence.

FRIENDS HELPING FRIENDS

The Transportation Reimbursement and Information Project of Riverside, California, is a non-profit, social assistance program with volunteer drivers/escorts. It is organized with a "friends helping friends" approach to driver recruitment in that riders recruit their own drivers. The program provides reimbursement for mileage. The reimbursement is given to the riders who in turn give it to their drivers. The driver recruitment and reimbursement methods are intended to empower the rider, to eliminate the need to purchase vehicles, and to reduce the need to organize and support a volunteer driver group.

ELDER EXPERIENCE TRAVEL

The San Felipe Elderly Transportation Program is a non-profit program operated through the senior center in the San Felipe Pueblo, New Mexico. The program consists of one van that was donated by the San Felipe Pueblo Casino, which continues to support the program by providing inexpensive gasoline. The program serves 90 older adults, charges no fees for service, and is the only transportation available for many of the riders. In addition to providing rides for nutrition and health care services, it also provides transportation for shopping and social activities. Further, periodic transportation is provided to religious events and to distant places such as the Grand Canyon and Juarez, Mexico. The distant travel has provided a mechanism for elders to join their wisdom with travel experiences and thus enhance their role as village elders in the eyes of their grandchildren.

PROVIDER DONATION MOBILIZATION

Shepherd's Center Escort of Kalamazoo, Michigan is an interfaith transportation program sponsored by 42 churches. It provides rides for medical appointments only and is a volunteer driver program with limited staff. It does not charge fees for transportation and accepts donations from riders and from service providers. The program does not explicitly solicit donations. However, drivers who escort riders to doctor's offices and other medical services leave an information card about the program and its service to the community, thus giving service providers the opportunity to contribute to a cause that is in their best interest and in the best interests of their patients.

DRIVER ESCORT SUPPORT

Jefferson County Service Organization of Oskaloosa, Kansas is a nonprofit agency that is the sole provider of transportation in the county. Eighty-five percent of the riders are seniors and most are age 75 years or older. Although many of its riders still drive their cars, they depend on the service for longer-distance rides to medical appointments. The majority of drivers are retired, and as most rides involve long distances, drivers usually stay with passengers until they are ready to return home. In addition to providing transportation, drivers also help schedule and record medical appointments and help with shopping and with carrying groceries and other packages.

VOLUNTEER MOBILIZATION

Located in Portland, Oregon, Ride Connection provides a concierge service in which volunteers ride on vehicles and provide information as well as physical escort assistance to seniors and the disabled. To accomplish this, partners mobilize volunteers to act as escorts for frail riders being transported on a vehicle driven by someone else. For example, if a vehicle is bringing more than one person to a destination, the escort may help one person into the building while the driver is operating the lift for another rider. The escort may also help obtain directions from a rider without the driver needing to be distracted.

The rural typography, geography, and population density combine to make it difficult to achieve standard measurements of efficient and effective rural transportation service delivery. At the same time, the senior friendliness, innovative approaches, specialized options, and supportive transportation services that are provided by many rural transportation services suggest a customer focus and human service orientation. One reason may be that many of today's rural transportation service providers got their start in the human service sector, especially in senior services. Also, much of the early financial support for such programs was contributed by local, state, and national human service agencies.

It also is worth noting that the U.S. Administration on Aging (AoA) provided considerable start-up and operations for many of the early senior transportation programs in rural areas. AoA's involvement was initiated by the National Eldercare Institute in the 1970s and 1980s, which recognized that transportation was key to the ability of seniors to access their services and activities in the community. Subsequently, a large number of the senior transportation programs evolved into the sole transportation service provider in many rural communities and counties. Today, AoA is the repository of information from those early initiatives.

CONCLUSIONS

The conclusion of this chapter reviews many of the problems inherent in senior transportation in rural America and presents recommendations for future action.

Problem: Rural elders' geographic distribution and that of their destinations make it necessary for them to travel great distances, for long periods of time, at times that are not normal business hours.

Solution: Encourage rural transit services to create flexible schedules, to organize low cost operations, and expand their service areas beyond the immediate community and county.

Problem: Community leaders often have difficulty understanding the transportation needs of seniors and lack financial commitment to meet those needs.

Solution: Change the perception and lack of commitment by clearly defining the benefit of providing transportation services to seniors, clearly stating the message about the need and benefit, and selecting the messenger with the necessary professional or political status to ensure that the message is heard.

Problem: Community leaders often make the assumption that if transportation options are available, transportation needs are met. Even when several options are available, that assumption may not be true.

Solution: Educate community leaders about the access problems faced by seniors when trying to use transit services.

Problem: Senior transportation programs often limit their services to specific program or service destinations such as a nutrition site, a senior center, or a medical visit.

Solution: Advocate for the expansion of senior transportation services beyond specific program destinations so that they can meet the quality-of-life needs of seniors.

Problem: Transportation providers say that the population they are serving is not the age 65 years or older population, but rather the age 85 years or older population. Mobility and mental limitations often have their onset in the early and mid-80s, and thus the projected increase in the age 85 years or older population will present great challenges to transportation providers.

Solution: Expand research and informational materials development about the relationships between age, physical and mental limitations, and transportation access.

Problem: Providers say that curb-to-curb transportation cannot meet the needs of a large number of their senior riders.

Solution: Initiate the design and development of efficient and economical methods for providing supportive transportation in the form of door-to-door and door-through-door service, transportation escorts and special attendants.

Problem: Because of the high cost of driver salaries, the involvement of volunteers, especially volunteer drivers, is said to be the hope of the future in providing low cost transportation services for seniors. Many transportation providers in rural communities are anxious to involve volunteers as drivers but say it is difficult to find volunteers.

Solution: Undertake research on successful volunteer driver programs to better understand how to involve volunteers in providing transportation to seniors.

Problem: Transit providers and volunteers express concerns about using personal automobiles, driving to and from destinations, and providing supportive transportation. Quite often the concern is about liability.

Solution: Identify methods for insuring volunteer driving programs and supportive transportation services.

Finally, what can be said about the plight of Mrs. Smith and Mr. Jones? Both of them required frequent travel to distant health services and to what might be considered recreational, educational, or social activities.

The use of private autos and vans, the availability of single passenger rides, and the involvement of volunteer drivers could eliminate their dependence on high occupancy vehicles and point-to-point transit routes. In effect, it could make transportation more efficient and less costly for Mrs. Smith and Mr. Jones and their transportation services. The availability of door-to-door service and escorts could make it possible for both of them to access the vehicle with someone to support them and without having to walk long distances. Further, the availability of rides for any purpose could make it possible for them to get to essential destinations as well as make quality-of-life trips. These and other such solutions make a compelling case for awareness and action.

In conclusion, transportation presents many challenges for seniors and transit services in rural America. Transportation for seniors is not only the domain of the public and paratransit systems but also the domain of community groups, clubs, senior centers' meal programs, and private providers. The government cannot do everything; we need to explore new, low-cost methods for designing and organizing community-supported transportation programs. If we continue to support and expand innovative public transit, paratransit, and community-based efforts to meet the transportation needs of seniors, perhaps one day the tapestry of transportation options in rural America will fulfill the promise of the 5 As of Senior Friendly Transportation.

REFERENCES

Bernier, B., & Seekins, T. (1999). Rural transportation voucher program for people with disabilities: Three case studies. *Journal of Transportation and Statistics, 2*(1), 61–70.

Bull, C. N., Krout, J. A., Rathbone-McCuan, E., & Shreffler, M. J. (2001). Access and issues of equity in remote/rural areas. *Journal of Rural Health, 17,* 356–359.

Foley, D. J., Heimovcitz, H. K., Guralnik, J. M., & Brock, D. B. (2002). Driving life expectancy of persons aged 70 years and older in the United States. *American Journal of Public Health, 92,* 1284–1289.

General Accounting Office. (2004). *Transportation-disadvantaged seniors: Efforts to enhance senior mobility could benefit from additional guidance and information.* Report to the Chairman, Special Committee on Aging, U.S. Senate.

Glasgow, N. (2000). Older Americans' patterns of driving and using other transportation. *Rural America, 15*(3), 26–31.

Kerschner, H. K. (2001). *The ties that bind* (White paper on STPs). Pasadena, CA: Beverly Foundation.

Kerschner, H., & Aizenberg, R. (1999). *Attitudes of drivers, non drivers and caregivers about giving up the keys* (Focus Group Report). Pasadena, CA: Beverly Foundation.

Kerschner, H., & Aizenberg, R. (2001). *Supplemental transportation programs for seniors.* Washington, DC: Beverly Foundation and AAA Foundation for Traffic Safety.

Kerschner, H., & Pang, E. (2005). *Volunteer drivers: the hope of the future* (Report on STAR Search 2004). Pasadena, CA: Beverly Foundation.

Kerschner, H., & Westphal, E. (2004). *Supplemental transportation programs for seniors: A report on STPs in America.* Washington, DC: Beverly Foundation and AAA Foundation for Traffic Safety.

Krout, J. A. (1994). An overview of older rural populations and community-based services. In J. A. Krout (Ed.), *Providing community-based services to the rural elderly* (pp. 3–18). Thousand Oaks, CA: Sage.

Ricketts, T. C., Johnson-Webb, K. D., & Randolph, R. K. (1999). Populations in rural America. In T. C. Ricketts III (Ed.), *Rural health in the United States* (pp. 7–24). New York: Oxford University Press.

Rogers, C. C. (2002). Rural health issues for the older population. *Rural America, 17*(2), 30–36.

Rosenbloom, S. (2002, July/August). Facing societal challenges: The need for new paradigms in rural transit service. *Community Transportation*, pp. 16–27.

U.S. Department of Transportation. (1997). *Improving transportation for a maturing society* (Publication No. P10-97-01). Washington, DC: U.S. Government Printing Office.

PART IV

Moving Forward: Technology and System Change

Transforming Rural Health Care

The Role of Technology

Linda Redford and Ryan Spaulding

Access to traditional health care services can be problematic for older adults or disabled individuals regardless of where they reside. Physical frailty, inability to get or use transportation resources, and financial limitations are significant barriers to care for both urban and rural elders. For rural residents these barriers are further compounded by geographic distance and inadequate health care infrastructures. Specialty medical care, intensive rehabilitation therapies, and emergency care, to name a few, are health care services in short supply outside of urban communities. Many communities in rural America have no primary care practitioners or hospitals and residents must travel considerable distances to access even basic primary care.

Traditional models of in-person, hands-on health care delivery appear unlikely to be the answer to all of the care needs in rural areas. Demographic shifts, economic pressures, and shortages of health care personnel, combined with federal and state policies aimed at controlling health care costs, continue to destabilize rural health infrastructures (Ormond, Wallin, & Goldenson, 2000). Health information technologies (HIT), such as interactive televideo (ITV) for telemedicine or telehealth and the Internet are showing promise as adjuncts to existing resources that can support and expand the capabilities of rural providers. In addition,

HIT can help providers keep abreast of current health care information, provide health care practitioners and patients access to needed specialty consultation and care, and minimize patients' need to travel long distances for specialty services.

This chapter provides an overview of the many barriers to quality health care found in rural America, followed by a comprehensive examination of the various technologies that are being deployed to alleviate them. Numerous examples of how the technologies are applied for specific health care needs are provided, such as the transmission of digital files of medical procedures from remote locations to consulting medical specialists for analysis and the use of home telemonitoring devices for patients with unstable acute and chronic conditions. The ways in which ITV and the Internet are used to educate health care professionals on the latest health information and treatments are also presented. In addition, an overview is provided of how traditional telehealth technologies, such as ITV, are now being integrated with the Internet to provide a more ubiquitous and less costly technological infrastructure for the delivery of health care and health information.

Finally, implementation issues are discussed, including such topics as insurance reimbursement of telehealth services, technological considerations, Health Insurance Portability and Accountability Act (HIPAA) implications, and the human factors involved in developing health information technologies. Overall, this chapter offers readers a broad understanding of why health technologies are needed in rural areas, how they are helpful in addressing health disparities, and what needs to be done to make them more accessible.

CURRENT ISSUES IN RURAL HEALTH CARE

The problems in rural health care are a reflection of broader economic and demographic pressures facing rural communities today. The migration of rural young to urban areas has been an increasing trend over the last several decades, resulting in eroding tax bases, inadequate labor pools, and general economic decline in vast numbers of rural communities (Rogers, 2002a). Rural counties, particularly those not adjacent to metropolitan areas, often have an aged and aging population. In such counties, it is not uncommon for almost a fifth of the population to be age 65 years or older, with a very high percent of these individuals age 85 years or older. In addition to an aging population, rural communities tend to have a higher percentage of persons living in poverty, with the elderly being heavily represented in this group (Rogers, 2002b; Tarmann, 2003).

Advanced age and poverty, separately and in combination, place people at greater risk for chronic illnesses and subsequently at a greater need for health care services. When in need of health care, rural elders are more likely to be dependent on local rural health systems due to the logistics and cost of traveling to urban areas for care. At the same time, the young and more mobile rural residents often bypass the rural health system and go to urban areas for care. This behavior appears to be fueled by a number of factors, including an apparent lack of confidence in rural health providers and a belief that specialty care is desirable (U.S. Department of Health and Human Services, 2003). This is a phenomenon that must be addressed in rural health care, as this trend tends to exacerbate the economic woes and instability of rural health infrastructures. Rural providers find themselves more dependent on revenues from public insurance (i.e., Medicare for older adults and Medicaid for the poor), leaving them potentially more vulnerable to vicissitudes of public policy and more likely to abandon rural practice (Rosenthal & Fox, 2000). Many rural hospitals have had to close or undergo restructuring to survive, health providers have left rural areas leaving gaps in health services, and rural communities continue to experience serious difficulties in recruiting and retaining new providers.

Rural residents who are unable or have great difficulty traveling long distances for care, typically the old, the disabled, and the poor, face dwindling options for care in many rural communities (Ormond, Zuckerman, & Lhila, 2000; University of Washington, 2000). Although those unable to travel for care are the most disadvantaged, inadequacies in our rural health systems can impact anyone. The insufficient funding of ambulance services, inadequate training of emergency personnel, and reductions in hospital-based emergency and acute care services threaten both those who live in and those who travel through rural areas (Institute of Medicine, 2005; University of North Dakota, 2005). The lack of readily available care also results in people waiting longer to get care. Delays in care frequently result in longer hospitalizations and higher costs of care, costs that are passed on to all health care consumers.

The litany of problems facing rural health care are cause for concern, but these problems should also be viewed as an incentive for us to rethink how health care can be provided and ways that technology can extend and expand the capabilities of our existing health care workforce and resources. The following sections address some of the ways that technology is currently impacting rural disparities in health care and how emerging technologies hold promise for more far reaching impacts.

APPLICATIONS OF TECHNOLOGY IN HEALTH CARE

Interactive Televideo in the Delivery of Primary and Specialty Medical Care

ITV has been and continues to be a significant innovation for delivering health care and health education. As easy as dialing the telephone, health professionals can connect with facilities anywhere in the world that have similar ITV equipment. ITV, often referred to as telemedicine or telehealth, has been available for many years and has typically been configured as room-based systems. Room-based units consist of a camera unit, a monitor, and usually a video recorder and can be easily connected with other compatible units via special lines and a telephone connection. Persons at both ends of the connection can see, hear, and speak to each other. This means a patient in a rural community and a physician or other health care provider across the state, the nation, or the world can see and converse with one another. With special ITV compatible medical equipment, a health care provider can examine the patient and, in many cases, make a diagnosis, recommend treatment, and monitor the progress of treatment much as would be done in a routine office visit.

Some specific examples highlight the range of ITV applications in health care delivery. For instance, rural residents with heart problems and those recovering from cardiac surgery who reside hundreds of miles from Kansas University (KU) Medical Center have been evaluated and received follow-up via ITV for more than 14 years. Telepsychiatry has been available from KU Medical Center and numerous other centers throughout the country for over a decade. This service has been vital to addressing the dearth of mental health services in rural communities and studies have shown it to be well accepted by patients (Rohland, Saleh, Rohrer, & Romitti, 2000; Zarate et al., 1997).

Real-time consultations are one approach to telemedicine, but the store and forward capacity of ITV units also allows for asynchronous consultations in situations that are not urgent. X-rays are currently sent via ITV to radiologists hundreds or thousands of miles away to be read and evaluated at the radiologist's convenience. Dermascopes attached to ITV units allow high quality pictures of rashes and lesions to be recorded and sent to dermatologists for later examination and diagnosis. The Veterans Affairs Centers in Michigan and Georgia recently studied the use of ITV to provide wound care. A store and forward system was used with a nurse coordinator taking pictures of the wound and collecting other clinical information then was forwarded to Veterans Affairs physicians for diagnosis and treatment recommendations (Kim, Lowery, Hamill, & Wilkins, 2004). Such applications have potential for improving care and outcomes for elders in urban and rural areas who are not ambulatory and cannot easily reach medical facilities for care of acute or chronic wounds.

In addition to the examples above, a study conducted by the Telemedicine Research Center (2004) provides the latest available information on telemedicine activity in the United States. Representatives from 88 telehealth networks across the United States reported providing over 85,000 patient-provider teleconsultations in 2003. Although the most active specialties continued to be those listed in earlier studies, such as mental health, cardiology, dermatology, and orthopedics, data indicated significant growth in emergency and obstetric/gynecologic teleconsultation volume. The most active programs cited by the study were found in five states: Arizona, California, Tennessee, Texas, and Vermont. For more telemedicine information, including an extensive bibliographic catalog and descriptions on telemedicine and telehealth programs in the United States and around the world, another resource is the Telemedicine Information Exchange at http://tie.telemed.org.

Interactive Televideo in the Delivery of Interdisciplinary Health Care

Telemedicine applications involving consultation among primary care physicians and medical specialists are numerous and well established, but many new applications are appearing. A growing area for telehealth is in the support of advanced practice nurses, such as nurse practitioners and physician assistants who are filling the gaps in rural health care. Nurse practitioners and physician assistants are knowledgeable and skilled in providing much of the primary care needed in rural areas. With physician backup, they also play a vital role in meeting the acute and emergency health needs of rural communities. In North Dakota, physician assistants began staffing rural emergency rooms in 1995. They play an integral role in facilitating emergency teleconsultations with consulting physicians in the Dakota Telemedicine system in Bismarck, North Dakota (Lambrecht, 1998). Through such consultations, they are able to provide necessary treatment for many ill and injured patients, while stabilizing others for transfer to urban tertiary care centers.

In many rural communities, nurses and nurse practitioners are the major source of health care for rural elders. At times they work side-by-side with busy rural physicians and at other times serve as the only health care provider in a clinic or emergency room. Nurse practitioners provide routine care under standing orders from physicians. In complicated or emergency situations, the nurse practitioners can connect through ITV with physicians or other health care specialists for consultation and assistance. By being able to see the patient, a physician can verbally direct or visually demonstrate a treatment that is needed.

In a recent case in Texas, an advanced practice nurse in an emergency room administered intravenous thrombolytic therapy to a patient suffering an acute ischemic stroke under the direction of an emergency room physician and Stroke Team physicians based at an urban medical center (Choi, et al., 2004). This therapy dissolves the clot that is obstructing blood flow to a portion of the brain. If given within a short time after the onset of the stroke, there is a good chance it will reverse the symptoms caused by the stroke and reduce the likelihood of permanent disability. If a patient has to wait to be transferred to an urban area to receive the treatment, the likelihood of full recovery is negligible.

In Washington state, nurses in remote areas are able to dispense prescription medications by having ITV connections to pharmacists in an urban area. The nurse sends the urban hospital pharmacist a scanned copy of the medication to be administered and enters the prescription into a computer. The pharmacist approves the medication and authorizes the nurse to dispense the medication via an automated dispensing device (Peterson & Anderson, 2004). This means a patient can begin treatment immediately rather than waiting until the medication arrives by mail from a pharmacy hundreds of miles away.

The use of ITV for physicians, other primary care providers, and allied health professionals to consult with health professionals from other disciplines is broadening access to needed expertise and treatment. For example, the Center for Telemedicine and Telehealth at KU Medical Center collaborates with speech-language pathologists to conduct swallowing evaluations transmitted live from remote sites. For these examinations, the digital fluoroscope at the remote facility is connected to the ITV equipment, thus transferring the live image to the speech-language pathologists at the distant site as if it were being viewed on the digital fluoroscope itself. The speech-language pathologist is able to assess swallowing problems and instruct rural providers on approaches to assist the patient in swallowing and reducing the risk of choking. A similar service also provided by KU Medical Center involves the transmission of live echocardiograms through ITV from a hospital in central Kansas to KU Medical Center cardiologists for diagnosis and treatment recommendations. These can be viewed synchronously or can be recorded for asynchronous viewing, depending on the urgency of the situation and the availability of the specialists.

Telehealth in Nursing Homes

Use of telehealth technologies in nursing facilities is a relatively recent development, but holds considerable promise for improving the care and comfort of nursing facility residents, while reducing costs of care. Wakefield, Buresh, Flanagan, and Kienzle (2004) found that telemedicine consultations conducted to a skilled nursing facility resulted in alleviation of the need for transfer of the resident to a physician or hospital in 72% of cases. A study of a wound care program conducted via ITV between a nursing facility and an acute care facility showed the cost of an average wound teleconsultation to be about half the cost of a traditional in-person visit with transportation (Pringle-Specht, Wakefield, & Flanagan, 2001).

In addition, teleconsultation eliminated the need to transport residents and subject them to an average of 8.5 hours of transport and waiting to receive care. These findings support other studies that show telehealth eliminates patient discomfort associated with transport, reduces treatment delays, lowers transportation costs, and decreases the number of unnecessary emergency room visits (U.S. Department of Health and Human Services, 2001). On-site assessment and consultation also allows the nursing facility nurse to interact directly with the treating physician or other providers, thereby improving communication regarding the problem under evaluation and the care recommendations.

Telehealth in Home Health Care

The application of ITV in home health care is one of the fastest growing telehealth contexts. Telemonitoring devices are now available that allow health care providers in a central office to conduct home health visits via ITV connections. Current devices bring high-resolution images and audio through not much more than a telephone line and a computer monitor. Home health care facilities, such as the one at Kaiser Permanente in Sacramento, California, provide ITV connections to the homes of patients miles away (Johnson, Weeler, Deuser, & Sousa, 2000). A home health nurse sitting in the video room at the home health agency connects to a computer in the home of a patient and can visually assess the patient, obtain vital signs, and evaluate several other clinical measures. Some of the latest telemedicine devices offer blood pressure cuffs, scales, thermometers, stethoscopes to monitor heart and lung sounds, blood glucose monitors, oximeters to measure the oxygen saturation in the blood, and spirometers to assess the lung status of persons with asthma symptoms or other lung conditions.

It is also possible to instruct and visually monitor patients and family members in treatment procedures and therapies. For example, nurses can instruct patients in drawing and administering their insulin and observe them doing the activity. Physical therapists can demonstrate rehabilitation and strengthening exercises and observe patients performing these activities. Rural patients can then benefit from more frequent therapy than would usually be available in a rural area.

The University of New York at Stony Brook, in collaboration with two home health agencies, studied the use of a telehealth device to monitor vital signs of patients with congestive heart failure recently discharged from the hospital to home health (Lehmann & Giacini, 2004). The patients measured their blood pressure, weight, and blood oxygen saturation (O^2 saturation) daily and the results were transmitted to the home health agencies. Each morning, patients were instructed to report any weight gain, edema, shortness of breath, or other possible symptoms of heart failure. Electronic stethoscopes were used to record heart or lung sounds if the patient experienced any breathing or cardiac changes. This study showed that the use of telehealth reduced hospitalizations among congestive heart failure patients and improved patient compliance with treatment regimens. It also provided evidence of the potential value of telehealth technology for high risk patients in rural areas where frequent home visits by nurses are not feasible. A rural home health nurse is now able to "see," assess, and educate more patients in one day than was possible in a week of home visits. Information on the technology available for home care applications and some programs currently providing home care via televideo can be found at http://telehealth.hrsa.gov/pubs/tech/home.htm.

USE OF TECHNOLOGY IN EDUCATION FOR RURAL HEALTH PROFESSIONALS

Education via ITV and the Internet

ITV technology and the Internet make both continuing education and academic programs for career advancement more accessible to rural health professionals. Rural providers can participate in scheduled academic courses, continuing education programs, conferences, grand rounds presentations, and other educational programs provided by leading educational institutions without leaving their communities. In addition, health promotion and health problem management programs are provided for the general public via ITV. This gives rural residents the opportunity to participate in health education programs, see demonstrations of exercises or therapies, and query experts.

The Geriatric Education Centers (GECs), funded by the Bureau of Health Professions, Health Resources and Services Administration, Department of Health and Human Services are among the organizations capitalizing on technology to deliver education to health providers over large geographic areas. The GECs are located in over 40 major medical centers throughout the country and offer a variety of ITV and online educational programs to train health care professionals in geriatrics and keep them abreast of the latest advances in geriatric care. The Central Plains GEC at KU Medical Center provides bi-monthly ITV lectures and demonstrations to rural health professionals throughout Kansas and surrounding states, as well as asynchronous Web-based educational modules (see http://coa.kumc.edu/GEC/LoginMain.asp). These educational offerings provide health professionals the latest knowledge and research information relating to geriatric care and promote the translation of evidence-based geriatric care into practice. ITV applications are also used for peer support and project consultation to health professionals in certificate programs offered by the Central Plains GEC. These programs are designed to prepare health professionals in leadership and mentoring roles in organizations serving older clients.

The Arkansas GEC of the University of Arkansas Medical Center, broadcasts quarterly two-hour educational programs to health professionals on a variety of topics in geriatrics/gerontology (see http://www.agec.org/programs/vtc.asp). These programs are broadcast throughout the state through the Rural Hospital Network, the Area Health Education Centers, and independent receiver sites. They provide current clinical updates and continuing education credits to rural health care providers who would otherwise have to travel several hours to participate in programs originating at the university.

Although ITV applications have a long history in the educational field and are still used as an adjunct in many educational programs, the dependence on special lines and the cost of line-based programming has proven a hindrance for broad applications of this option. On the other hand, the Internet has virtually exploded as a venue for educational programs. Universities and private vendors throughout the country now offer a plethora of academic and continuing education programs online.

The Montana GEC offers online modules and case studies that cover a wide array of topics, ranging from "Web-based Teaching" to "Neurological Problems and Case Studies" (http://mtgec.montana.edu/modsyl.htm). These modules are offered on a monthly basis. Moreover, this GEC offers some online courses for academic credit. Information about all ITV and online educational resources in geriatrics available through the GECs is available on the Health Resources and Services Administration Web site at http://bhpr.hrsa.gov/geriatric/resources/HRSAdefault.asp.

The School of Nursing at KU Medical Center has offered graduate level nurse practitioner education online for almost a decade. This has increased rural nurses' access to graduate nursing programs and has played a major role in increasing the number of nurse practitioners in rural communities in Kansas. Today, there are more than 350 nurse practitioners in Kansas, as compared with 26 in 1994. Graduate certificate programs and Registered Nurse to Bachelor of Science in Nursing degree programs are now being offered online.

Mount Aloysius College in Pennsylvania is working, with funding from the Office of Naval Research, to develop a Virtual Clinical Practicum for nursing students in rural and remote areas (Grady & Berkebile, 2004). This prototype will provide nursing students the opportunity to gain clinical skills in the absence of accessible physical clinical sites. Clinical faculty and clinical simulations will be brought to students through technology.

Until recently, the majority of Internet applications for education provided for little interactivity, except through the use of text-based WebBoards. This technology allows individuals to interact through the use of text messaging. There are limitations to such low-end Internet applications, but they have been a popular option in distance learning. They are, however, rapidly becoming outmoded as high-speed lines permit high quality video and audio interaction. Use of peripheral equipment with computers is further expanding educational options, such as the Virtual Clinical Practicum at Mount Aloysius.

With increasing access to high-speed lines and video streaming solutions, the Internet is becoming the medium of choice over traditional ITV for educational offerings. It has numerous advantages, not the least of which are lower costs for the transmission and receipt of programming, elimination of the need to run additional lines or purchase additional equipment, and elimination of the "middle man" for scheduling multipoint transmissions.

A number of resources are available that provide or catalog online education programs for health professionals. The Group on Educational Affairs and the Association of American Medical Colleges Division of Medical Education, in conjunction with the Virginia Commonwealth University School of Medicine, has developed a Web-based repository for medical education curriculum and assessment materials. The resource is titled MedEdPORTAL Cube and is found at http://www.aamc.org/mededportal. The materials are organized in a Cube. Its three dimensions serve to organize the peer reviewed teaching and/or assessment materials using three primary axes: Accreditation Council for Graduate Medical Education Competencies, Levels of Medical Education (Undergraduate, Graduate, Continuing Education), and Locations for Medical Education.

Another site providing information on online education programs for health professionals is Medscape (http://www.medscape.com). For public health information and education covering both clinical and social sciences perspectives, the resources available at http://www.train. org, which is a project of the Public Health Foundation, are valuable. In addition, numerous national organizations, companies, and universities provide online education. In some instances, the online programs are available free-of-charge or at a nominal cost.

Linking Internet and Interactive Televideo Capabilities

Webcasting has moved the Internet closer to ITV capabilities. Webcasts involve the transmission of a video signal to a Web site where participants can login and view the live event. Webcasts typically allow participants the opportunity to watch the broadcast from the convenience of their office or home computers. The federal government used Webcasts extensively after the September 11 attacks and the anthrax incidents to disseminate information about bioterrorism issues. This use continues today with a broader range of topics. The Veterans Administration and an increasing number of universities are also using Webcasting for educational events.

The capabilities of the Internet are now being expanded far beyond the early Webcast technology to become a truly real-time interactive media. Early Webcasts provided one-way video and audio and participants were required to call in or e-mail questions or comments. Today, with Voice over Internet Protocol (VoIP) and affordable Web cameras that transfer video shots of participants across the Internet, instructors and learners, as well as clinicians and patients, may interact with as if they were in the same room.

The integration of ITV, using traditional ITV equipment and the Internet, is an even greater leap toward improvement of rural health care delivery and education for rural health professionals. By providing ITV over the Internet, high-quality videoconferences can be conducted in virtually any location that a personal computer would typically be found, including desktops, conference rooms, clinics, and even homes. All of the capabilities of room-based telemedicine and telehealth discussed previously are now becoming available via the Internet. Thus, health professionals can provide ITV consultations from the convenience of their own offices while maintaining proximity to their e-mail, patient records, telephones, and other necessities. Leveraging these two technologies offers tremendous potential for meeting health care needs where the delivery of human services, provision of educational programs, and dissemination of information are compromised by such factors as low-density populations, large geographic distances, rough terrain, and provider shortages.

Merging the Internet and ITV has particular advantages for education. A major obstacle to the use of ITV in education has been the telecommunication line charges on the Integrated Services Digital Network

(ISDN) system. Also known as the H.320 protocol, ISDN calls can incur long distance charges ranging from $50 per hour to more than $150 per hour. This has greatly hampered instate education programs and has made most multi-state programs prohibitive from a monetary standpoint. Using Internet Protocols (IP), or the H.323 standard, virtually eliminates the line charges and allows greater access for all health professionals and health organizations. Though many programs are migrating to IP for videoconferencing, the migration is slow and not all programs or sites have made the transition. However, IP-ISDN calls are still possible by employing a multi-point control unit—commonly called a "bridge"—that will facilitate the call between two different types of lines. In addition, videoconferences involving multiple sites can also be bridged whether the sites are all IP-based, ISDN-based, or a combination of both.

The Wireless Future

Wireless options are poised to further revolutionize the technological options available for education and clinical care. Although wireless linkage to the Internet has become commonplace in most urban and suburban communities, the freedom from dependence on lines remains an impractical and expensive alternative for many rural and remote communities. With the integration of ITV and the Internet via line-based systems just beginning to expand, it may take some time for wireless options to be widely available. Once they are available, the possibilities for educational and clinical applications are endless.

German researchers have developed a wireless armband that can monitor and transmit vital signs on patients to health care providers in distant locations (Versweyveld, 2004). This will allow health care providers to continuously monitor the heart rate, blood oxygen saturation, temperature, and other vital signs of sick or older frail patients while they move around the hospital, their homes, or the community. This would mean that patients requiring monitoring would no longer be tethered to lines or restricted to mobility over a limited area. The reduction in hospital stays and the improvement in quality of life for patients could be dramatic. Further, such a device could prove useful in the treatment of patients in disaster situations where immediate transport to medical facilities is not possible and the infrastructure for usual communication between the field and medical facilities is compromised. With the addition of wireless video capabilities, treatment options could be greatly expanded.

Another prototype is being tested for use in swiftly moving vehicles (Versweyveld, 1999). This device provides a wireless link between a paramedic in an ambulance and the emergency room staff while a patient is being transported to a hospital. The patient's vital signs can be monitored and emergency room staff may in the future receive video images of the patient that will allow them to guide necessary treatment procedures before the patient reaches the hospital. In a less dramatic scenario, this technology could expand the use of mobile clinics to reach patients in rural and remote communities. Such clinics could be staffed by nurse practitioners and physician assistants with wireless linkages to backup physicians and specialists in urban communities for needed consultation and treatment recommendations.

The applications of such technology for education are numerous. Not only would this mean health care providers could access educational programs essentially anytime and anywhere, it would also provide opportunities for education and consultation more tightly linked to practice issues. Providers in a home or community settings could link to mentors or consultants for guidance and education as needs arise.

BARRIERS TO THE USE OF TECHNOLOGY

Though the use of technology for the delivery of health care and health information has many benefits, the widespread, rapid adoption of it is met with a similar number of impediments. In addition to a potentially expensive initial investment often required to obtain telehealth equipment, there are important policy issues that have not kept pace with the rapid growth of technological capability. These issues range from reimbursement for technology facilitated clinical consultations to the role human factors play in the adoption of an innovation. Some of the primary concerns of the telehealth community are covered in the next several paragraphs.

Reimbursement

Reimbursement has traditionally been one of the main barriers to utilization of ITV and Internet technologies in health care, though developments in reimbursement coverage over the last several years may prove promising for the growth of telemedicine. The first development was the implementation of the Balanced Budget Act of 1997, which significantly expanded the ability of the Health Care Financing Administration (HCFA) (now called Centers for Medicare and Medicaid Services [CMS]) to reimburse telehealth activities despite containing several important restrictions. To address these limitations, the Medicare, Medicaid, and State Children's Health Insurance Program Benefits Improvement and Protection Act (BIPA) of 2000 (HR 5661) was passed and became effective on

October 1, 2001. The main differences between the Balanced Budget Act of 1997 and the BIPA of 2000 included the elimination of presenter requirements, a nominal originating site fee, and elimination of fee splitting. Refined and expanded eligible site criteria also were outlined, including critical access hospitals, rural health clinics, federally qualified health centers, and hospitals. As some telehealth observers predicted, this legislation provided an environment for other insurers to follow suit in providing telehealth coverage. Now, over 100 private payers in 25 states reimburse for telemedicine services. In addition, telemedicine reimbursement is available from Blue Cross/Blue Shield in 21 states, and from Medicaid in 22 states (American Telemedicine Association and AMD Telemedicine, 2004). Additional insurers will likely follow the lead of those that currently reimburse for telemedicine; improving the possibility that telemedicine will be adopted more widely and will be sustainable over the long-term.

Despite the good news, there is still more work to be done on the reimbursement issue. Regrettably, some of the more innovative applications for which there is growing demand are noticeably absent from current reimbursement policies. Obtaining reimbursement for physicians providing teleconsultations to mental health centers is currently prohibited. Similarly, teleconsultations that originate from nursing homes or from patients' homes for home monitoring purposes are not billable. Even though there has been a growth of online health consultations between patients and providers, the health insurance industry has not been quick to respond with reimbursement policies. One notable exception is a recently enacted policy through Blue Cross/Blue Shield of Florida for routine, Web-based consultations (Healthcare IT News, 2004). Information about the effect this policy has had on Web consultations is not yet available.

Technical Infrastructure

While most reports on the future of telehealth and the Internet point to the increasing capabilities of technology to enhance services, typically at reduced costs, the availability and affordability of evolving technologies are often a barrier for underserved populations most desperately needing access. Many of the most rural and remote communities who could benefit from telecommunication technologies do not have the technical infrastructure to effectively access and use such technology. Consider, for example, that many rural hospitals do not have Internet access or may have only one Internet access point in their facility. Even when rural health care providers want services, there may not be a telecommunication provider in the county that offers services such as ISDN for high-speed connectivity. In other cases, local telecommunication providers resist an outside telecommunication provider bringing such services into their area—even when they do not provide comparable services. Tele-home health projects in Kansas that use regular telephone lines to provide low-bandwidth video-calls between practitioners and patients have been hampered by the absence of standard telephone services in rural communities. For instance, the existence of two-party lines and rotary-only services in rural patients' homes has impeded the use of the home health telemedicine device.

Inherent in the issues outlined above is the consideration of common technical standards. As the interactive video world is in its relative infancy, standards for providing services from one proprietary system to another can be challenging. With the acceptance of H.320 telecommunication standard, many of these problems dissolved by the late 1990s, however, many rural areas still have very dated technologies. With the transition from the H.320 to H.323 (from telephone lines to IP lines), standardization concerns are once again an issue, as not all organizations have migrated to IP and remain on older, H.320-based technologies. As the capabilities and availability of public, private, and independent telecommunications providers pervade the market, standardization will become an increasing consideration.

Licensure

Telemedicine licensure is a critical issue facing policy makers. When a practitioner consults with a patient using telemedicine technology, questions surface regarding where the consult physically occurs. Is it reasonable to assume that the care occurred where the patient was located or should the consulting site be the point of service? Or should a completely new model exist? Implications for these questions become critical for telemedicine licensure, particularly when practitioners reside in a state different from the patient. In the United States, licensure laws for health care are typically regulated on the state level and telemedicine licensure laws have generally reflected this same approach. This raises concerns about interstate telemedicine services. Today, just over half of the states have licensure laws that may be considered restrictive to interstate activity. In most cases, a practitioner is required to be licensed in their own state as well as the state where the patient is residing. Critics to the policy explain that it is highly unlikely that a practitioner will become licensed in the referring state when only a handful of patients may be consulted for specialty or second opinion services. In response, a formidable lobby exists at the federal level to sponsor legislation for "general" or "special purpose" licensure across states. Opponents to general licensure cite concerns about the impact it may have on existing rural health care delivery systems, referral networks, and localized health care (U.S. Department of Commerce, 2001). Nonetheless, due to the efforts of the American Telemedicine Association, the Center for Telemedicine Law, and many other telemedicine providers and organizations, two bills that would allow telemedicine practitioners to provider service across state lines are currently pending in Congress (Center for Telemedicine Law, 2003).

Privacy

Privacy concerns are at the forefront of telemedicine challenges, and in many ways are the most difficult to articulate. The various types of technology and evolving delivery models continue to complicate the issue. Furthermore, perceptions from users regarding privacy, security, and confidentiality are very real obstacles to overcome.

HIPAA is beginning to address privacy concerns in health care delivery. The standards outlined in the policy include "electronic transaction standards for electronic exchange of health information for administrative purposes; standards for the privacy of individually identifiable health information; a national provider identifier; an employer identifier; and secure electronic signatures, among others." Implications of the Act are only beginning to be recognized. However, it seems clear that HIPAA will have significant effects on health care in general and on current and future telehealth initiatives. As privacy has been a formidable concern of the telemedicine industry since its inception, the policy may support and reassure industry efforts. On the other hand, if the policy is overly burdensome, it could effectively dismantle existing telehealth services and thwart new ones.

Though additional privacy steps have been taken as a result of the HIPAA rule, HIPAA has to date not been a significant barrier to providing telehealth services. In fact, ITV consultations are actually exempt from the HIPAA rule. This is because an interactive video consultation is not considered patient information that exists in an electronic form prior to the consultation, nor is it stored afterward. Similarly, faxes, telephone calls, or messages left on voicemail are not covered by HIPAA for the same reasons (U.S. Department of Health and Human Services, 2003). However, store-and-forward transmissions, such as x-rays, echocardiograms or ultrasounds, need to be de-identified of patient information or encrypted during the transmission process.

In addition to de-identification of patient records, the KU Medical Center takes several additional precautions in its telemedicine practice, despite the exemption of videoconferencing from the HIPAA rule. First, any telehealth patient from a rural community receives the HIPAA-required

Notice of Privacy Practices from KU Medical Center *and* from the local community hospital. Further telemedicine video conferences are conducted over private or dedicated Internet lines and are encrypted with the latest encryption standards for enhanced protection. E-mailing conducted for telemedicine purposes is devoid of specific patient information and fax machines for receiving patient records are located in secure areas and any hard copies that are retained are kept in locked cabinets. With these and other precautions in place, no known breaches of patient privacy have occurred as a result of KU Medical Center's telemedicine services. Due to the relative infancy of the HIPAA rule, no national data could be found regarding telemedicine-related privacy intrusions, though it will likely be available in the near future.

The Human Element

With all the possibilities and potentials of telecommunication and information technologies in health care, one caution must be noted. We need a better understanding of telecommunications technologies as a mode of health and human services delivery within a social context. The human element of acceptance, comfort, and trust of technology cannot be underestimated. Conrath, Dunn, and Higgins (1983, p. 201) issued the following warning:

> A technology does not stand alone. Neither should it be evaluated alone. Its use takes place in a social context, and has an effect on that system. To assume otherwise, or to assume the consequences are irrelevant, or to assume that they can only be good, is to place man as the servant of machine. Conscious effort has to be made to insure that the situation is the reverse.

As these authors stated, innovations occur in a human context, so people are the most important considerations when introducing new ideas and the resulting acceptance and adoption of those ideas. Telemedicine is no different. A telemedicine service driven by technology is certain to fail. Instead, telemedicine service should be designed by responding to a health care need with an appropriate technology.

With his landmark publication *Diffusion of Innovations*, Rogers (1962) described five characteristics that potential adopters must recognize for an innovation to be widely adopted. Those characteristics include a relative advantage, observability, trialability, compatibility, and low complexity. In other words, an adopter must believe that the innovation is useful, easy to use, and obviously beneficial. With telemedicine, the benefits to patients are clear, including access to needed health care, reduced travel, and increased convenience. However, for the physicians who provide telemedicine service and who are the primary adopters of the technology, the advantages are not nearly as clear. In one of the few available telemedicine adoption studies available, Spaulding, Russo, Cook, and Doolittle (2005) showed that rural physicians who perceived an advantage to both them and their patients were more likely to be adopters of telemedicine. In contrast, rural physicians who recognized a benefit to patients only or no benefit at all were less likely to be adopters. Thus, one conclusion that can be drawn is that telemedicine champions need to more effectively consider the needs of the health care practitioners.

CONCLUSIONS

The technology is available today to significantly reduce isolation and poor access to basic health care, specialty care, emergency care, health professional and paraprofessional education, and health information which have plagued rural areas for decades. Telehealth technologies have begun to alter and erase some of the separations in rural and urban care and the disparities in health care access. For well over a decade, ITV has offered links for patients and rural providers to urban specialists and to educational opportunities. Still, our traditional ITV approaches have required special equipment and lines that are non-existent in vast areas of the country. Therefore, ITV alone has done relatively little to improve access to care or educational opportunities on a large scale basis.

The Internet is changing this picture. It has dramatically improved access to education and health information. Academic health professional programs and private vendors throughout the country now offer online access to the latest health information, continuing education, and to academic programs that train rural individuals in health care occupations without requiring them to leave their home communities. Both real-time and access-on-demand educational and informational opportunities allow rural health providers access to the latest protocols for care, the latest research on new treatment strategies, new products, and new drugs.

Until recently, security concerns and technological limitations hampered use of the Internet for many telehealth applications, particularly real-time patient and physician interactions. The newer computer-based applications available through high-speed cable and wireless systems are now poised to dramatically expand the possibilities for health care delivery to rural communities. Medical specialists and other health care providers are now able to interact by sight and sound with other health care practitioners and patients from their office or home computers. This not only makes telehealth more convenient for practitioners, which increases their likelihood of using the technology, but also greatly expands the applications and accessibility of this technology for rural health care.

Despite the phenomenal opportunities technology now offers, the lack of monies and political will to adequately develop the needed technical infrastructure, policies, and reimbursement environment to support and sustain these technologies continue to present significant challenges. Coordinated and concerted efforts are needed among providers, policy makers, and technology developers to ensure that regulatory and reimbursement policies and the technical infrastructure will effectively support, rather than further dismantle rural health care. Even greater efforts will be necessary to forge partnerships among health care providers, payers, and consumers to ensure that the possibilities of telecommunications technologies in rural health care are optimized without jeopardizing the quality of care or the human contact necessary to the well-being and satisfaction of patients and health care providers alike.

REFERENCES

American Telemedicine Association and AMD Telemedicine. (2004). *Private payer reimbursement information directory*. Retrieved April 21, 2004, from http://www.amdtelemedicine.com/private_payer/index.cfm

Center for Telemedicine Law. (2003). *Telemedicine Licensure Report*. Retrieved July 8, 2005, from http://telehealth.hrsa.gov/lincensure.htm

Choi, J., Wojner, A., Cale, P., Gergen, P., Degioanni, J., & Grotta, J. (2004). Telemedicine physician providers: Augmented acute stroke care delivery in rural Texas: An initial experience. *Telemedicine Journal and e-Health*, 10(Suppl. 2), S90–S94.

Conrath, D., Dunn, E., & Higgins, C. (1983). *Evaluating telecommunications technology in medicine*. Dedham, MA: Artech House.

Grady, J., & Berkebile, C. (2004). Nursing telehealth applications initiative: a research project for nursing education and practice. *Home Health Care Technology Report*, 1(6), 81, 86, 96.

Healthcare IT News. (2004, November). *Early adopters offer online consult reimbursement plans*. Retrieved April 21, 2004, from http://www.healthcareitnews.com/NewsArticleView.aspx?ContentID=1853&ContentTypeID=3&IssueID=12

Institute of Medicine. (2005). *Quality through collaboration: The future of rural health*. Washington, DC: The National Academies.

Johnson, B., Weeler, L., Deuser, J., & Sousa, K. (2000). Outcomes of the Kaiser Permanente tele-home health research project. *Archives of Family Medicine*, 9, 40–45.

Kim, H., Lowery, J., Hamill, J., & Wilkins, E. (2004). Patient attitudes toward a web-based system for monitoring chronic wounds. *Telemedicine Journal and e-Health, 10*(Suppl. 2), S26–S34.

Lambrecht, C. J. (1998). Telemedicine in trauma care. *Telemedicine Today Magazine, 2,* 25.

Lehmann, C., & Giacini, J. M. (2004). Pilot study: The impact of technology on home bound congestive heart failure patients. *Home Health Care Technology Report, 4*(50), 59–60.

Ormond, B., Wallin, S., & Goldenson, S. (2000). *Supporting the Rural Health Care Safety Net.* Retrieved May 15, 2005, from http://www.urban.org/url.cfm?ID=309437

Ormond, B., Zuckerman, S., & Lhila, A. (2000). *Rural/urban differences in health care are not uniform across states.* Retrieved July 1, 2005, from http://www.urban.org/url.cfm?ID=309533

Peterson, C., & Anderson, H. (2004). *Telepharmacy telemedicine technical assistance documents: A guide to getting started in telemedicine.* Retrieved January 30, 2005, from http://www.muhealth.org/~telehealth/geninfo/A%20Guide%20to%20Getting%20Started%20in%20Telemedicine.pdf

Pringle-Specht, J., Wakefield, B., & Flanagan, J. (2001). Evaluating the cost of one telehealth application connecting an acute and long-term care setting. *Journal of Gerontological Nursing, 27*(1), 34–40.

Rogers, C. (2002a). *Rural population and migration: Rural elderly.* Retrieved June 26, 2005, from http://www.ers.usda.gov/briefing/population/elderly

Rogers, C. (2002b). The older population in 21st century rural America. *Rural America, 173,* 2–10. Retrieved June 6, 2005, from http://www.ers.usda.gov/Briefing/Population/elderly

Rogers, E. M. (1962). *Diffusion of Innovation.* New York: Free.

Rohland, B., Saleh, S., Rohrer, J., & Romitti, P. (2000). Acceptability of telepsychiatry to a rural population. *Psychiatric Services, 51,* 672–674.

Rosenthal, T., & Fox, C. (2000). Access to health care for the rural elderly. *Journal of the American Medical Association, 284,* 2034–2036.

Spaulding, R. J., Russo, T., Cook, D. J., & Doolittle, G. C. (2005). Diffusion theory and telemedicine adoption by Kansas healthcare providers: Critical factors in telemedicine adoption for improved patient access. *Journal of Telemedicine and Telecare, 11*(Suppl. 1), S1–S3.

Tarmann, A. (2003, August). *Older Americans: A growth industry for rural areas?* Retrieved July 3, 2005, from http://www.prb.org/Template.cfm?Section=PRB&template=/ContentManagement/ContentDisplay.cfm&ContentID=9252

Telemedicine Research Center. (2004). *2004 TRC report on U.S. telemedicine activity.* Kingston, NJ: Civic Research Institute.

University of North Dakota, Center for Rural Health. (2005). *Emergency medical services.* Retrieved July 10, 2005, from http://www.med.und.nodak.edu/depts/rural/ems/overview

University of Washington, Health Policy Analysis Program. (2000, August). *Rural health policy: Where do we go from here?* Retrieved January 10, 2005, from http://www.users.qwest.net/~wwahec/LandscapeReport.html

U.S. Department of Health and Human Services. (2001). *Report to congress on telemedicine*. Retrieved August 10, 2005, from http://telehealth.hrsa.gov/pubs/report2001/main.htm

U.S. Department of Health and Human Services. (2003). Health insurance reform: Security standards; Final rule. *Federal Register, 68*, 8333–8381.

U.S. Department of Health and Human Services, National Advisory Committee on Rural Health and Human Services. (2003). *Health care quality: The rural context*. Retrieved June 10, 2005, from http://ruralcommittee.hrsa.gov/QR03.htm

Versweyveld, L. (1999). The newly emerging concept of next generation wireless and mobile telemedicine systems. *Virtual Medical Worlds*. Retrieved September 29, 2005, from http://www.hoise.com/vmw/99/articles/vmw/LV-VM-05-99-16.html

Versweyveld, L. (2004). German researchers aim to set patients free with wireless telemedicine applications. *Virtual Medical Worlds*. Retrieved September 29, 2005, from http://www.hoise.com/vmw/04/articles/vmw/LV-VM-04-04-27.html

Wakefield, B., Buresh, K., Flanagan, J., & Kienzle, M. (2004). Interactive video specialty consultations in long-term care. *Journal of the American Geriatrics Society, 52*, 789–793.

Zarate, C., Weinstock, L., Cukor, P., Morabito, C., Leahy, L., Burns, C., & Baer, L. (1997). Applicability of telemedicine for assessing patients with schizophrenia: Acceptance and reliability. *Journal of Clinical Psychiatry, 58*(1), 22–25.

CHAPTER TWELVE

Public Policy and Rural Aging

David K. Brown and Robert Blancato

Estimates are that approximately 65 million Americans live in rural areas and significant population shifts are changing the racial and ethnic characteristics of rural communities. Demographic diversity is among the issues driving the need for new policy approaches that are rural specific in areas such as transportation, housing choices, long-term care options, and income support (U.S. Department of Health and Human Resources, 2003). Paramount among the realities of service delivery in America is that rural communities often do not have adequate organizational resources to develop and sustain programs that meet complex and long-term health and social needs. Although coordination and integration of services for older persons is a universal challenge, it is a particular problem in rural areas because extant policy and resources do not adequately address challenges of low population size and density, increasing community diversity, lack of infrastructure, and ongoing service demands. Such demands are outstripping the supply of resources to meet escalating need.

Health and social services are critical to the well-being of rural residents. These services struggle to survive due to weak service delivery infrastructure, inadequate funding, economic underdevelopment, undifferentiated local political institutions, and lack of effective coordination. Cultural barriers in many communities can decrease rural residents' willingness to use the available services. For these and other reasons, policy makers, practitioners, and service providers are placing increased emphasis on the challenges and opportunities to overcome these and similar barriers and better meet the complex health and human service needs of rural populations.

Underlying rural challenges are fragmented and uncoordinated public policies, programs, and services that are scattered across hundreds of jurisdictions on the state and federal level. We believe a sustainable framework of public policy for rural older adults focused on service availability and delivery can be developed if existing policies are changed to be more sensitive and supportive. This will require more finely targeted resources to rural areas and rural-sensitive regulations that fit current realities of non-urban settings. To that end, the goal of this chapter is to examine the drawbacks of existing policies and identify policy changes that will better met the needs of rural elders.

FEDERAL PROGRAMS

To get the services they need, rural older adults are heavily dependent on public entitlements such as the Older Americans Act (OAA), Medicare, Medicaid, and Social Security. Fluharty (2002) estimates that 20% of personal income in rural areas comes from federal sources; rural economies are sustained by this support. Because rural seniors are generally less healthy than older urban cohorts, they are heavier users of prescription drugs, although at the same time less able to pay due to a lack of insurance coverage and lower incomes.

Older Americans Act

Major legislation addressing the need to provide an integrated program of social services to the nation's older adults was embodied in the OAA, passed in 1965. The OAA provides a range of home- and community-based services such as congregate and home-delivered meals, transportation, homemaker services, an ombudsmen program focusing on institutionalized older adults, legal assistance, employment assistance, and caretaker services.

Under terms of the legislation, states must develop an intrastate funding formula, which takes into account the geographic distribution of individuals age 60 years or older in a given state, and those in the greatest social and economic need (socially or culturally isolated persons, and those living below poverty guidelines) paying particular attention to low income minorities. Rural factors can also be built into this formula. The formula is the device that funds Area Agencies on Aging (AAAs) in the program. These AAAs serve as planning and resource development agencies with a focus on pooling resources and advocating for older people living in their planning and services. In turn, AAAs largely contract with proximate senior centers and nutrition sites which actually provide the services. This "network" has remained fairly stable and effective for three decades.

The intrastate funding formula has been a source of legal conflict over the years, precipitating legal action in Florida, Virginia, and California (Brown, 1997). Krout (1994) has assessed the impact of the intrastate funding formula on rural AAAs, finding that these AAAs have smaller budgets and staff than urban counterparts, while serving geographically larger planning and services areas. Krout has found that almost half the states have a rural factor in their intrastate funding formula but allocate only a small percentage of the formula to this item.

The OAA remains a major system of social support for older Americans. Programs sponsored by the OAA, both home- and community-based, have been vital to helping provide services to rural elders. In the 2000 reauthorization of the OAA, rural incentives were detailed. Provisions in the interstate funding formula have maintained at least stable funding and increases in some states. In addition, U.S. Department of Agriculture cash allotment procedures have been streamlined in congregate and home-delivered meals programs. Significantly, $125 million has been made available to the National Family Caregiver Support program (Title III-E and Title VI-C). This program provides training, counseling, and respite services to family members and others who provide caregiving support services to dependent older adults. Though funding is small, all states have implemented these provisions, and monies have filtered down to AAAs and county-based providers.

Medicare and Medicaid

It has been amply demonstrated that the great safety net programs of Medicare and Medicaid are compelling and substantive sources of health and income protection for rural older people (Ricketts, 1999). Within broad guidelines, states administer the Medicaid program, which pays for medical assistance for clients with low incomes. States establish eligibility, determine the scope of services, and set reimbursement to providers. Because rural older adults are heavy users of the program, policy issues on the state level are necessary. States can also offer optional programs, such as in-home care, targeting individuals deemed needy.

Medicaid expenditures reached $245 billion in fiscal year 2002 and are increasing faster than spending for Medicare and other state programs. Medicaid pays for almost half of all nursing home care and supports home- and community-based services under special waiver programs. In addition, the program pays for most publicly financed mental health care and is a major source of funding for hospitals that serve low income, uninsured patients. The program also funds Medicare premiums, coinsurance, and deductibles for low income older adults and persons with disabilities, which is significant to rural clients who qualify for both programs (Smith, 2002).

Two trends in the program are seemingly on a collision course. On the one hand, rural older adults continue to be the heaviest users of the Medicaid program, given lower incomes in rural areas and a noticeable lack of private health insurance. On the other hand, states are determined to rein in ever-increasing health care costs which are not sustainable into the future. The National Governors Association (2003) has posited a number of reforms to control Medicaid costs which may or may not protect clients in rural areas. These initiatives include the following: (a) changes in purchasing and pricing arrangements, (b) minimizing fraud and abuse, (c) coordinating with private insurance providers to create more affordable small group products, (d) shifting from nursing home to community-based care to reduce the former costs, (e) promoting disease prevention, (f) reducing provider reimbursement rates (which may be counter-productive in rural areas where subsidy inducements are needed to attract providers), and (g) providing options for managing prescription drug costs and/or reducing benefit coverage. As in other safety net programs, reform is atop the policy agenda. Service providers and advocates need to pay careful attention to the impacts these measures will have on clients in the near future.

The Medicare program has likewise been reformed with the addition of a prescription drug benefit which contains a "doughnut hole," or a suspension of coverage, from between $2,250 and $5,100 of costs. There is relief in the program with financial inducements to attract rural doctors and home health agencies, and increased reimbursement rates to rural hospitals. Much will depend on how health plans are devised for rural clients, which will attract them to enroll (Families USA, 2004).

Managed Care

With the passage of the Balanced Budget Amendment of 1997, states were granted extended authority to enroll greater numbers of clients, particularly Medicaid beneficiaries, in managed care programs. Though definitions of managed care abound, most stress the following characteristics: fixed, negotiated price or capitated services through a managed care organization; an enrolled membership that primarily receives acute care services; and use of a preferred physician, care manager, or other health care official who serves as a gatekeeper over the prescribed care received by enrollees (Brown, 1997). Managed care is an approach to health care delivery which seeks to use an alternative to open-ended, fee-for-service practice by controlling (some say reducing) utilization, compressing access, and stressing disease prevention. Estes has referred to managed care as the "blunt instrument of rationing," which is likely to deprive consumers of control over the components of care they receive (1999, p. 142).

A 1996 study by the Rural Research Policy Institute of managed care penetration in rural areas and the state's response to it found only limited managed care activity in rural areas. Yet, states continue to expand legislative initiatives for Medicaid managed care plans. At the same time, rural communities have noted difficulties recruiting and retaining primary care providers in managed care settings. Financial sustainability of rural providers is a key issue. States have addressed the problem partly by forming purchasing cooperatives to enlarge the risk pool in rural areas and to increase purchasing power in negotiations with providers.

Along the way, several pitfalls to managed care have been noted including the loss of a customary doctor, restricted access to specialty care, restricted access to medication, and an incentive to underserve (Kane, Starr, & Baker, 1996). States have seized on managed care as a mechanism to integrate acute and long-term care with the hope of slowing the growth of costs. Shifting services from institutional to home- and community-based long-term care, along with reducing the number of providers and capping service hours and reimbursement, are among strategies now being tested for implementation in several states. States under managed care can also shift the care-risk burden from state government to managed care organizations. Some states taking the lead in this best practice scenario are New York, Texas, Washington, Wisconsin, California, Colorado, and Massachusetts (Weiner & Stevenson, 1998).

The forces of utilization and costs, driven by managed care schemes, have profound implications for rural older adults. Fundamentally, the jury is still out on the success of managed care organizations in penetrating rural places. Barriers include low numbers of enrollees in rural areas, resulting in underfinanced risk pools, low adjusted average per capita cost rates of reimbursement, and low physician availability, making managed care organizations in rural areas less attractive for potential members than in urban areas, and more chronic illness and lower income of rural people.

Social Security

Social Security remains the major foundation of federal transfers to rural elders. The program is the major source of income, at least half, for 66% of aged beneficiaries and the only source of income for 22% of current retirees (Social Security Administration, 2004). Several issues affect older rural beneficiaries of the Social Security program. Because benefits are pegged to earned income, the program is designed to benefit steady, unbroken employment. Sporadic or part-time employment prevalent in rural areas can result in a break of contributions and rupture in earned benefits. Adequacy and equity provisions in the program to guarantee a consistent floor of benefits can serve to maintain a minimum level of income for life. Suggestions to raise the current retirement age and the recent push by the Bush administration to shift workers' contributions to personal savings accounts require close scrutiny from advocates as to impacts of these measures on the rural older population. The major issue at hand is the debate over diminishing the role of the federal government in entitlements and placing greater fiscal and administration support for safety net benefits in the hands of individuals, local levels of government, and/or the private sector. The eventual consequences of these trends are not fully understood as yet, but rural beneficiaries, who are highly dependent on these programs, are in the eye of the storm.

DEVOLVING FEDERAL ROLES TO THE STATES

Spiraling costs and a conservative swing to federal policy in the country have resurrected a new look at the process of devolution. In essence, the devolutionist approach, which gained new emphasis during the Contract with America of the mid-1990s, seeks to limit and control the ongoing role of central government in funding and regulating entitlement programs, particularly Medicaid, Medicare, and Social Security (Brown, 1999). Devolutionists would decentralize authority in these programs and spin off increased authority and regulatory decision-making to the state and local units of government. Devolution would mandate a resorting of state–federal relations in the implementation and funding of safety net programs for older Americans. This ideologically based school of thought contends that the federal entitlements are over-generous to current older beneficiaries to the point that the economic future of younger Americans is in jeopardy.

Several currents flow from this argument. First, the target population at the root of the problem is the older population, the largest consumers of health care and long-term care benefits. An element of victim-blaming is thus directed to older adults since, it follows, they are at fault for living longer, for needing ongoing and expensive long-term institutional and community-based care, and for being numerous, vocal and skillful advocates who have achieved a prominent national level of political power and influence. Advocates for older adults would respond that this group earned their benefits the old-fashioned way—they accessed the political system and successfully shaped public policy on their own behalf and are unwilling to give up their hard-fought benefits.

A second aspect the devolutionist assault on old-age benefits assumes is an intergenerational rivalry and class segmentation, which inevitably pits younger cohorts against the growing older population. Increasing claims on the income of younger generations to continue funding benefits could result in an aging backlash, already manifest in calls for the privatization of Medicare benefits and Social Security contributions. The stakes of this aspect of the debate strike at the fundamental principle of social insurance policy—the traditional legitimacy Americans have given to the notion that generations are economically bonded and interdependent, and that successive cohorts are willing to bear the costs of the allocation of benefits from younger to older generations. This is the core value that holds the intergenerational contract of entitlements together. If these values are eroded, intergenerational polarization will become a policy premise of the future and the social contract between government and older adults will be broken. In this manner, heretofore sacrosanct programs become policy targets.

The devolutionist position further holds that entitlements are best left in the hands of state and local constituents. Federal government is too big, too intrusive, and inherently wasteful of taxpayer dollars. Particularly in the Social Security program, tax payers should control their own health care and retirement investment dollars, rather than chafing under a national, universal, and compulsory program that takes taxable income, passes it on to another generation, and gives little or no voice to the wage earner. The specific impact of the devolutionist approach upon rural programs and services is not clear at this point. However, the safety net of entitlements, particularly income protection and health care, critical in rural areas, is the target of devolutionists. Additionally, placing greater fiscal burden on state and local areas that can hardly manage Medicaid budgets as it is, does not bode well for rural clients. The issue is what level of government can uphold and sustain safety net programs for the most needy and vulnerable older adults. Without a strong federal presence, in our view, the great safety net programs would be significantly damaged by a devolutionist approach which does not make provision for the vulnerability of rural areas and older people who live there. Addressing spiraling costs in entitlement programs and reigning in escalating demand is necessary, but not at the expense of rural areas and those who are most vulnerable among us.

POLICY INNOVATIONS

The managed care and devolutionist movements in funding and service delivery to older adults may well shape the future of safety net programs. Major responsibility for restructuring service system design in rural areas in any case will fall to state and local levels. Orloff (1998) has suggested major issues on the rural agenda include provider recruitment and retention, telemedicine capacity, long-term care options, and community-based managed care systems development. Additionally, many rural and more remote areas have been designated as health professional shortage areas by the Health Resources and Services Administration. Economic disadvantage, isolation from peers, and lack of amenities such as schools and recreation and cultural opportunities contribute to making rural and frontier areas unattractive to health care professionals and weakens the health care provider infrastructure.

Controlling Costs

On the long-term care side, states have taken innovative measures driven by the need to control costs. The key to these reforms is a partnership between states and their rural communities. North Dakota serves as a best practice example of these performance partnerships, which, under a state grant program, helps near-failing nursing homes convert to assisted living facilities. Another example is the Rocky Mountain Health Maintenance Organization (HMO) which structures its managed care plan to outreach to rural residents and the indigent. This HMO has created a risk-sharing arrangement with rural communities and local providers. In another arrangement, Rocky Mountain has created internal physician report cards to be shared among plan providers, which has resulted in improved practice patterns, outcomes, and cost-effectiveness (Orloff, 1998). As these examples show, the real innovation and best practice is taking place on the state and local levels. State–local partnerships are a sleeping giant where the real potential for change and innovation in rural areas rests.

Consumer-Directed Programs

In September 2004, 11 states received approximately $250,000 each from the Robert Wood Johnson Foundation and the Department of Health and Human Services to implement a novel Cash and Counseling program. In West Virginia, the program is known as Mountaineer Choice. Cash and Counseling gives Medicaid beneficiaries choice and control over their personal care needs. It provides a self-directed, individualized budget to recipients of Medicaid personal care services. Participants use the money to hire their own caregivers or purchase items—such as chair lifts or touch lamps—that help them live independently. Each person's budget is comparable to the value of services that he or she would have received from an agency. Consulting and bookkeeping services are available to help participants weigh their options and keep up with required paperwork. The program is entirely voluntary. If a participant wants to continue receiving personal care services through a Medicaid-contracted agency, that option remains available to them.

An independent evaluation of the original three-state Cash and Counseling programs by Mathematica Policy Research Inc. found that in all three participating states, when Medicaid beneficiaries of various ages and disabilities were given the opportunity to direct their own supportive services and hire their own caregivers, their quality of life improved, satisfaction with services increased, unmet needs for care were reduced, and access to home care increased—without compromising beneficiaries' health or safety (relative to randomly assigned control groups that received services from agencies). Although the effects on the use and costs of Medicaid services are not yet available for all three Cash and Counseling programs, results from one evaluation show that by the second year of enrollment, the consumer-directed option cost no more than agency care due to lower spending for nursing home and other Medicaid services (Foster, Brown, Phillips, Schore, & Carlson, 2003; Carlson et al., 2005).

In other consumer-directed programs, clients decide services they want, the workers they want to hire, and the scheduling of service delivery. In some areas, a fiscal intermediary such as a care manager can provide training to workers, assist clients in managing workers, assist with paperwork when clients use vouchers or cash to reimburse provides, and fill out necessary forms to document program activity. In terms of best practices, as part of a three-year project among 13 states, the National Association of State Units on Aging and the National Council on Aging are seeking to develop consumer and policy maker partnerships to assess home- and community-based services to form and implement a consumer direction reform agenda. Public forums and focus groups in each state will address issues such as barriers to consumer choice and control of their program.

ECONOMIC DEVELOPMENT: KEY TO SERVICE DELIVERY

The authors would argue that economic development and the strength and sustainability of the delivery of health care and social support services go hand in hand. Briefly put, the efficiency and effectiveness of human services delivery is a function of the economic strength of communities sponsoring these programs. The major challenge facing rural communities is how to inspire a take-off of the economic development which would provide the means to build necessary infrastructure. Infrastructure development, including roads, hospitals, schools, sewer and water systems, and sanitation systems, help provide a surplus economy to invest in health care and social services.

Seemingly, a revival of economic innovation and social and cultural values is slowly emerging in rural America, moving beyond the stereotypes of rural places as geographically and socially isolated, culturally fatalistic, and dependent on the largesse of federal transfers (McGranahan, 2003). Rural areas are on the move and stand poised on the threshold of a developmental take-off to greater prospects and well-being. Strategically, the time has come to advance an agenda of public policy for rural America to address major challenges in economic development and the design of local service delivery systems in health care and social services for seniors and others.

Economic development is an exercise in political development. That is, there must be a willful, conscious decision by a given community to commit to a process of social change to improve political capacity and guide and direct economic transformation. Economic development is defined as a process of institution-building, whereby semi-skilled subsistence employment is replaced by technologically oriented jobs which pay surplus income. Investment capacity is enlarged so that developing communities can improve and build infrastructure—roads, medical facilities, schools, and adequate housing. Political decision-making is more sophisticated so that public authorities can make successful claims on financial support from central government. Values shift and place a premium on merit and achievement, and the sociopolitical distribution of resources smoothes out the relative disadvantage historically felt by under-developed areas. As economic capacity is enhanced by the development process, so is human and physical infrastructure improved to reify the level of health and human services delivery to a standard which meets client needs, at least most of the time (Brown, 2004). Such a change in rural economic development would require a dedicated commitment on the federal level to give fiscal and political authority to the states which can then inspire development on the local level.

As noted earlier, the economic and sociopolitical landscape of rural communities is changing. Whitener (2005) has pointed out that rural communities are no longer dominated by farms and agriculture as the foundation for their economies, and they are looking for non-farm sources of economic growth. Today, less than 10% of rural people live on farms, and only 14% of the rural workforce is employed in farming. These emerging economies now look to manufacturing, services, tourism, and government operations as the new engines driving rural economies. Improving wages and living standards, and upgrading infrastructure such as roads, schools, and health facilities, are targeted as growth priorities. Human resources development is also receiving a new emphasis through training education and supplying technologically based employment skills. Age-related programs and services need to be closely aligned with these trends so that priorities for rural older adults are not left out of the equation. This is a major challenge facing advocates for older adults in rural places.

Bayard (2005) provides a comprehensive review of many rural state-based initiatives in economic development. To review them is beyond the scope of this chapter, but it is clear that states and rural communities are on the move. Most of these development initiatives have the following goals in common:

- building a skilled workforce through training and education;
- promoting research through local colleges and universities;
- encouraging private sector engagement;
- supporting local entrepreneurs by providing fiscal incentives for job growth; and
- developing marketing innovations and supporting small business development.

States are also engaging in vigorous marketing of what they have to offer in terms of working conditions, leisure amenities, climate advantages, and sustained economic opportunity. Again, the aging network in these states needs to join hands and champion economic growth plans and programs for rural America.

RECOMMENDATIONS

The following recommendations are offered for consideration to move the rural agenda forward, if only in a modest way. First, regardless of the shape and form of safety-net entitlements in the future, the federal government needs to continue to strengthen its contract of commitments to rural areas and the seniors who live there. Benefits need to be indexed for those with the greatest need, as advocated by the Rural Task Force report to former Department of Health and Human Services Secretary Tommy Thompson in July 2002. The Department of Health and Human Services needs to follow up the report with clear implementation strategies.

A second recommendation is for state and local political and administrative institutions to be reinvented to advantage rural areas. For example, state–county partnerships need to be created in all states, using

county associations and associations of rural mayors to form economic
development laboratories to streamline and overhaul local political institutions, city charters and the like, and to remove costly and overlapping
legal and regulatory barriers to development. The local private sector is an
indispensable ally. State legislators who do not have them need to create
rural development policy committees or sub-committees within their
bodies. Rural advocates will thereby have clearly definable constituent
representatives to work with. Unincorporated places and special districts
should be targeted outreach areas for training, education, and information on how to grow local economies. Also, local supportive services such
as those offered under the OAA and programs addressing housing and
transportation need to be more highly valued and funded. As a society,
dependency—a reality to some degree of old age—needs to be prioritized
and supported as well as independence. The stigma of dependency needs
to be removed and rural innovation models may well guide the way.

Third, the aging network needs to become a proactive partner in local
development efforts. After all, infrastructure enhancements such as job
growth, roads, schools, sewer, and water systems all work to the advantage
of seniors. For instance, AAAs directors or staff should seek positions sitting
on regional development and planning councils congruent with their planning and services areas. These groups seek grants and economic assistance
to do the development planning work on a host of projects including transportation, housing, land use, capital infrastructure, and similar issues which
impact all individuals. Aging advocates need to access these key policy
making and implementation bodies, especially in rural areas. The aging
network has been historically underrepresented at the policy and planning
table where these issues are discussed and operationalized. Such an advocacy strategy is well within the broad mandate of the OAA, which directs
State Units on Aging and AAAs to be proactive and take leadership on all
issues in the community which impact the lives of older persons.

Many of the best program ideas in this chapter and book have con-
structively used community and technical colleges, four-year institutions,
and universities to develop training, education, and skill-building programs for rural individuals. Together with these efforts, university-based
Geriatric Education Centers need to provide outreach to small rural
hospitals and other rural health care practitioners in their states with
training, teaching, continuing education, and technical assistance interventions to upgrade skill and knowledge of health care providers. The
national aging network, under the direction of the Administration on
Aging, is strategically positioned, particularly on the local level, to forge
closer ties with health care providers in rural areas. Best practices reform
of social insurance programs such as Medicare need to ensure parity for
rural beneficiaries by providing inducements to attract provider plans to

rural areas. Payment systems need to adequately compensate the paucity of health care providers in rural areas and provide incentives to increase the supply and access of health and social services practitioners.

Enhanced transportation to reach the remotest clients, medical assistance and information through technology, mobilizing caregiver support systems, and ongoing and persistent training and education for rural health care professionals are areas that should be targeted for increasing funding. These aspects continually invigorate capacity and infrastructure for service delivery. Federal legislation, such as the Transportation Equity Act, might institute a rural impact analysis into the reauthorization process to help identify critical areas of highest need for targeting funding. The recent report by the Commission on Affordable Housing and Health Facility Needs for Seniors in the 21st Century (2002) recommends, among other priorities, that more support be given to Section 504—rural home repair and modification. Other recommendations from the report on housing loan programs need to be studied carefully and action taken. Advocates need to seek and organize funding in order to support ongoing research data collection and retrieval to assess and upgrade the needs of rural elders. Such research efforts need to be immediately transferred into practice and service.

Finally, advocates for economic development and health and social services reform in rural areas need to include the participation and civic engagement of elders as they shape priorities and agendas for the future. Advocates need to support resolutions passed at the 2005 White House Conference on Aging, which address some of the issues on reaching rural seniors presented here (White House Conference on Aging, 2005).

CONCLUSIONS

The new demographic and economic trends in rural areas, such as the shift from farming as the dominant economic activity to diverse manufacturing efforts and greater global competition, exacerbates the need for rural areas to create rural development strategies for the future. Major issues include development of interactive business environments through infrastructure improvements such as roads, schools, and sewer and water systems, attracting tourism, capitalizing on natural amenities such as climate, scenic beauty, and opportunities for leisure and recreation. At the same time, these communities are struggling to manage and develop human services delivery provisions to address spiraling unmet need.

At the policy table, rural areas are at a competitive disadvantage due to a number of factors including population patterns which have diminished rural clout and the reversal of population flow to rural areas resulting from the flight of manufacturing jobs to third-world locales (Longino, 2003). The rural economic system transition, from farm-based economies to niche-based manufacturing and service activities, presents daunting challenges to rural communities (Whitener, 2005). Rural places also suffer from inadequate advocacy systems to articulate policy needs, which are built on fragmented political and economic institutions. Inadequate and underdeveloped economies equate with weakened political institutions and public decision-making, which makes it difficult to develop coordinated, focused, and articulate advocacy efforts to influence decision makers.

Our review of existing policies and programs suggests that successful, innovative, and best practice programs share at least four common characteristics. First, these programs seek out and serve unmet need and assist clients not previously served. Second, programs bring together new fiscal packages and/or arrangements to integrate funding in a way which can sustain programs. State and local innovations in managed care schemes cited earlier are a case in point. Third, new agency and networking coalitions emerge to shape service delivery. Fourth, program evaluations and outcome measures are developed to assess the impact of programs on clients and communities.

Rural aging policy is at a critical juncture since major currents of so-called "reform" such as the new Medicare prescription drug program, hyping personal savings accounts in Social Security, and the devolutionist approach to entitlements, are aimed at dismantling or diminishing the role of federal government, which has undergirded these programs for decades. These movements are also occurring at the same time rural areas are struggling with issues of economic development and reinventing community infrastructure and policy strategy to better accommodate needed changes in delivery systems of care. The major issues of inspiring a rural economic development take-off, while at the same time innovations in health care and social support services will shape the future policy agenda. These issues are rising in the face of significant federal and state reform to control costs and shift the burden to local areas and individuals. How the moving parts of the rural advocacy network responds to these challenges is a key issue for the ongoing rural aging policy agenda.

REFERENCES

Bayard, M. (2005, January 24). *Enhancing competitiveness: A review of recent state economic development initiatives* (Issue Brief). Washington, DC: National Governors Association Center for Best Practices. Retrieved October 12, 2005, from http://www.nga.org

Brown, D. (1997). *Introduction to public policy: An aging perspective.* Landham, MD: University Press of America.

Brown, D. (1999). A context for teaching aging-related public policy. *Journal of Educational Gerontology, 25,* 711–722.

Brown, D. (2004, September). *Aging in rural America. Shaping a vision for the future.* Paper presented to the National Policy Committee of the 2005 White House Conference on Aging, Washington, DC.

Carlson, B. L., Dale, S., Foster, L., Brown, R., Phillips, B., & Schore, J. (2005, May). *Effect of consumer direction on adults' personal care and well-being in Arkansas, New Jersey, and Florida.* Final Report. Princeton, N.J.: Mathematica Policy Research, Inc.

Commission on Affordable Housing and Health Facility Needs for Seniors in the 21st Century. (2002, June). *A quiet crisis in America: A report to Congress.* Washington, DC: Author. Retrieved February 13, 2006, from http://govinfo.library.unt.edu/seniorscommission/pages/final_report/finalreport.pdf

Estes, C. (1999). The aging enterprise. In M. Minkler & C. Estes (Eds.), *Critical gerontology: Perspectives from the political and moral* economy (pp. 135–146). Amityville, NY: Baywood.

Families USA. (2004). *Approximately half of Americans in Medicare are at risk of losing coverage when the new law is implemented.* (Special Report). Washington, DC: Author.

Fluharty, C. (2002, January 18). *Toward a community-based rural policy for our nation: Exploiting new rural realities and federal policies.* Paper presented to the Texas Office of Rural Community Affairs, Jefferson, TX.

Foster, L., Brown, R., Phillips, B., Schore, J., & Carlson, B. L., (2003). Improving the quality of Medicaid personal assistance through consumer direction. *Health Affairs,* W3-162–175.

Kane, R., Starr, L., & Baker, M. (Eds.). (1996). *Managed care: Handbook for the aging network.* Minneapolis, MN: University of Minnesota, National LTC Center.

Krout, J. (1994). Rural aging community-based services. In R. Coward, C. Bull, G. Kukulka, & J. Galliher (Eds.), *Health services for rural elders* (pp. 84–107). New York: Springer Publishing.

Longino, C. F. (2003). Demographics and resettlement impacts on rural services. In R. Ham, R. T. Goins, & D. Brown (Eds.), *Best practices in service delivery to the rural elderly* (pp. 23–31). Morgantown, WV: West Virginia University, Center on Aging.

McGranahan, D. (2003). How people make a living in rural America. In D. Brown, & L. Swanson (Eds.), *Challenges for rural America in the twenty-first century* (pp. 135–151). University Park, PA: Pennsylvania State University.

National Governors Association Center for Best Practices. (2003). *State actions to control health care costs.* Washington, DC: Author.

Older Americans Act of 1965, Public Law 89-73. Washington, DC: Administration on Aging.

Orloff, T. (1998). *State challenges and opportunities in rural and frontier health care delivery.* Washington, DC: National Governors Association.

Ricketts, T. (1999). (Ed.). *Rural health in the United States*. New York: Oxford University Press.

Smith, V. (2002, March 15). *Making Medicaid better*. National Governors Association Center for Best Practices. Retrieved October 12, 2005, from http://www.nga.org

Social Security Administration. (2004). *Fast facts and figures about Social Security*. Washington, DC: Social Security Administration, Office of Research, Education, and Statistics.

U.S. Department of Health and Human Services. (2003). *One department serving rural America*. Washington, DC: Author.

Weiner, J., & Stevenson, D. (1998). State policy on long-term care for the elderly. *Health Affairs, 17*(3), 81–100.

White House Conference on Aging. (2005, December). 50 Resolutions as Voted by 2005 WHCoA Delegates. Retrieved February 14, 2006, from http://www.whcoa.gov/about/resolutions/whcoa_voting_results.pdf

Whitener, L. (2005). *Policy options for a changing rural America: Amber waves*. Washington, DC: U.S. Department of Agriculture, Economic Research Service.

CHAPTER THIRTEEN

Summary and Conclusions

John A. Krout and R. Turner Goins

This book has examined issues surrounding the provision of health and social services to older adults living in rural areas. Our aim has been to discuss these issues in a contemporary light with emphasis on emerging trends and policies that will affect services to rural elders nationwide and to provide examples of successful rural program approaches. We have not attempted to discuss every discrete service that can be found in the menu of programs available to older adults, nor have we provided a detailed accounting of long-term care because it is such a complicated topic and would require a book of its own.

To understand the nature of the challenges facing rural service provision and thus the steps that need be taken to meet them, we began the book by identifying factors that underlie service planning, support, and delivery beginning with population dynamics and the make-up of rural older adults. Longstanding barriers to the development and provision of many rural services still exist, which have also been identified and discussed. Policy, more precisely the lack of inclusion of rural realities in many federal policy approaches, is central to an understanding of the "whys" of the current service disadvantages experienced by rural elders. Changing policy assumptions and priorities are an important part of the rural service delivery fix. Fundamental to the well being of rural elders and at the core of rural health service delivery are the dominant American health care management and reimbursement approaches (i.e., managed care), so these have been given considerable attention as well.

In addition to health issues, several specific service arenas have been
included. Finally, emerging policy approaches in Medicare, the financing of acute and long-term care, and the role of technology in rural
health will all play important roles in the future of aging services in
rural America.

The purpose of this chapter is to pull together and distill the many
valuable facts and ideas presented by chapter authors and provide an
overarching view of rural service delivery to rural older persons. We also
aim to identify the major themes from the contributions in this book
that will help us better understand and respond to rural aging service
delivery in terms of research, policy, and practice.

SETTING THE STAGE

In chapter 1 Goins and Krout cover the well-known story of the multiple jeopardies faced by rural elders; being poorer, sicker, and living
in smaller communities that have historically not been well served by
America's health and social service system. Rural elders have fewer resources with which to access needed services and rural communities do
not support a sufficient range of service options. Population loss and a
lack of economies of scale make rural places less able to attract service
options. Although the story has been told many times, it has not made it
to "prime time" on the national political stage. Good data on service deficiencies and their impact are lacking and the term "rural" carries many
definitions. Thus, comparing findings from various studies and government data sets is tricky. Most rural aging research looks at ecological
factors such as population size, density, and integration with urban economic markets as indicators of rurality and do not look at socio-cultural
variables. In short, we still do not have a good empirical or conceptual
grasp of the everyday reality of being old in rural America and how rural
living impacts the various processes associated with aging. Many rural
studies focus on urban comparisons without any identification of how
and why living in rural as opposed to urban places matters. In short, we
lack adequate conceptual frameworks to guide our empirical analyses.
The insights of the subspecialty known as environmental gerontology,
by and large, have not been applied to residential differences.

Goins and Krout also note that far too little information is available
on the impacts of rural services, and best practice information is particularly sparse. There is a need for more research on basic questions about
the status of rural elders, their need for services, and the programs that
most effectively meet their needs. The increasing diversity of rural elders,

based on both community type and demographic characteristics, needs to be explored much more fully. Researchers and policy makers must work together to identify a national agenda for rural aging research and service assessment.

Krout and Bull provide an overview of what has become accepted as the rural service disadvantage for older adults. Social and health care services are less available and accessible to rural elders, even though a variety of indicators show that their need for such services is as great or greater than found among suburban or urban elders. The recognition and understanding of this fact is hampered by myths of rural aging that portray elders as living in bucolic settings with high levels of community and family support, which reduce the need for formal service. Krout and Bull note that rural elders face environmental press from a variety of sources. In addition to stagnant or declining population, the lack of economic resources characterizing much of rural America contributes significantly to the rural service disadvantage. Finally, the lack of resources of rural elders and the communities they live in are exacerbated by federal policies that do not adequately recognize or support rural services.

Nonetheless, Krout and Bull point out that many dedicated professionals work hard to ensure quality services are made available to rural elders. Working within the constraints of inadequate funding, the aging services network created by the Older Americans Act (OAA), for example, has worked to provide a variety of community-based services such as nutrition, transportation, health promotion, recreation, and legal aid. Successful service delivery to rural elders involves addressing the A words: Availability, Accessibility, Affordability, Awareness, Appropriateness, and Adequacy. Successful rural services do not develop by accident. Krout and Bull note that providers need to adjust program approaches to fit specific rural community values and resources and take advantage of existing networks of formal and informal support.

SETTING THE STAGE: SUMMARY

- Variation in the definitions used for rural have retarded the growth of a sophisticated and comprehensive understanding of aging in rural communities. Much of what is known is descriptive and lacking in conceptual underpinnings. As a result, we have an incomplete picture of how living in a rural setting impacts the aging experience and differs from other residential environments.

- Research to date has fairly consistently shown that rural elders compared to their urban counterparts are disadvantaged on health and other measures of well being, especially income, housing, and long-term care options, and transportation.
- Barriers to service development and delivery in rural areas include long distances, lack of population size, lack of economies of scale, and lack of individual and community resources to support the full continuum of service options needed to allow elders to live as independently as possible.
- Although market forces and population patterns underlie many of these barriers, government policies in areas such as health care, housing, and transportation also are a factor.
- Successful service delivery to rural elders involves addressing availability, accessibility, affordability, awareness, appropriateness, and adequacy.

POPULATION DYNAMICS

Demography may not be destiny, but 20th century demographic trends in this country have done much to shape the reality of service delivery in rural America. As Bradley and Longino point out, the major population shift in this country since industrialization began has been from rural to urban, and we might add since World War II from central city to suburb. The movement of large numbers of young persons to cities in response to the growth of economic opportunities there and the concomitant decline in rural areas lead to low population densities and small towns that no longer can support the array and complexity of services found in more densely populated places. Although rural population loss followed lost job opportunities and declining economic bases, it has also created those very problems. Rural population declines have dampened economic growth, which in turn has led to more population loss. Thus, for many years, much of rural America has been caught in a circle of depopulation and economic decline that has changed the composition of rural populations and led to a decline in local resources. Since population migration is selective by age, education, and economic status, the rural populations left behind generally have been older and less advantaged.

These demographic realities underlie many of the service delivery issues discussed in this book. Authors repeatedly note that research has shown services for older rural adults are less available and accessible than in more urban areas. Critical masses of people or consumers are required in today's economy for services to be available in a community, be it housing, transportation, shopping, or health care. Without enough elders to reach economies of scale, services gravitate to larger places, leaving smaller towns underserved. This is especially true in health care, wherever growing costs have led to the increasing concentration of health care services and decreasing availability of basic health and social services for rural elders and their families.

The depopulation of many rural areas has affected individual communities, but has also had a cumulative effect that has left entire parts of states without small cities that in turn support goods and services needed by rural residents. As the American population increasingly concentrated in mid- and large-sized cities and then spread to suburbs and contiguous nonmetropolitan counties, more remote areas became even less relevant in the national economy and less well served. Politically, especially in the U.S. Congress, rural areas have seen their representation diluted with population shifts to big cities and suburbs. There is little to suggest that this situation will change.

As Bradley and Longino note, the much-heralded (by demographers at least) rural population turnaround of the mid-20th century was short lived. Some rural retirement counties have fared better, retaining more of their younger population as well as attracting somewhat younger and more economically advantaged older in-migrants. Also, Bradley and Longino argue that although the question is complicated, existing data support the contention that overall, older in-migrants provide an economic boost to receiving communities that are not overwhelmed by demands for services. These retirement communities, however, tend to be adjacent to metropolitan counties so it would appear that relatively few elder migrants find the more rural locations attractive, despite the image of retirement to the picturesque countryside that we see in many magazines. Even more interesting is Bradley and Longino's documentation using data from the U.S. Census that metropolitan destinations are the most prevalent among older migrants, although older persons going to nonmetropolitan destinations are more likely to start from nonmetropolitan origins. Data presented by these authors show that the preference among even older migrants is to move to larger places. In fact, they find that as the size of place of origin moves further down the community size scale, the likelihood of moving to a place further up the scale increases.

Another demographic factor is that of population composition. The "who" of the older population has significant effects on service needs and delivery responses to those needs. A number of authors refer to data that show today's rural older population tends to have less formal education and considerably less income than their urban counterparts. Thus, rural elders have fewer personal resources to meet their needs and to pay for services such as housing, transportation, ancillary health, and long-term care largely not covered by federal programs (the major exception being Medicaid coverage for nursing home care). Fewer resources for rural elders reflect and contribute to resource deficits in rural communities that affect people of all ages and the ability of families to provide intergenerational support. One aspect of population composition is the age distribution of the older population itself. Nationally, rural areas are older in this regard. Rarely talked about in discussions of rural aging issues is the likely impact of the growth of the rural older population due to the aging-in-place of the baby boom generation (people born between 1946 and 1964). Although many rural communities are not growing in terms of overall population, they will increasingly become older as this national trend unfolds.

The aspect of population composition that is garnering more attention is that of race and ethnicity. Rural areas nationwide are more than 90% White, but as Goins, Mitchell, and Wu note, this statistic masks important regional and local variation and the increasing diversity of rural America. For example, over 90% of older rural African Americans live in the South and Southeast and these elders are largely concentrated in just seven states. Because of immigration and higher than average fertility rates, only 5% of Hispanics are age 65 years or over and less than 7% of that group lives in rural places. However, there is considerable diversity in the makeup of the older Hispanic population and Hispanics in the Southwest are much more likely to live in rural communities. Looking to the future, Goins and colleagues point out that the increasing size of the Hispanic population, now more numerous than African Americans, means the number of rural Hispanics, especially Mexican Americans, will likely grow dramatically.

While studies are sparse, the findings have been clear. Rural non-White elders are more disadvantaged on almost every indicator of well being than their rural White counterparts, be it housing, health, or transportation and experience even greater problems in service availability and accessibility. Older rural African Americans, for instance, suffered from overt as well as covert racism during their younger years which has contributed to the cumulative disadvantage they experience in meeting the health and social needs that come with old age. Many older rural American Indians and Alaska Natives (AI/ANs) have lived their entire lives on reservations with high rates of poverty, poor education and housing, and high rates of health and mental health problems. In terms of service access, long-term care services and options are particularly lacking for rural older AI/ANs. Despite cultural norms that honor elders, years of economic disadvantage and unfulfilled federal policies have undermined the ability of AI/AN families to meet intergenerational obligations. Rural Hispanics have been found to be poorer and more likely to suffer functional limitations than non-Hispanic Whites. Strong norms of filial obligation supporting familial care have contributed to lower levels of formal service use among Hispanic elders, but so have availability and access disadvantages. However, studies suggest that Hispanic families have been unable to meet the needs of their elders and require more assistance from the formal service community.

A major impediment to more effective service and policy responses to the needs of older rural minorities is the lack of good data on which to base these responses. Despite recent efforts by some federal agencies, analyses of racial and ethnic comparisons for older adults in important areas such as health are limited largely to secondary databases which have small numbers of rural respondents and hence do not capture the true diversity of rural older minority living circumstances. Without better data, advocates for the needs of older rural minorities will be hard pressed to make convincing arguments for increased and more targeted resources to meet the needs of this often overlooked population.

The challenge of providing more and better service to older rural minorities goes much deeper than the need for more and better data. Rural programs that do provide needed services to this population often have to compete with urban interests that seek, legitimately, to gain more resources for the older adults they serve. Advocates for minority needs, in general, represent groups that are younger than the White population and hence may focus less on aging issues (despite the coming boom of minority elders). Political representation of rural older minorities is even more diluted than that of rural interests in general. Rural minority elders with their high rates of poverty and geographic dispersion do not present a potent base of support for advocacy. National aging advocacy organizations have, by and large, not been effective voices for the interests of rural elders in general and rural minority elders in particular. Finally, the commonly held belief, not always supported by research, that minority families have and act on stronger norms of filial responsibility for caregiving of elders may have lessened the sense of urgency among service providers to target programs to minority elders.

As was noted earlier in this chapter, we do not view demography as destiny. It is true that the demographic and economic clout of rural areas has declined nationally as America has become increasingly urbanized and suburbanized. Rural people face challenges in maintaining health and well being across the life span and rural communities face challenges in maintaining and increasing their population and economic bases. It is also true that older rural minorities, in particular, have fewer resources and greater needs for service that are often inadequate. But, as we will discuss toward the end of this chapter, technology that eliminates the need for proximity to service expertise has been shown to be effective and holds promise to meet some of the health care needs of increasing numbers of rural elders.

POPULATION: SUMMARY

- Population loss has been a key contributor to the decline in rural economic and social resources and the ability of rural individuals and communities to meet the needs of persons as they age. This is especially true for more remote rural communities. Rural areas close to metropolitan centers have generally fared much better benefiting from job growth as well as greater service availability.
- The development and support of services for rural elders are not likely to increase without government policies and rural communities addressing the circle of population loss and economic decline that have characterized much of rural America since World War II.
- There is little to suggest that a national rural population revival is likely to occur even though some rural communities are witnessing in-migration of older retirees.
- Rural areas generally have less diverse populations in terms of race and ethnicity, but there are important regional concentrations of non-White rural elders.
- The increasing diversity of America's population is occurring in rural America and will change the make-up of rural elders.
- Minority rural elders have greater service needs and fewer resources with which to meet those needs. By and large, services to meet their needs are inadequate and are likely to become even more so as the numbers of older rural minorities increase.
- Appropriate and adequate policy and program development for older rural minorities is significantly hampered by a paucity of good data.

HEALTH, NUTRITION, AND HEALTH CARE
FINANCING POLICY

Three of the chapters in this book explicitly addressed rural health and health care issues. The first chapter in this section by Sharkey and Bolin provides an overview of health and nutrition problems experienced by older rural adults. Although there have been inconsistent findings on rural–urban differences in health, disease, and functional ability, we agree with Sharkey and Bolin that the bulk of the evidence supports the conclusion that the health of rural older persons is poorer. Rural older adults are more likely to report functional limitations and to experience health conditions linked to disability and premature death (e.g., diabetes, hypertension, obesity, nutritional deficiencies). Previous researchers have too often simply looked at rural–urban differences in morbidity and mortality and not closely at the aspects of rural environments responsible for them. Sharkey and Bolin help us understand the complex factors underlying the health of rural elders and its impact on everyday living through a discussion of the factors that make up chronic disease management. This shift in emphasis away from personal health behaviors and compositional factors is a welcomed perspective and underscores the complexity, not only of the problem of the poor health and nutrition of rural elders, but also of their solution. As Sharkey and Bolin discuss, a variety of community and health system factors contribute to improved outcomes in the care of chronic health problems. To understand the health status of rural or urban elders, one must include all of these factors and how they interact and connect to support healthy behavior on the part of individuals. We also need better information on effective community-based programs and services that promote healthy behaviors and respond to health problems. Unfortunately, as Sharkey and Bolin note, barriers to the availability and accessibility of health care reduce the ability of rural health care providers and elders to comply with important aspects of chronic care management.

Sharkey and Bolin's discussion of food insecurity also illustrates the role that community factors play in the health of older rural adults. Community factors such as the availability of grocery stores, transportation to access food, and programs that assist older individuals with food education and availability must be considered. Individual economic resources and health also play important roles. These and other factors affect the adequacy of personal and community resources and the accessibility, availability, and affordability of food, which determine food security and ultimately nutritional health. The complexity of factors that combine to ultimately influence nutritional health illustrates just how difficult it can be to respond to health problems of rural elders. Most health issues are multidimensional in their origin and require solutions that are also multidimensional. One of the best known food programs for elders in rural areas is Title III-C of the OAA that provides congregate or in-home meals. Despite the importance of these programs, they do not and were not intended to address the health and nutrition needs of elders comprehensively and are illustrative of the community-based program approach in our country that tends to fragment rather than integrate services. Nonetheless, Sharkey and Bolin note that partnerships in many rural communities are at work to overcome these barriers. Some of these involve demonstration projects funded and sponsored by the Administration on Aging (AoA) and national aging advocacy organizations.

Moving from health status to health care, there is little debate among researchers on the rural disadvantage when it comes to the availability and accessibility of health care, especially specialty medical care. It is unclear exactly how much of a role this disadvantage plays in the health problems of rural elders, but it is clear that a lack of access to such care combined with factors such as food insecurity and a lack of health promotion and disease prevention programs negatively impact the physical and psychological well being of rural elders. Population loss and economic decline have certainly played a role in the health care troubles of rural America. Increasingly expensive health care technology and trends in health care provider concentration in fewer, larger corporations are just a few factors that have led to rural hospital closures and the migration of services to more populated areas.

Federal health care funding policy has also been a significant factor in the diminution of rural health care. The development of managed care did not occur in a policy vacuum but was spurred on by the desire of the federal government to squeeze savings out of a health care system that seemed to have an insatiable appetite for increased costs. Alternatives to nursing home care such as assisted living were not only market driven, but also part of an attempt to slow the growth of Medicaid spending at the federal, state, and local government levels. Unfortunately, these developments have not been to the advantage of rural elders. Generally, managed care options are scarce in rural America as are alternatives to nursing homes as long-term care living arrangements. It is telling that the one health care option that is more available in rural compared to urban areas is that of nursing home care; alternatives such as affordable assisted living and home care are not. Demographic factors, such as the lack of rural economies of scale due to smaller markets, play a significant role in this situation, as does health care policy in America.

The chapter by Coburn, Loux, and Bolda drives home these problems and also delves into an important and often overlooked aspect of rural health care: the role of hospitals in long-term care. They point out that rural and urban long-term care systems differ in terms of services offered, with rural areas relying more heavily on nursing homes than home care and assisted living options. As a result, long-term care service use patterns among rural and urban elders differ. One important but often overlooked provider of long-term care in rural areas is the hospital. The implementation of the Medicare Prospective Payment System spurred rural hospitals to develop new services such as skilled nursing facilities, home health services, and swing-beds. Later, in response to managed care and market pressures, rural hospitals developed rural health care networks. Federal health care reimbursement policy since then has changed frequently and these changes have impacted the nature of services provided by rural hospitals. For example, the Balanced Budget Act of 1997 and other Medicare reimbursement changes reduced the payments to rural hospitals for new services such as skilled nursing care.

Although 40% of rural hospitals offer skilled nursing care and close to 25% have hospice beds, Coburn et al. report that more recently, the proportion of rural hospitals providing post-acute and long-term care has stagnated and the proportion offering home health services has declined to under 50%. Rural hospitals have used diversification, networking, and service integration to maintain acute care services and offer more long-term care options in an environment of shifting federal policy and competitive private market forces. A variety of factors have acted as impediments to these efforts including: smaller financial and organizational capacity; difficulties in achieving economies of scale; location in regions with fewer providers and services; and service populations who are often older and poorer. When all is said and done, these authors are not optimistic regarding the ability of rural hospitals to drive the expansion and integration of acute and long-term care service as a means to better care for older persons in their communities.

Mueller and McBride analyze one of the most recent policy shifts in federal health care for older adults, the Medicare Prescription Drug, Improvement and Modernization Act (MMA) of late 2003. They examine the impact of the provisions of the MMA on rural elders by looking at five principles: equity, quality, choices, access, and cost. They conclude that rural elders are likely to benefit more than their urban counterparts, primarily because rural elders are more disadvantaged under current policies. Mueller and McBride note that rural elders are less likely to have prescription drug coverage, have higher out-of-pocket expenses, have lower household incomes, lack Medigap coverage, and are in poorer health. All of these are deficiencies that the MMA addresses. Because the MMA is so new, information on best practices is lacking. Mueller and McBride identify areas where these are likely to emerge such as beneficiary education and enrollment, coordination with Medicaid and state pharmacy assistance programs, and care management. These authors see the changes brought by the MMA as having significant impacts on the health of rural Medicare enrollees through a variety of avenues. They also acknowledge that significant challenges exist to realizing those benefits.

HEALTH AND HEALTH CARE: SUMMARY

- Research supports the argument that rural elders have poorer health than their urban counterparts.
- The factors contributing to these health problems are complex and include lifestyle, economic resources, work environments, and nutrition.
- A lack of availability, accessibility, and affordability of health promotion and disease prevention, as well as acute and chronic disease treatment services, also contribute to the disadvantaged health status of rural elders.
- Rural elders generally find a narrower range of health and long-term care services in their communities and specialty care is increasingly available only in larger hospitals.
- A variety of factors serve as barriers to health care services in rural areas. These include population loss and a lack of economic growth in rural communities, as well as trends in America's health care system such as the reliance on managed care and the increasingly large amount of human and economic capital required to provide quality health care.
- Although federal health care funding policy has contributed to this service disadvantage, it also plays a significant role in decreasing it. Thus, the MMA holds the promise of benefiting rural elders disproportionately, partly because they are disadvantaged under current policies.

SELECTED SERVICES

A book on service delivery has any number of services to examine. In addition to health and long-term care services, we thought it would be valuable to look at services in three areas critical to the well being of rural elders. The first, caregiving, acknowledges the critical importance of informal family and friends as service providers and looks at services which support informal care providers. The other two service areas, housing and transportation, are critical to the ability of rural elders to remain independent and maintain their well being. Accessible and affordable transportation options are essential for rural elders who do not have cars or are unable to drive. Adequate housing and housing options for more frail elders are also key services as they can, on the one hand, facilitate successful aging in place or, if inadequate, lead to a greater need for other services and even premature nursing home placement.

Wagner and Niles-Yokum note a point often overlooked in caregiving research. This is that with the general rural disadvantage in home- and community-based health and social services, informal caregiving issues and challenges take on even greater importance for rural than for nonrural elders. Unfortunately, they also correctly point out that the amount of research on rural caregiving is sparse indeed. These authors note that a number of factors present challenges to caregiving in rural areas. One is demographic because rural areas have higher percents of old persons, largely a result of the out-migration of middle-age and young adults—the very persons who would fill both formal and informal caregiving roles. Second, rural elders are also less healthy and poorer than urban elders, which increases the likelihood that they will need caregiving. Third, rural and small town elders can find themselves living considerable distances from their adult children, who have moved away to urban centers for economic and social opportunities. Fourth, Wagner and Niles-Yokum indicate that there are reasons to expect care norms and patterns to differ between rural and urban areas, including expectations for caregiving and the use of fictive kin, but state that research on these issues is lacking. Finally, these authors note that limited access to formal care in rural areas likely influences the interface between formal and informal care but is not well understood. They raise the concern that the lack of formal services in rural areas can put additional strain on family caregivers and lead to inappropriate nursing home placement. Wagner and Niles-Yokum close their chapter with a discussion of how to build a supportive community context for rural family caregiving to elders. They conclude that while many gaps exist in our understanding of rural caregiving, much of what we do know suggests that significant residential differences do exist in its context and dynamics.

Folts, Muir, Peacock, Nash, and Jones provide a comprehensive overview of housing, which is a fundamental element in the well being of rural elders. Housing is often overlooked as a service, largely because in America it is seen as an individual responsibility and housing issues rarely make headlines. However, housing quality and options are important to the ability of older persons to maintain independence and quality of life. Folts and colleagues consider rural housing first within the context of federal housing policy. Not only is funding for housing programs very low, it also is based on an urban perspective and urban biases which leave many rural housing needs unmet. The authors note that the increasing presence of retirement communities in America has not generally benefited rural older populations because they have tended to require location near urban amenities and largely serve higher-than-average income elders. Many popular housing options like assisted living and continuing care retirement communities are not geographically or economically feasible for elders living in more remote areas. Finally, Folts et al. note that several housing best practices are especially applicable to many older rural populations including home sharing, share-a-home, and cooperative living. These are small scale, use housing stock that already exists in rural communities, and allow rural elders to maintain residence in communities where they have lived over the years.

The last service discussed in the book is transportation, the one service that generally tops the list as an unmet need of rural adults, both among service professionals and the general public. Kerschner discusses rural transportation and rural elders in the context of the importance of transportation availability to all aspects of quality of life and the consequences of elders not being able to provide for their own transit. Many smaller communities lack not just health services, but even grocery stores, pharmacies, banks, post offices, and retail shopping, and the distances to these services can be considerable. This makes travel by personal vehicle expensive and elders who do not drive or have family/friends to drive them face the challenge of using transportation services. Kerschner notes data that report almost two-thirds of America's rural population live in areas with no public transportation or paratransit or experience inadequate transportation. Her chapter focuses on a variety of solutions to the transportation challenges faced by rural elders, including promoting senior friendliness, adapting existing options, creating new options, and providing supportive services. Innovative approaches have also been shown to be effective and represent tailored responses to specific community situations that use local resources, especially nonprofit agencies and volunteers.

SERVICES: SUMMARY

- Many of the same demographic factors that are affecting the delivery and quality of formal services affect informal care providers. Rural diversity, rural values and sensitivities, lack of community resources, geographic distance, and access to information are just a few.
- Federal resources devoted specifically to services for caregivers of older adults tend to be sparse and programs do not reflect rural realities. Private sector services also tend to underserve rural areas because of the lack of economies of scale and smaller markets.
- Federal aging service policies and program emphases need to do a better job of taking rural realities and needs into account and provide the resources and flexibility to rural health and social service providers, which are necessary to create programs that reflect community values and organizational resources.
- Effective service approaches often incorporate local community needs and resource systems, such as nonprofits and volunteers, and these should be provided more funding through existing federal and state programs.

TECHNOLOGY: SUMMARY

This last section of the book introduces the application of telemedicine as a service delivery vehicle that transcends reliance on physical proximity between consumer and provider. Redford and Spaulding examine another approach to improving the delivery of health care services to rural elders: the use of technology. Whether dealing with acute or chronic conditions, hospital or individual providers, preventive or follow-up care, rural elders often must overcome barriers of availability, accessibility, and affordability to receive needed health care. Telemedicine, or telehealth—specifically interactive televideo and the Internet—is increasingly viewed as a cost-effective way to overcome these barriers, especially those of access and availability. It is also being used in the training of practicing rural health care professionals and those preparing to enter a variety of health professions. The use of such technologies can overcome distance and the lack of medical specialists, as well as the lack of equipment and facilities that treatment providers require to practice effectively. Telemedical approaches can overcome the contraction of rural health care systems in the face of changing public reimbursement policies and market forces.

Redford and Spaulding provide numerous examples of effective application of interactive television-based technology to the health care issues of rural elders. These practices tend to concentrate in a small number of states that are geographically large or have large numbers or proportions of older people living in rural areas, or both. The Internet has expanded access to interactive television by significantly reducing its cost. Redford and Spaulding see this linkage as one of the most important innovations in the ability to use technology to help meet the health care needs of rural elders. However, these authors also acknowledge that the use of technology in the provision of health care and health education in rural areas faces some of the same barriers as traditional methods. Although recent policy changes have increased the federal coverage of telemedicine, reimbursement is still a fundamental problem for providing services via telemedicine.

In rural areas the technical infrastructure needed for telemedicine can be unavailable or very expensive. Many rural health care providers simply do not have the resources or high-speed connections that make sophisticated applications possible. Like others, people in rural areas who want to use telemedicine face issues of licensure, quality control, privacy, and finding the proper balance of distance and in-person health care. Nonetheless, the use of technology in the delivery of health care to rural elders is a significant development—one that the authors believe will continue to expand.

Although technology will not in and of itself level the health care playing field for rural elders, various forms of telemedicine have been shown to bring needed health services to rural areas where the traditional face-to-face delivery of care is prohibited by distance and cost.

CONCLUSIONS

There are programs at all levels of government that do successfully meet the needs of rural elders. The aging services network of State Units on Aging and Area Agencies on Aging established and funded by the OAA has worked to develop and support home- and community-based programs for rural older adults. Advocates for rural needs have worked to ensure that the OAA directs resources to these programs. However, the overall amount of program dollars in the OAA is little more than a billion dollars and OAA has experienced flat funding for many years even while the number of elders (defined as age 60 years and older) has increased. This is very little money, given the large number of programs supported by the OAA. Issues of funding and delivering community-based programs, especially the challenge of doing so in rural areas, are constantly overshadowed by the big ticket and politically visible issues of Medicare, Social Security, and Medicaid. Long-term care, especially that which is provided outside of nursing homes by family members and practitioners, has largely been consigned to the periphery of public discourse and political debate. Rural issues in general, and the needs of older adults in particular, are not high political priorities at the federal and state level. The fragmentation of federal funding for home- and community-based services for older adults further dilutes their potential impact.

Rural population trends and their impact on the economic fortunes and service capacity of rural communities present significant barriers to the development and implementation of programs for rural elders. There is little to suggest that the stagnation in rural population growth will change, small pockets of rural in-migration notwithstanding, and more remote rural areas are likely to continue to depopulate. Many rural communities face further economic decline and loss of people who otherwise would fill caregivng roles as family members or professionals. Rural populations are changing in other ways and will likely become more diverse ethnically and racially. Thus, service providers will be challenged to find the resources and appropriate program approaches to meet the needs of this changing older population.

Inadequate public funding based on demographic, economic, and political factors has led to a lack of availability of many important aging services in rural America. The realities of low population density both intensify the need for transportation services and partially account for their absence or inadequacy in rural places. The same can be said for many other services. Behavior patterns among rural elders such as poor nutrition and a lack of interest in healthy lifestyles increase the challenges faced by rural service providers. Chapter authors have repeatedly noted that there is a dearth of good data both on the dimensions and characteristics of rural elder's service needs and also on the elements that make rural programs effective and sustainable.

All is not bleak, however. We know that many successful service delivery approaches and programs for rural elders are in operation around the United States. Some of the chapters have focused on general aspects or characteristics of such programs while others have given specific examples of their content and operation. There is even some

hope that policy change at the federal level, such as the MMA, will have
positive impacts on the service needs of rural elders. The successful use of
telemedicine suggests that the stereotypes of rural elders as mistrustful
of outsiders and less accepting of change are overdrawn. By and large,
however, the rural service delivery approaches which have emerged as
effective and appropriate are not high tech, but rather use local community resources and indigenous support networks. This theme is reflected in service approaches in nutrition, caregiving support, housing,
and transportation.

So where does this leave us? Certainly the need for more resources
to support existing services and program innovation is clear. There is also
the need for more and better data on the service needs of rural elders,
especially how they vary between communities and regions. Because
rural issues have tended to be seen as homogeneous in the past, it is
very important to learn more about how these needs differ based on the
demographic characteristics of the rural people in question. We know
that the ethnic and racial diversity of the older rural population will
increase in the near future. However, virtually no attention is being paid
to the fact that as rural baby boomers age, traditional models of service
delivery will need to change for rural elders in general. It is unlikely that
the same service approaches that worked with older rural adults who
are now in their 80's will work for rural baby boomers when they reach
their 60's. Regardless, the perceptions of need and program preferences
of rural elders must stand as the core for service content and delivery.

Federal health and human service policies, as well as the hundreds
of federal and state programs that provide funding and oversight for services, need to be examined critically with an eye toward their adequacy,
applicability, and effectiveness in rural communities. In addition to looking at the impact of resources and regulations, greater attention needs to
be given to assembling best practices of programs for rural elders. Many
communities and organizations can point to programs that are making
a difference, but information on these is generally known only at the
local or, at best, the state level. Thus, information on program operation
and success that could be used in other communities for the training of
existing and future practitioners is not easily accessed. State and national
conferences of a variety of professional organizations provide forums
for such sharing, but these efforts do not lead to a cumulative or coordinated approach to knowledge development and dissemination.

We lack a central clearinghouse at any level for information on
rural aging needs and services. Some 15 years ago, the AoA funded a national resource center on rural aging that published booklets on service
issues and service approaches on a wide variety of rural aging topics, but

no similar initiative has emerged since. A national focal point for such information, as well as a national dialogue and dissemination effort on needed rural aging research and service delivery issues, is required if we are to move beyond the current state of fragmented knowledge and service efforts. Perhaps a consortium of government, foundation, business, and academic sources could join forces to make this need a reality. Such a commitment is necessary to ensure that dedicated professionals, volunteers, and family members are successful in their efforts to help maintain the highest possible quality of life for rural elders.

Index

Page numbers followed by f or t indicate
figures and tables, respectively.

AAA. *See* Area Agencies on Aging
AARP, 68, 132, 134, 148, 151
Access, 131–132
Accessibility, of services, 28
Activities of Daily Living (ADL), 66,
 67, 68, 148
Acute health conditions, 80
Adequacy, of services, 28
ADL. *See* Activities of Daily Living
Administration on Aging (AoA), 31,
 64–65, 93, 194, 247
Adult children, 150–151
Adult day care, 24, 104, 110, 184
Adults, older, in rural settings,
 13–15
Adverse drug reactions, 83
Affordability, of services, 28
African Americans, 56–61
 health services for, 60
 noncondition-specific health
  outcomes of, 58t
 service delivery and, 59
Age, working v. retirement, 42t, 43t
Aging Services Network, 93
AgrAbility Project, 156
AHA. *See* American Hospital
 Association
AHEAD. *See* Asset and Health
 Dynamics Among the Oldest
 Old
AI. *See* American Indians
Alabama, 59
Alaska, 10
Alaska Natives (AN), 61–65, 244

long-term care service provisions
 for, 65
Alzheimer's Demonstration Grants,
 157
Alzheimer's disease, 82, 191
Amenity migrants, 39, 45, 48
America, rural, 12–13
American Hospital Association
 (AHA), 107–108
American Housing Survey, 164
American Indians (AI), 61–65, 244
 long-term care service provisions
  for, 65
American Telemedicine Association,
 216
Annual Rural Geriatric Conference,
 156
AoA. *See* Administration on Aging
Appalachia, 47, 87
Appropriateness, of services, 28
Area Agencies on Aging (AAA),
 24–25, 30, 224–225, 234
Area Health Education Centers, 209
Arizona, 61, 205
Arkansas, 87, 156
Arkansas GEC, 87, 209
Arthritis, 80, 81t, 83
Asian, 15
Asset and Health Dynamics Among
 the Oldest Old (AHEAD), 68
Assistance migrants, 39
Assistant Secretary for Planning and
 Evaluation (ASPE), 156
Assisted living, 106–107

Association of American Medical
    Colleges Division of Medical
    Education, 210
Asthma, 137, 207
Availability, of services, 28
Awareness, of services, 28

Baby boom, 51
Balanced Budget Act (BBA), 104,
    108, 214, 226, 249
Balanced Budget Refinement
    Act, 108
BBA. *See* Balanced Budget Act
Behavior, defining, 5
Benchmarking, 11
Beneficiary education, 133–134
Beneficiary enrollment, 133–134
Benefits Improvement and
    Protection Act (BIPA), 108, 213
Best practices
    defining, 11–12
    for housing, 171–173
    MMA and, 132–137
    for nutritional health, 93
Beverly Foundation, 190, 191
Blindness, 82
Blue Cross/Blue Shield, 214
BMI. *See* Body mass index
Body mass index (BMI), 87
Bolda, Elise J., 248
Bolin, Jane N., 246–247
Bradley, John E., 242–243
Brain drain, 57
Bull, C. Neil, 241
Bureau for Indian Affairs, 64
Bureau of Health Professions,
    Health Resources, and Services
    Administration, 208–209

California, 61, 192, 205, 207,
    225, 227
Cancer, 81t
Cardiovascular disease, 82
Care management, 136–137
Care oriented retirement
    communities (CORCs), 169,
    170–171

Caregiving, 145–160
    consumer-directed models of,
        156–157
    demographic factors in, 148–149
    design factors for, 154–155
    distance, 149–150
    educational services for, 156
    formal v. informal, 152–154
    informal, 146–148
    initiatives, 155–158
    outreach models for, 157–158
    patterns, 150–152
    proximity, 149–150
    research on, 158–159
    respite models, 157–158
    rural, 148–149
    supportive context for, 154–155
Case management, 136, 159
Cash and counseling demonstration
    evaluation (CCDE), 156
Caucasian(s), noncondition-specific
    health outcomes of, 58t
CBSAs. *See* Core Based Statistical
    Areas
CCDE. *See* Cash and counseling
    demonstration evaluation
Census, 66, 243
    1960, 37–38
    2000, 38, 41
Center for Telemedicine and
    TeleHealth, 206
Center for Telemedicine Law, 216
Center on an Aging Society,
    151, 153
Centers for Medicare and Medicaid,
    127, 133, 156–157
Central Plains GEC, 209
Central Savannah River Area Rural
    Day Care Program, 157
Choice, 128–129
    MMA and, 128–129
Chronic care, 84, 85, 93, 118,
    128, 247
Chronic care model, 84, 85f, 93, 94
Chronic disease management,
    84–86, 93, 94, 247
Chronic disease model, 85

Chronic health conditions, 80
  comparison rates of, 81t
  management of, 84–86
Chronic obstructive pulmonary
  disease, 137
Civil War, migration after, 56
Clawback state payment, 134
Coburn, Andrew F., 248
Colorado, 68, 227
Commission on Affordable Housing
  Health Facility Needs for
  Seniors in the 21st Century, 235
Community-based long-term care
  services, 64, 65, 68, 114, 227
Community-based services, 14, 17,
  24, 25, 27, 60, 92, 105, 106,
  107, 115, 145, 152, 188, 225,
  231, 241, 255
Composition, of rural community, 5
Congestive heart failure, 137, 208
Congressional Budget Office,
  132, 134
Consumer Price Index, 90
Consumer-directed models, of
  caregiving, 156–157
Consumer-directed programs,
  230–231
Continuing care retirement
  communities, 170, 252
Contract with America, 228
Cooperative living arrangements,
  175–176
Coordination, 119
Coordination and Advocacy for
  Rural Elders, 157
COPE. See Project Care Option and
  Public Education
CORCs. See Care oriented
  retirement communities
Core Based Statistical Areas (CBSA),
  6, 7t, 10
Cornell University, 48
Costs, of Medicare, 129–130
  MMA and, 130–131
Counterstream migration, 49
Critical access hospitals, 110–112,
  125

Cuban-Americans, 66
Culture, of rural community, 5
Current Population Survey, 89–90

Dakota Telemedicine system, 205
Data collection, 69–70
Dementia, 82
Demographics, 242–245
  caregiving and, 148–149
  of rural aging, 164–165
  of U.S. households, 164t
Department of Housing and Urban
  Development (HUD), 166,
  168, 172
Department of Transport (DOT), 186
Depopulation, rural, 38
Depression, 82–83
Destination needs, 184
DETERMINE checklist, 86
Devolution, 228
DHHS, 133
Diabetes, 81t, 82
Diffusion of Innovations (Rogers),
  217
Disability, 41–42
Disability migrants, 39
Disablement Process, 79
Disease, among AI/AN populations,
  61–62
Distance caregiving, 149–150
District of Columbia, 61
Diversification, 112–118
  forces shaping, 112–113
DOT. See Department of Transport
Driving, 185, 186
  after age 74, 186t
Drug-drug interactions, 83
Drug-nutrient interactions, 83

Ecology, defining, 5
Economic development, 25
  after World War II, 37–38
  defined, 232
  public policy and, 231–233
  retirement and, 48–49
Economic Research Service, 48
Economic resources, defining, 5

Education, 56–57
  beneficiary, 133–134
  for caregiving, 156
  Internet, 208–211
  ITV, 208–211
Elder Care Initiative, 64
ElderLink, Inc., 157
Elderly Nutrition Program, 91
Emancipation, 56
Emphysema, 81t
End stage renal disease, 82
Enrollment, beneficiary, 133–134
Environmental press, 23
Equal access, 62
Equity, 124–125
  MMA and, 125–126
Extension Service Centers, 155

Falls, 83
Family Caregiver Support, 65
Farmers Home Administration,
    167–168, 168
Fear of falling, 83
Federal housing policies, 166–176
Federal Office of Rural Health
    Policy, 11
Federal programs, 224–228
  managed care, 226–227
  Medicaid, 225–226
  Medicare, 225–226
  Older Americans Act, 224–225
  Social Security, 227–228
Fictive kin, 150–151
Flex Monitoring Team, 110
Florida, 10, 49, 128, 133, 137, 156,
    174, 214, 225
Folts, Edward, 252
Food choice, 89
Food prices, 90
Food security, 89–90
Food Stamp Program, 91
Food sufficiency, 89–90
Formal care, informal care v., 152–154

GECs. See Geriatric Education Centers
Geisinger Rural Aging Study, 88
Geographic isolation, 26

Georgia, 59, 128, 157, 204
Geriatric Education Centers (GECs),
    208–209. See also Arkansas
    GEC; Central Plains GEC;
    Montana GEC
Goins, R. Turner, 240, 244
Government Accounting Office, 131
Great Migration, 56

H.320, 212, 215
HCFA. See Health Care Financing
    Administration
Health care, 201–219, 246–250.
    See also Interdisciplinary health
    care; Primary health care;
    Specialty health care
  current issues in, 202–203
Health Care Financing
    Administration (HCFA), 213
Health care providers, rural,
    85–86
Health informative technologies
    (HIT), 201
Health Insurance Portability and
    Accountability Act (HIPAA),
    202, 216–217
Health Maintenance Organizations
    (HMO), 129, 230
Health problems, 80–84
  acute, 80
  best practices for, 93
  chronic, 80, 84–86
  depression, 82–83
  diabetes, 82
  heart disease, 81–82
  mental illness, 82–83
  model programs for, 93
  polypharmacy, 83–84
Health Resources and Services
    Administration, 208, 209, 230
Health services, 3–4, 79, 81
  African Americans and, 60
  Alaskan Natives, 61–65
  American Indians, 61–65
  challenges to issues of, 92
Heart disease, 81–82, 81t
Hemophilia, 137

H-EPESE. *See* Hispanic Established
    Populations for Epidemiological
    Studies of the Elderly
HIPAA. *See* Health Insurance
    Portability and Accountability Act
Hispanic Established Populations for
    Epidemiological Studies of the
    Elderly (H-EPESE), 68
Hispanics, 66–69, 244
    immigration of, 67
HIT. *See* Health informative
    technologies
HMO. *See* Health Maintenance
    Organizations
Home care, 64, 103, 118, 153, 208,
    225, 231, 244, 248, 249
Home health care, 106, 109f
    telehealth in, 207–208
Home maintenance, 90
Home sharing, 173–176
Home-delivered meals, 59
Homeownership, 176, 177
Homestead Housing Center, 176
Hospice, 108, 110, 112, 114, 249
Hospitals, 103–120
    critical access, 110–112
    diversification, 112–118
    financial pressures on, 116
    home health services provided
        by, 109f
    inpatient services provided
        by, 109f
    in long-term care, 107–112
Housing
    adequate, 163–164
    assistance programs, 178
    best practices, 171–173
    cooperative living arrangements,
        175–176
    CORCs, 170–171
    demographics of, 164–165
    developments, 172
    federal policies for, 166–176
    home sharing and, 173–174
    LORCs, 170
    models, 178
    NORCs, 169–170

    personal barriers to, 176
    political barriers to, 177
    Share-A-Home, 174–175
    social barriers to, 177
Housing and Urban Development
    (HUD)
    242 Hospital Mortgage Insurance
        program, 118
    best practice and, 172
    Section 8, 166–167
    Section 202, 166–167
    Section 255, 166
    Section 502, 168
    Section 504, 168
    Section 515, 168
Housing Assistance Council, 165, 167
HUD. *See* Housing and Urban
    Development
HUD 242 Hospital Mortgage
    Insurance Program, 118
Human service infrastructures, 26
Hypertension, 81t

IADL. *See* Instrumental activity of
    daily living
Idaho, 88
IHS. *See* Indian Health Service
Immigration, of Hispanics, 67
Incentives, 118, 119–120
Independence Choice Programs, 156
Indian Country, 62, 64, 65
Indian Health Service (IHS), 63
    Long-Term Care Work Group, 64
Informal caregiving, 146–148
    formal care v., 152–154
Inpatient services, 109f
Institute of Medicine, 126
Instrumental activity of daily living
    (IADL), 66, 67
Integrated Services Digital Network
    (ISDN), 212–213, 214, 218–219
Interactive televideo (ITV), 201–202
    education and, 208–211
    in home health care, 207–208
    in interdisciplinary health care,
        205–207
    Internet and, 211–212

Interactive televideo (ITV) (*Continued*)
    in nursing homes, 206–207
    in primary and specialty medical
        care, 204–205
Interdisciplinary health care, ITV in,
    205–207
Internet
    education and, 208–211
    ITV and, 211–212
    wireless, 212–213
Internet Protocols (IP), 212
Iowa, 136
    Medicaid program of, 136
IP. *See* Internet Protocols
ISDN. *See* Integrated Services Digital
    Network
Isolation, 26
ITV. *See* Interactive televideo

Jones, Katherine L., 252

Kaiser Permanente, 207
Kansas, 193, 204, 206, 209, 210, 215
Kansas University Medical Center, 204
Kentucky, 88
Kerschner, Helen, 253
Krout, John A., 240–241

Leisure oriented retirement
    communities (LORCs),
    169, 170
Leisure World, 175
Licensure, 215–216
Life expectancy, of women, 147
Life-care retirement communities, 170
Linkage, 119
Literacy, 28, 134
Loans, 168
Longino, Charles F., 242–243
Long-term care, 103–120
    assisted living, 106–107
    critical access hospitals and,
        110–112
    home health care, 106
    hospitals in, 107–112
    integration of, 112–118
    nursing homes and, 105

Long-Term Care Work Group, 64
LORCs. *See* Leisure oriented
    retirement communities
Loss of function, 79
    framework for progressive, 80
Louisiana, 59, 87
Loux, Stephenie L., 248

Maine, 156
Malnutrition, 81
Managed care, 226–227
Maryland, 137
Massachusetts, 227
Mathematic Policy Research Inc.,
    231
McBride, Timothy D., 249
Meal patterns, 88
Meals-on-Wheels, 152
MedEdPORTAL Cube, 210
Medicaid, 63, 64, 118, 119,
    225–226, 254
    in Iowa, 136
    state pharmacy assistance
        programs and, 134–136
Medicare, 63, 64, 83, 119, 225–226,
    229, 236, 249, 254
    + Choice program, 125, 126, 129
    access and, 131–132
    Advantage plans, 126, 130, 138
    analyzing changes in, 124–132
    costs and, 129–131
    equity and, 124–125
    Modernization Act, 104
    modernization act, 85
    Part D of, 136
    policy changes, 103–104
    Prescription Drug, Improvement,
        and Modernization Act, 108,
        123, 125–126
    Prospective Payment System,
        103, 248
    quality and, 126–127
Medicare Current Beneficiary
    Survey, 62
MedPAC, 131
Medscape, 210–211
Mental illness, 82–83

Metropolitan Statistical Areas, 6
Mexican-Americans, 66, 68, 86,
    90, 244
Michigan, 193, 204
Micropolitan Statistical Areas, 6, 7t,
    9t, 10
Midwest, 26, 56, 176
Migrants
    amenity, 39, 45, 48
    assistance, 39
    counterstream, 49
    disability, 39
    economic impact of, 48–49
    leaving urban areas, 42
    long-term, 50
    provincial, 40
    provincial return, 40, 45
    retirement, 48–49
    retirement settings of, 43–44
    rural-to-urban, 45–46
    settling in rural areas, 42
Migration impact, 47–48
Minnesota, 118
Minority elders, 55–70
    African Americans, 56–61
Mississippi, 59, 87, 128, 136, 137
Mitchell, Jim, 244
MMA. See Prescription
    Drug, Improvement, and
    Modernization Act
Mobility status, elders defined by, 46t
Model programs, for nutritional
    health, 93
Montana, 10, 88
Montana GEC, 209
Morning Meals on Wheels Pilot
    Program, 93
Mount Aloysius College, 210
Mueller, Keith J., 249
Muir, Kenneth B., 252
Myths, 12

Nash, Bradley, 252
National Alliance for Caregiving,
    148, 151
National Association of State Units
    on Aging, 231

National Committee on Vital Health
    Statistics, 70
National Conference of State
    Legislature, 136
National Congress of American
    Indians, 56n1
National Council on Aging, 93, 231
National Eldercare Institute, 194
National Family Caregivers Support
    Act, 146–147, 155, 225
National Governor's Association
    (NGA), 147, 226
National Health Interview, 82
National Long Term Care Survey,
    Informal Caregiver Supplement
    to, 151
National Rural Health Alliance
    (NRHA) of Australia, 11
National Rural Health
    Association, 69
National Survey of Hispanic Elderly
    People, 68
National Tribal Chairmen's
    Association, 56n1
Native Americans. See American
    Indians
Naturally occurring retirement
    communities (NORCs), 169–170
Networking, 112–118
New Jersey, 156
New Mexico, 192
New York, 10, 22, 227
NGA. See National Governor's
    Association
Niles-Yokum, Kelly J., 251
Noncondition-specific health
    outcomes, 58t
NORCs. See Naturally occurring
    retirement communities
North Carolina, 59, 86, 87, 90,
    91, 137
North Carolina Nutrition and
    Function Study, 87
North Dakota, 137, 203, 205, 230
Northeast, 56
NRHA. See National Rural Health
    Alliance

Nursing homes, 67
   long-term care and, 105
   in rural and urban areas, 105f
   telehealth in, 206–207
Nutrition Screening Initiative, 86
Nutritional health, 246–250
   best practices for, 93
   challenges to issues of, 92
   deficiencies, 88–89
   model programs for, 93
   obesity, 87
   programs, 91–92
   risk, 86
   self-management of, 89–92

Obesity, 81, 87
Office of Management and Budget
      (OMB), 6, 10
Office of Naval Research, 210
Office of Rural Health Policy, 11,
      31, 85
Oklahoma, 61, 128, 156
Older adults, in rural settings,
      13–15
Older Americans Act, 59, 64,
      224–225, 234, 241, 247, 254
   Nutrition Programs, 86
   Title III-C, 64
   Title VI, 64, 65
Olmstead Decision, 157
OMB. See Office of Management
      and Budget
Ombudsmen, 224
Oregon, 193
Organizations, defining, 5
Outreach models, for caregiving,
      157–158
Overweight, 87

PACE programs, 116, 119
Paratransit, 189
Peacock, James R., 252
Pennsylvania, 87, 128, 133, 210
PHC-T-36, 41
Political development, 232
Polypharmacy, 80, 83–84
Population bases, 117–118, 246

Population dynamics, 242–245
Post-acute care, 103–104, 113, 118
Poverty rates, 15, 149
PPS. See Prospective Payment
   System
Preferred Provider Organizations,
   129
Prescription Drug, Improvement,
      and Modernization Act
      (MMA), 108, 123, 135,
      249, 255
   access and, 131–132
   beneficiaries of, 138
   best practices from, 132–137
   care management, 136–137
   changes made by, 137–138
   choice and, 128–129
   costs and, 130–131
   equity and, 125–126
   quality and, 127–128
   Title IV, 125
Pricewaterhouse Coopers, 132
Primary health care, ITV in,
      204–205
Privacy, 216–217
Private Fee-For-Service plans, 129
Profile of Older Americans, 165
Programs for All-inclusive Care
      for the Elderly (PACE), 116,
      117, 119
Project Care Option and Public
      Education (COPE), 157
Prospective Payment System (PPS),
   103
Provider donation mobilization,
   193
Provincial migrants, 40
Provincial return migrants, 40, 45
Proximity caregiving, 149–150
Public housing, 166, 167, 172
Public policy, 62, 179, 223–236,
      239–240
   consumer-directed programs,
      230–231
   controlling costs of, 230
   economic development and,
      231–233

federal programs, 224–228
federal roles in, 228–229
innovations in, 230–231
recommendations of, 233–235
Public transit, 187
Public Use Microdata Areas
    (PUMAs), 41, 42t, 43t
    destination and origin, 44t
Public Use Microdata Sample
    (PUMS), 40, 61
Puerto Ricans, 66, 67
PUMAs. *See* Public Use Microdata
    Areas
PUMS. *See* Public Use Microdata
    Sample

Quality, 126–127
    MMA and, 127–128

Race, 55–56
    data on, 69–70
Real Choice System Change Grants,
    156–157
Real-time consultations, 204
Redford, Linda, 249
Regional Education about Choices
    in Health, 133–134
Reimbursement, for telemedicine,
    213–214
Renal disease, 82
Resettlement
    data for study on, 40–41
    impact of, 47–52
    measures for study on, 41
    results of study on, 42–47
Resources, defining, 5
Respiratory disease, 81
Respite models, for caregiving,
    157–158
Retirement
    age of, 42t, 43t
    economic impact of, 48–49
    migrant preferences for, 43–44
    migration, 47–49
    rural, 39–40
RHS. *See* Rural Housing Service
Ride Connection, 193

Robert Wood Johnson Foundation,
    155, 156
Rocky Mountain Health
    Maintenance Organization, 230
RUPRI. *See* Rural Policy Research
    Institute
Rural
    defining, 3, 5–10, 117–118
    terminology of, 7t–9t
Rural aging, myths of, 12–15
Rural America, 12–13
Rural communities, changes in,
    232–233
Rural elders
    programs for, 29–31
    service needs of, 22–24
Rural Healthy People 2010 Project,
    11–12, 81, 92
Rural Hospital Flexibility Program,
    110
Rural Housing Service (RHS), 168
Rural locations, studying, 4
Rural migration, 38–39
Rural Policy Research Institute
    (RUPRI), 123
Rural Research Policy Institute,
    227
Rural services. *See* Service delivery

San Felipe Elderly Transportation
    Program, 192
San Luis Valley Health and Aging
    Study, 68
SCHIP, 108
School of Nursing, 208–209
Section 8, 166–167
Section 202, 166–167
Section 255, 166
Section 502, 168
Section 504, 168
Section 515, 168
Section 521, 168
Self-management of nutritional
    health, 89–92
Service availability
    community size and, 185t
    transportation, 184–185

Service delivery, 16, 21–36
  adequacy of, 28
  affordability of, 28
  African Americans and, 56–61
  appropriateness of, 28
  availability of, 28
  awareness of, 28
  barriers to, 25–27
  future research in, 30–31
  limited, 117
  migration impact on, 47–52
  needs for, 22–24
  planning and implementing,
    27–29
  programs, 29–31
  rural hospital, 111f
  types of, 24–25
Service integration, 112–118, 119
  benefits of, 114
  challenges to, 116–117
  clinical, 115
  defined, 113
  functional, 115
  hands-off, 116
  population served, 114–115
  strategies for, 114
  types of, 115–116
Share-A-Home, 173, 174–175, 178
Sharkey, Joseph R., 246–247
Shepherd's Center Escort, 193
Skilled nursing facilities, 104, 105,
    107, 108, 110, 112, 113, 114,
    118, 135, 207, 249
Slavery, 56
Small populations, 117–118
Social networks, 150–151
Social resources, defining, 5
Social Security, 23–24, 227–228,
    229, 236, 254
Social Security Act, 64
  Title XX, 64
Social services, 3–4
Sole Community Hospitals, 125
South, 56, 57, 59, 244
South Carolina, 59, 157
Southeast, 56, 57, 59, 244
Southern rural areas, 57

Southwest, 68, 244
SPAPs. See State pharmacy
    assistance programs
Spaulding, Ryan, 249
Specialty health care, ITV in,
    204–205
Spousal care, 151–152
State Health Insurance Assistance
    Programs, 133
State pharmacy assistance programs
    (SPAPs), 134–136
State policy, 118
State Units on Aging, 234
Stereotypes, 12, 13, 23, 160
STPs. See Supplemental
    transportation programs
Stroke, 81t, 82, 206
Stroke Team physicians, 206
Substance abuse, 81, 82
Supplemental Security Income,
    23–24
Supplemental transportation
    programs (STPs), 190–191
  characteristics of, 190t
Supportive context, for rural
    caregiving, 154–155

Technical infrastructure, 214–215
Technology
  barriers to use of, 213–218
  human element, 217–218
  licensure and, 215–216
  privacy and, 216–217
  reimbursement and, 213–214
  technical infrastructure and,
    214–215
Telemedicine Information
    Exchange, 205
Telemedicine Research Center, 205
Telepsychiatry, 204
Tennessee, 128, 205
Texas, 56, 86, 90, 137, 205,
    206, 227
Thompson, Tommy, 233
Tie That Binds, 184f
Title III-C, 248
Title III-E, 225

Title IV, 125
Title VI, 64, 225
Title XX, 64
Transfer Act of 1954, 63
Transportation, 183–184, 203
  adapting existing options, 189
  destination needs, 184
  driver escort support, 193
  driving option, 186–187
  elder experience travel, 192
  friends helping friends, 192
  needs, 186t
  new options, 190–191
  promising practices, 192–194
  provider donation mobilization, 193
  public transit, 187
  senior friendliness in, 188
  service availability, 184–185
  service challenge, 185–187
  solutions to, 188–194
  supportive services, 191–192
  tie of, 184f
  volunteer mobilization, 193–194
Transportation Equity Act, 235
Transportation Reimbursement and Information Project (TRIP), 192

University of New York at Stony Brook, 208
Urban, definition of, 6
U.S. Census Bureau, 6, 7
U.S. Congress, 31
U.S. Department of Agriculture (USDA), 48
  Community Facilities Program, 118
  Security Survey Module, 89–90
U.S. Department of Agriculture Food Security Survey Module, 89–90

U.S. Department of Health and Human Services, 63, 70, 131
U.S. Select Committee on Aging, 146
USDA. See U.S. Department of Agriculture
Utah, 137

Vermont, 205
Veterans Administration, 210
Veterans Affairs Centers, 204
Veterans Health Administration, 157
Virginia, 59, 136, 210, 225, 230
Virginia Commonwealth University School of Medicine, 210
Virtual Clinical Practicum, 210
Vitamin deficiencies, 88
Voice over Internet Protocol (VoIP), 212
VoIP. See Voice over Internet Protocol
Volunteer mobilization, 193–194

Wagner, Donna L., 251
Wagner's chronic care model, 84, 85f
Washington, 206, 227
Web-based teaching, 209
WebBoards, 210
West Virginia, 87, 137
White House Conference on Aging, 235
Wireless Internet, 212–213
Wisconsin, 118, 227
Women, 15
  life expectancies of, 147
Working age, 42t, 43t
World War II, 21, 51
  economic growth after, 37–38
Wu, Bei, 244
Wyoming, 88